MASCULINITY, CONSUMERISM AND THE POST-NATIONAL INDIAN CITY

Drawing upon historical analysis, ethnographic research and analyses of popular culture, this book brings together two topics that have great bearing on contemporary Indian life but have rarely been discussed within the same analytical framework, namely the cultures of masculinity and those of the city.

This book explores relationships between masculinity and urban life through an interdisciplinary and multi-sited approach. The contexts include elite nationalist imaginations of the city and modernity; the manner in which working class men negotiate the city as a site of desire and aspirations of social mobility; masculinity and religion; sexualised visions of the city in popular-culture texts – such as Hindi language pulp fiction – that circulate as quotidian fantasies of the city as a site of thrill, danger and the 'necessity' of men's control over women; and representations of the political leader as a global masculine type who will lead a previously emasculated nation to future economic and cultural glory.

Imagining the city as a series of interconnected spaces, *Masculinity, Consumerism and the Post-national Indian City* explores how several such connections – between the home and the street, family and public spaces, religious and non-religious contexts, for example – bear upon the topic of masculinity and produce lived social reality. This exploration of the making of contemporary male subjectivity is also, of course, an exploration of gender as a relationship.

The book foregrounds the city as the *mise en scène* of the making (and un-making) of masculine cultures, thereby theorising both gender and urban life. It explores how ideas of family life, educational processes, sexuality, notions of 'tradition' and 'modernity', consumerism, religiosity, rural–urban migration and 'strong' masculinity as a political trope are intertwined with the cultures of urban masculinity.

Sanjay Srivastava is an anthropologist and British Academy Global Professor in the Department of Anthropology and Sociology at SOAS, University of London. He is also Visiting Research Professor in the Department of Sociology, Shiv Nadar University, Delhi-NCR. His research interests include urban cultures, consumerism, middle-class cultures and the relationship between new forms of work and identity. His publications include *Constructing Post-colonial India: National Character and the Doon School* (1998); *Sexual Sites, Seminal Attitudes: Sexualities, Masculinities and Culture in South Asia* (edited, 2004); *Passionate Modernity: Sexuality, Class and Consumption in India* (2007); *Entangled Urbanism: Slum, Gated Community and Shopping Mall in Delhi in Gurgaon* (2015), *(Hi)Stories of Desire: Sexualities and Culture in Modern India* (co-edited, 2019) and *Critical Themes in Indian Sociology* (co-edited, 2019).

Masculinity, Consumerism and the Post-national Indian City

Streets, Neighbourhoods, Home

Sanjay Srivastava

CAMBRIDGE
UNIVERSITY PRESS

CAMBRIDGE
UNIVERSITY PRESS

University Printing House, Cambridge CB2 8BS, United Kingdom

One Liberty Plaza, 20th Floor, New York, NY 10006, USA

477 Williamstown Road, Port Melbourne, vic 3207, Australia

314 to 321, 3rd Floor, Plot No.3, Splendor Forum, Jasola District Centre, New Delhi 110025, India

103 Penang Road, #05–06/07, Visioncrest Commercial, Singapore 238467

Cambridge University Press is part of the University of Cambridge.

It furthers the University's mission by disseminating knowledge in the pursuit of education, learning and research at the highest international levels of excellence.

www.cambridge.org
Information on this title: www.cambridge.org/9781009179867

© Sanjay Srivastava 2022

First published 2022

Printed in India by Thomson Press India Ltd.

A catalogue record for this publication is available from the British Library

ISBN 978-1-009-17986-7 Hardback

In memory of Annapurna Srivastava (1931–2021)

Contents

Figures

Acknowledgements

The key themes in this book have emerged from conversations with friends and colleagues over a number of years. Each has contributed in ways that are unquantifiable but real. Beyond academic engagements, I also wish to acknowledge those who have provided hospitality and care. I am grateful to the following for comments on drafts of chapters; contribution to shaping my thinking on cities, masculinities and the cultures of Indian modernity; and help and encouragement in many other ways: Janaki Abraham, Zaid Al Baset, Michael Allen, Joseph Alter, Anu Aneja, Yasmeen Arif, Amita Baviskar, Ritajyoti Bandyopadhyay, Srimati Basu, Jeremy Beckett, the late Ian Bedford, Christiane Brosius, Maitrayee Chaudhury, Radhika Chopra, Romit Chowdhury, Lawrence Cohen, Claire Colomb, Gillian Cowlishaw, Abhijit Das, Veena Das, Steve Derné, Michael Dwyer, Rachel Dwyer, the late Tom Ernst, Tanweer Fazal, Martin Fuchs, Nandini Gooptu, Thomas Blom Hansen, Surinder Jodhka, Radha Khan, the late Viv and Alex Kondos, Mangesh Kulkarni, Nita Kumar, Ratheesh Kumar, Alison Leitch, Rose Lilley, Antje Linkenbach, Neil Maclean, T. N. Madan, Nita Mathur, Subhash Mendhapurkar, Sudesh Mishra, Caroline Osella, Filippo Osella, Francesca Orsini, Stephen Legg, Deepak Mehta, Len Palmer, Kim Paul, Shilpa Phadke, Ujithra Ponniah, Helen Quinn, Kalpana Ram, Raka Ray, Rahul Roy, Srila Roy, Veenapani Seksaria, Manisha Sethi, Bikram Sharma, Sanjay Singh, Satish Kumar Singh, Sunila Srivastava, Ilika Srivastava-Khan, Ishana Srivastava-Khan, Renny Thomas, Patricia Uberoi, Mathew Varghese and Sumita Verma. I also extend my thanks to the two anonymous reviewers for their constructive and generous engagements with the manuscript.

Qudsiya Ahmed at Cambridge University Press initiated discussion on the manuscript and Anwesha Rana saw it through to publication. It has been a pleasure to work with them and I thank them both for their enthusiasm and professionalism. Finally, I am grateful to Fuzail Siddiqi and Aniruddha De for meticulous copyediting that has improved the manuscript in many ways and to Sohini Ghosh for assistance with the cover and post-production processes.

I am grateful to the British Academy for its Global Professorship grant (2019) that was crucial in completing this book. I am also thankful for the support received from the Indian Council for Social Science Research (ICSSR) under the 'Collaborative Research Programme on Urban Transformation in India' (2018) and a National Research Foundation of Korea Grant funded by the Korean government (NRF 2017S1A6A3A02079749).

1

Introduction

Masculinity, Modernity, Urbanity

Introduction: Men in Cities

From July to August, many parts of north India witness the *kanwariya* pilgrimage activity that relates to the worship of the god Shiva (Figure 1.1). Pilgrims collect water from the River Ganges and bring it back to their local Shiva temples. The water is carried in containers that are slung on shoulder contraptions that are known as *kanwar*s. From being a relatively small-scale affair, over the past decade or so, the pilgrimage has grown to one that involves several million participants.

Tented encampments are set up along the various pilgrimage routes. These serve as night shelters and offer food, sleeping and toilet facilities. The camps are sponsored by a variety of bodies such as market-traders' organisations, village groups, urban 'residents'' welfare associations (RWAs) and private businesses. They are also sponsored by caste-specific associations. The encampments are usually set up on public land, and there is state support in building the boundary walls, hiring the tents and regular spraying of disinfectants. Increasingly, as I observed during the pilgrimage period in 2019, they are guarded by paramilitary and police personnel, in the light of what their organisers describe as 'terror threats'. The police play a significant role in the organisation of pilgrimage activity, including creating safe passageways and directing traffic around the pilgrim routes.

The *kanwariya* procession is an urban ritual par excellence, and I open with this vignette in order to provide an ethnographic example that captures the most significant themes of this book. While the pilgrimage might have

Figure 1.1   *Kanwariya* pilgrim, Gurugram, Haryana, 2019
Source: Author.

an ancient lineage, its place in contemporary times should be understood as part of the processes of the present. Shiva devotees marching along lanes, streets and highways, with security provided by the state, and food, water and rest facilities by a variety of neighbourhood organisations, tells us a great deal about relationships between masculinity, the city, religious identities, the state and new cultures of modernity.

We should begin with the idea of the entangled nature of urban processes (a theme explored in Srivastava 2015). In this context, a religious event, beyond its dimension as an aspect of subaltern 'protest' (V. Singh 2017), is also a window into an understanding of the nature of masculine presence in the city. Though women have also begun to take part in the pilgrimage, their numbers remain miniscule. Such large-scale public presence of women marching across cities – even in the cause of religious practice – would be considered both morally reprehensible and against gender propriety. This goes to the heart of the book's discussion of the nature of public spaces and urban ones in particular. Indian public places are significantly male, with men of all classes and other backgrounds exercising a monopoly over them. The *kanwariya* procession reinforces certain notions of masculinity and men's 'right' to public spaces. It naturalises the idea that men may have a right to public spaces in a way that women do not.

Second, there is a relationship between public spaces, *Hindu* men and the state. The annual march of the *kanwariya*s is part of a larger trend where the state allows certain kinds of disruptive public activities but not others. Consider, for example, a recent case in the city of Gurugram (which is also a district and was earlier known as Gurgaon) in the state of Haryana. Earlier a largely rural area, Gurugram lies on the southern borders of Delhi and, since the 1980s, has been a site of intense, privately sponsored urban developments, including offices of multinational corporations, shopping malls and gated residential communities (Brosius 2012; Srivastava 2015).

Since the 1980s, as the district became both increasingly urban and industrial, it attracted a large number of working-class migrants, many of them Muslim. There is, however, an inadequate number of mosques in the city to cater to their needs. Of the twenty-two mosques in Gurugram, just two are situated in localities that are easily accessible to its *new* Muslim population that is unable to travel far from its places of work; the businesses Muslims work for are mostly owned by Hindus, and they are unlikely to get regular permission to take periodic breaks from work. Further, there has been significant hostility to constructing mosques that are accessible to worshippers. Both Gurugram's majority population – Hindus – and the party in power at the state level (the Bharatiya Janata Party) have stymied efforts to build new mosques (Dey 2018). The nature of urban development in Gurugram has created an environment where Muslims have no choice but to offer prayers in the open.

On 20 April 2018, when a large number of Muslim men were offering *namaaz* in a vacant plot of land in the village of Wazirabad in Gurugram, the prayers were disrupted by members of a group known as the Sanyukt Hindu Sangharsh Samiti (United Hindus Campaign Committee). Soon after, the police registered a case against six men belonging to the organisation. On the following Monday, the United Hindus Campaign Committee organised a demonstration, seeking the quashing of the case against its members and delivered a letter to the chief minister of the state of Haryana with the demand that *namaaz* on public land in all parts of Gurugram must be banned as these were pretexts to (eventually) illegally occupy these lands and convert them into Muslim places of worship. The protestors also argued that the worshippers had shouted anti-India and pro-Pakistan slogans following the prayers.

As distinct from the case of the *kanwariya* pilgrims, Muslim men who seek to utilise public spaces for worship are not just thwarted by (Hindu) public opinion and the state but also stigmatised as populations who might both subvert public and national order. As the *kanwariya* and the *namaaz* episodes graphically illustrate, different kinds of men – in this case, Hindu and Muslim – occupy public spaces in different ways. And that – in this particular case – it should lead us to reflect upon the intersection of class (middle-class Hindus have opposed new mosques as they fear it may lead to declining land values), religious identity, subalternity and state action. I explore these particular themes in Chapters 5 and 7 that explicitly focus on the entanglements of religion, masculinity, the city and the state. This is a specific example of the multiple entanglements – of class, religion, consumer cultures, gender and urban processes, among others – that form the book's focus.

This book explores how cultures of masculinity define cities and how urban relations of dwelling, mobility, togetherness, work and leisure are affected by the ways in which men inhabit the city. It also investigates how men's identities are shaped by city-living and demonstrates that 'masculinity' and the 'city' are historically intertwined topics. Drawing upon historical analysis, ethnographic research and writings on popular culture, this book brings together two topics that have great bearing on contemporary forms of sociality but are not usually discussed within the same analytical framework, namely the cultures of masculinity and those of the city. While there have been writings on gender and the city – primarily focusing on relationships between the city and women (Phadke 2007; Massey 1996) – there is comparatively little sustained focus on the relationship between men, masculinity and urban spheres (but see Baas 2020; Chowdhury 2019; Osella and Osella 2006; Srivastava 2007).

This lacuna needs to be addressed if we are to understand gender as a *relationship* and the ways in which rapidly expanding urban spheres both shape it and are affected by it. This book is, then, an exploration of men as gendered beings, the specific social character of Indian cities and the ways in which these two contexts, taken together, narrate the social life of Indian modernity. In this way, also, it seeks to move away from frameworks of 'planetary urbanism' (Brenner and Schmid 2015) in order to demonstrate that *localised* historical and ethnographic focus is a crucial tool for understanding how specific spaces and populations become entangled in processes that unfold at national and transnational levels. To *not* begin with the messiness of particular places is to end up with universal theories regarding cities and their lifeways, a universalism that implicitly favours theoretical and analytical preoccupations of the Global North (Schindler 2017).

To study men as gendered beings is to explore relationships of power among genders. This way of understanding masculinity is also an exploration of the naturalisation of the category 'man' through which men have come to be regarded as both un-gendered and the 'universal subject of human history' (O'Hanlon 1997: 1).[1] The ways of being men deserve scrutiny to understand the processes through which the exercise of power is made invisible and unquestionable. This aspect is increasingly being explored in both academic and activist contexts around the world (Kulkarni 2019).

Before proceeding further, however, it is important to say something about the terms 'masculinity' and 'patriarchy' and the relationship between the two.[2] Masculinity refers to the *socially produced but embodied ways of being male.* Its manifestations include manners of speech, behaviour, gestures, social interaction, a division of tasks 'proper' to men and women, and an overall narrative that positions it as superior to its perceived antithesis, 'femininity'. For masculinity to be positioned in a relationship of superiority to feminine identity, however, it is a key requirement that the latter be represented as possessing characteristics that are the binary opposite of the former. In this sense, 'masculinity' and 'femininity' are not simply opposite and equal categories, such that (as is frequently asserted) 'each has its own sphere of activity' (Srivastava 2018: 35). Rather, they stand in a hierarchical relationship to each other and the 'feminine' acts as a *complement* to the masculine, being defined in a manner that produces masculine identity as a superior one. Finally, in this context, dominant or 'hegemonic' masculinity (Connell 2005) stands in a relationship not just to femininity but *also to those ways of being men* that are seen to deviate from the ideal. It is in this sense, then, that masculinity possesses both external (relating to women) characteristics and internal ones that relate to 'other' men.

We need also to differentiate the linked concepts of 'patriarchy' and 'masculinity'. Patriarchy refers to a *system* of social organisation that is fundamentally organised around the idea of men's superiority to women. Within this system, even those who may not approximate to the male ideal (such as homosexual men) still stand to benefit from the privileges attached to being men. Though it is difficult to posit simple definitions of 'patriarchy' and 'masculinity', we might say that patriarchy refers to the systemic relationship of power between men and women, whereas masculinity concerns both inter- and intra-gender relationships. And, while it cannot be argued that under patriarchy *all* forms of masculinity are equally valorised – in 1870, the colonial government in India sought to register all *hijra*s and *zanana*s (that is, non-castrated transvestites) and to make them ineligible to adopt a son or act as guardians to minors[3] – there is nevertheless an overwhelming consensus regarding the superiority of men over women. So, we might say that whereas patriarchy 'makes' men superior, masculinity is the process of producing superior men. This book is about the struggle to be 'superior' men in the city.

The ideas of 'making' and 'producing' are crucial to the study of masculinity, for they imply the historical and social nature of gender identities. Further, the fact that masculinity must consistently be reinforced says something about the tenuous hold of gender identities. Following from this, masculinity is *enacted* rather than expressed. When we say that something is 'expressed', we assume that it 'already exists'. Rather, as we will see in the book, it is produced through the acts of building and rebuilding, consolidation, representation and enforcement of masculine identities. This does not, of course, imply that existing formations of masculinity do not also contain instances of men's deviation from the dominant mode (see, for example, Chopra 2003); rather, it suggests that we still need to be attuned to whether such deviations disrupt existing frameworks or find ways of operating within them.

Of those recent discussions that have foregrounded enactment as a significant aspect of gender, the one that relates to 'performance' has been particularly influential. The theoretical discussion on gender as performance (or enactment) owes much to the work of Judith Butler (1999), who has sought to move the discussion of gender and sexuality from notions of 'depth' to 'surface'. Butler also argues against the separation of 'gender' and 'sexuality'. She suggests that '[t]he regulation of gender has always been part of the work of heterosexist normativity and to insist upon a radical separation of gender and sexuality is to miss the opportunity to analyze that particular operation of homophobic power' (Butler 1999: 186). These ideas – performance, the yoking of gender and sexuality within the same analytical framework – are important and will be discussed in different contexts in this chapter.

While a productive context of thought, it is also important to recognise the limits of 'performativity' as a framework of analysis. For, as Blackwood and Wieringa (1999) point out, '[a]lthough performance theory is interested in unravelling the workings of gender, it cannot explain how people of different races, classes, and cultures and in different historical periods experience their bodies and their sexuality' (Blackwood and Wieringa 1999: 14). In other words, gender identities on the ground must account for the social and historical contexts within which 'performing' subjects are nurtured, and this requires a more nuanced understanding of what makes the 'everyday'.

Keeping in mind the above, this book is organised around an approach that seeks to explore how cultures of masculinity shape and are shaped by urban processes across *several* performative contexts of everyday life. That is, what are the different sites where enactments of masculinity impact upon the city as a social agglomeration? The discussion unfolds through identifying the specific social and historical processes that produce the urban 'everyday' as far as performances of masculinity are concerned. The contexts that are explored include elite nationalist imaginations of the city and modernity during the early twentieth century; the manner in which poor men negotiate the city as a site of desire and aspirations of social mobility; masculinity, religion and urban life; sexualised visions of the city in popular culture texts – such as Hindi language pulp fiction – that circulate as quotidian fantasies of the city as a site of thrill, danger and the 'necessity' of men's control over women; and representations of the political leader as a global masculine type who will lead a previously emasculated nation to future economic and cultural glory.

The discussion of the book is committed to the idea that a significant aspect of understanding social relationships – such as class, caste, gender, sexuality and power – lies in exploring relationships between social identity and space. Our everyday lives – played out through a variety of freedoms and constraints – unfold upon and through specific spaces. Homes, offices, parks, shopping malls, streets, footpaths, bazaars – those threads that bind cities – are crucibles of urban social life. Additionally, spaces have a dual nature: they are both sites upon which different identities find voice and also sites of the formation and consolidation. That is, spaces are both objects and processes (Lefebvre 1991). So, for example, the home is commonly understood to be the domain of women, but it is also the space that defines the kinds of activities women may take part in. Similar arguments can be made for the other spaces I have listed earlier.

The city, as I have argued elsewhere (Srivastava 2015), is a series of entangled spaces. Rather than 'a collection of independent realms – the slum, the up-market gated community, the shopping mall, the "resettlement colony"', cities consist of 'a series of interconnected spaces and processes' (Srivastava 2015: iv). Imagining the city as a series of linked spaces, the book explores how several such connections – between the home and the street, family and public spaces, religious and non-religious contexts, for example – bear upon the topic of masculinity and produce lived social realities. These, as the book outlines, consists of the ways in which men in cities – nationalist leaders of another era, subaltern men, men as consumers and 'heads' of the family, those who belong to 'Hindu fundamentalist' organisations and others whose fantasies of the city are mediated through pulp fiction and 'footpath pornography' – imagine relationships between masculine cultures and urban cultures.

The key departure the book offers from other studies of masculinity (or masculinities) is the way it foregrounds the city as the *mise en scène* of the making (and un-making) of masculine cultures. Urbanisation in India is a vibrant site of an extraordinary cultural, social and economic churn, a context of new forms of both masculinities and anxieties about their place in the unsettling of hierarchies that cities can frequently produce (on articulations of masculine anxiety by 'men's rights activists' in India, see Basu 2015 and 2019).[4] This book captures these processes through an interdisciplinary and intersectional methodology that aims to provide an accessible account of masculine modernity.

But why focus explicitly on masculinity? Is not 'gender' a productive enough term? Gender has come to be seen to offer a means of renewing feminist discourse by encouraging a more relational approach to masculinity and femininity, as against the marginalisation inherent in the project of 'women's studies'. It also allows the investigation, problematisation and interrogation of masculinity, equally with 'femininity'. Notwithstanding these enabling possibilities, however, 'gender' tends to be used, in popular as well as academic discourses, as a synonym for 'women', its relational aspect obscured and the invitation to interrogate masculinities largely ignored. This book proceeds from the position that the study of masculinity is important in that it 'is simultaneously a place in gender *relations*, the practices through which men and women engage that place in gender, and the effects of these practices in bodily experiences, personality and culture' (Connell 2005: 71, emphasis added). Further, as the historian Rosalind O'Hanlon has pointed out, '[a] proper understanding of the field of power in which women have lived their lives demands that we look at men as gendered beings too' (O'Hanlon 1997: 1).

As several recent events show, there are significant reasons why we should study the different ways in which men occupy and shape cities. Urban spatial transformations – that might give off an air of a new world of possibilities – are, in fact, circumscribed by wider social norms that continue to affect how women, for example, are regarded. Gender continues to be a site of expression of 'Indian traditions' and 'morality' (see, for example, Bernroider 2018 on single women as tenants in Delhi), and it is important to understand how these concepts play out in relation to the city and the manner in which its spaces are affected by the politics of masculinity. While the city may be the grounds for the unfolding 'modern relationships', such ideas circulate in contexts 'where descent, succession and inheritance are in the male line; post-marital residence is "patrivirilocal" ... and authority resides with the senior males of the family or lineage' (Uberoi 2008: 245). What is the extent to which urban environments are contexts where the strictures of gendered behaviour are undone, and under what conditions do they continue to remain in place?

The brutal rape and violence inflicted upon the young woman known as Jyoti Singh in Delhi on 16 December 2012 is one of the several events through which we might think of relationships between city and gender. The twenty-three-year-old Singh was returning from a multiplex in a shopping mall and was accompanied by a male friend. As is the case with many young single women who migrate to large cities to pursue a better future, Singh worked in a lowly paid job (a call centre) in order to raise finance to train for the profession she hoped to enter, in her case, physiotherapy. The potential risk she was exposed to as a single woman in the city was magnified by the fact that someone of her background may not have been able to afford private transport for a late-night journey and opted for a public bus instead. She was raped and violently beaten by the bus driver and five of his companions. Two weeks after the assault, Singh died of her injuries. On the one hand, the city offers potential freedoms to women; however, on the other, the public woman is also the object of suspicion, harassment and violence. Singh's death stimulated a vigorous public debate over women's 'safety' in public spaces which, in turn, led to a variety of measures designed to ensure such safety. Chapter 6 analyses the safety discourse and its entanglements with cultures of masculinity in the city.

Masculinities, Public Spaces and Their Cultures

Relationships between space and human life provide significant insights into the nature of social relationships. However, spaces also have identities, and when we think about cities, in particular, we are led to reflect upon the significance of two relatively recent ideas in human history, namely the 'public' and the 'private'. Whether or not the public–private categorisation has existed in all societies across time, it is certainly true that the idea that each gender has a separate sphere to which it 'naturally' belongs has become part of modern common sense.

Increasingly, through several processes of modernity, the different-spheres-for-different-genders perspective and the public–private distinction has tended towards convergence. Scholarship on the topic has approached the issue in different ways. Given the historical specificity of the Indian situation – its systems of distinction and hierarchies, the colonial experience and the interplay between the two, for example – it is unlikely, however, that writings that address the European experience (Habermas 1987; Sennett 1976) can capture local complexities. Also, in 'classical' discussions on the topic, the relationship between gender and space has tended to be sidestepped (Fraser 1992; Pateman 1989). Both in terms of the dimensions of historical and contemporary specificity and gender, it is important to formulate our understanding of the Indian situation in terms other than those that might have been true of the European case, while nevertheless borrowing from scholarship on these contexts.

Let us begin with the idea that the categories of the public and the private play an important role in the beliefs we hold about how society works and *should* work. It is commonplace to understand certain spaces (say, the street) as public, and others (say, the home) as private. There is also the belief that spaces thus categorised have their own characteristics in terms of *behaviours* expected of those located in those spaces, as well as the 'natural' claims of certain groups to them (say, men against women). In this sense, Jyoti Singh was a woman out of place and her presence was a provocation to cultures of masculinity in Indian cities.

The idea of 'publicness' invokes its putative opposite, that is, 'privateness'. However, the 'public' and the 'private' are not simple opposites, each with its own independent set of characteristics. It is, in fact, important to understand the public and the private – as suggested for 'masculinity' and 'femininity' earlier – as complementary rather than oppositional spheres. Chapter 5, which focuses upon members of the Bajrang Dal – the foot-soldiers of the Hindu right-wing – and their relationship with urban spaces, should be read as an attempt to problematise this distinction. It explores the ways in which cultures of masculinity enfold both private and public aspects. It suggests that the public nature of the city cannot be understood without an understanding of the ways in which discourses of the private – on religion and gender, for example – circulate.

Following this, if we remember that the public sphere has historically been defined as that of men and the private of women, then it becomes easier to understand why the two operate as *complements* to bolster gendered power. So, if the public is presented as the domain of action, 'rationality', 'educated opinion' and a realm where important matters of social life can be discussed among the 'rightful' claimants to the public sphere – men – then the private is imagined as that sphere where men can find relief from the 'difficult' tasks of engaging and forming the public sphere (Chatterjee 1993a). The private is represented as the 'soft' sphere where other kinds of sensibilities – 'feminine' – come into play. Here, women rule according to their capacities: skill at maternal care and emotional response; lack of ability for 'rational' and 'scientific' thinking, engagements with concrete matters such as the state, and abstract matters such as philosophy (Seidler 1994).

According to this line of thought, then, the private sphere is a necessary complement to the public as it provides a shelter from the pressures of the public; the private is, then, in a binary relation to the public in as much as it demonstrates why the public is a superior realm. As the discussion of this book demonstrates, the city – an entity whose 'mental life' (Simmel 1971) is characterised by the mixing of multiple populations in *public* spaces – is the ideal ground for exploring this complementarity. Men, as they go about the business of seeking pleasure and fortune in the pell-mell of urban life, do not define their masculine identity through just being in public. Rather, both their identities and that of urban spaces – which gender belongs where and how each must behave within them – are defined by the relationship between the home and the world. The ways in which 'home life' and 'public life' define each other are explored in Chapters 3 and 4, which concern men who visit 'sex clinics' and read 'footpath pornography' and Hindi detective pulp fiction, and in Chapter 5, which focuses upon the young men of the Hindu right.

The discussion of the book also suggests, then, that a significant point relating to the public–private binary is the need to make a further distinction between the private and the *domestic*. A woman may well have autonomy over a private space (say, a single woman who can afford to rent her own flat), but not over the domestic one, inasmuch as this is the space shared with the husband and, possibly, an extended family. While these terms may frequently be used interchangeably, the distinction is an important one. The discussion of Chapter 6 suggests that measures relating to the safety of women frequently seek to erase this distinction. That is, the possibility of private autonomy is sought to be brought within the ambit of the discourse of domesticity.

The most significant interrogations of the public–private distinction have been via feminist thought. An important ground for the feminist objections pertains to the fact that, in addition to its 'women's sphere' connotations, the private has come to denote the sphere that is (or should be) immune to 'outside' intervention. An important corollary of this is the belief that domestic violence is an 'internal' matter and the state, or other non-state bodies, should stay out of the matters of private (family) life. These notions of the inner and the outer aspects of social life are significant contributors to debates that relate to masculinities and the public and private spaces of cities. And finally, in this context, we should also remember that while we may now come across greater instances of violence against women – both actual and symbolic – in public spaces, there is no evidence that the incidence was lower in the past.[5] The relative lack of attention to the topic in past years may be due to a situation where men had a more undisputed relationship to the public spaces of the city. And that in the present time, there are more women who seek to occupy – or find themselves – in such spaces because of several social, cultural and economic changes. These, as the following chapters explore, form the background against which men in cities engage with urban spaces and women as well as seek to control them.

The historic division of social life as 'public' and 'private' has, simultaneously, entailed a division of institutions as public and private. And this, in turn, has led to what might be referred to as the gendering of institutions. According to this logic, public institutions are understood to be the 'natural' preserve of men and hence have expected to operate according to a variety of masculinist ideologies.

The recent salience of residents' welfare associations (RWAs) that carry out a variety of administrative tasks in middle-class localities (Harriss 2007) is an important example of the consolidation of masculine cultures within urban bodies and institutions. RWAs tend to be not just male-dominated (Kamath and Vijayabaskar 2009) but frequently act to enforce rules of residence and mobility that affect women and have been appropriately described as a kind of 'moral policing' (Kaushik 2019). Chapter 6 explores some aspects of contemporary forms of 'moral policing' that unfolds by imagining the city as a 'technotopia' – a context where intensive use of technology is imagined as addressing deep-rooted social and economic disparities – and discourses of women's safety.

A variety of patriarchal privileges and masculinist ideals are normalised through institutions such as bureaucracies, schools, the legal system and the police. That is, there are significant linkages between discourses and ideologies formulated at institutional sites (whether public or private) and behaviours and expectations at non-institutional spaces such as streets and parks. Hence, if we are to address violence against women in specific instances (say, on the street, at a bus stop or in a park), then a proper understanding of how 'institutional' thinking produces ideas of the street and the park – about the 'rights' of men and the 'dangers' for women – is important.

Following from the above, the idea that the public sphere is a masculinised one is the starting point for exploring the relationship between gender and publicness. This throws light upon the causes and nature of gender-based violence in public spaces and the anxieties and aspirations of masculinity that shape urban spaces. To return to a point made earlier, one of the first things we might say about violence against women – and other groups (such as non-heterosexual people) – in public spaces is that it relates to ideas of 'natural' claims to such spaces. That is to say that once the 'private' is defined as the (inferior) complement to the 'public', some, more than others, are seen to properly belong to the latter. The most straightforward way of elaborating upon this is to say that heterosexual men are seen to have a greater (if not exclusive) claim upon public space. But it is not as simple as that, and a more nuanced understanding is required. To introduce a level of complexity into our understanding, we might say, for example, that upper-caste middle-class heterosexual men are likely to have greater sway over public spaces compared to women, lower-caste, non-middle-class men and non-heterosexual men.

Linked to this is the popular perception that there are *specific conditions* under which men and women may access public spaces. Hence, while it is generally understood that men's access to public spaces need not be tied to a purpose (that is, carrying out specific tasks), the idea of women 'loitering' (Phadke, Khan and Ranade 2011) in such spaces becomes both incomprehensible and condemnable. A 2007 study carried out in Mumbai that asked respondents to indicate how men and women utilise space summarises its findings as follows:

> ... it is always men who are found occupying public space at rest.... Women, on the other hand, are rarely found standing or waiting in public spaces – they move across space from one point to another in a purposeful movement.... Women occupy public space essentially as a transit between one private space and another. (Ranade 2007: 152)

The idea of the necessity of purposeful activity by women emanates from many sites, of which the domestic is one of the most powerful. And, just as significantly, gender combines with different kinds of social attributes in restricting or permitting physical mobility. A study by the School of Women's Studies at Jadavpur University (SWSJU) points out that while there exist different restrictions on women's mobility outside the home among various caste and class groups, 'restrictions over time are completely absent in the case of upper-caste men. The only condition for men is that they should inform a family member in case of delay, indicating a gendered ideology at play' (SWSJU 2010: 30). Further, the discourse of women and 'purpose' is reinforced by a complementary formulation that refers to the 'balance' a working woman must achieve between her paid work and household responsibilities. So, a woman's 'paid work was not objectionable, provided she took good care of her household responsibilities' (SWSJU 2010: 38). To achieve this 'balance', however, it is imperative that women spend only that time in the public sphere that serves the purpose of carrying out the responsibilities of paid work and, thereafter, retreating to the home for other duties. In their interviews with a wide cross-section of men and women in Kolkata, SWSJU researchers were told that should a woman be found wanting in her abilities to balance work and home life, she must get back to where she belongs – the home (SWSJU 2010). As we will see in Chapter 5, the perceived ability to exert control over space and time is significant for an understanding of how masculinity is both defined and reinforced. Men range over multiple spaces, unconstrained by temporal regulations, and the apparent ability to best the capricious nature of the city through masculine capacities defines both male identity and the city as the playground of masculinity.

Spaces, as we know (Lefebvre 1991; Massey 1994), are not 'natural' in their attributes, and have a social character. In the Indian case, this relates to the specifics of local histories, which include religious belief, social distinctions such as caste and gender *and* – very significantly – the ways in which *regionally specific capitalism* engages with and produces constantly changing forms of social life. In very significant ways, this book is about the social life of cities within the crucible of capitalism. Each chapter is organised around this theme. However, the book's discussion is not an exploration of 'neoliberalism', the concept that is frequently deployed to explain a 'reconceptualized state project' (Gooptu 2013: 8) within which many activities carried out by the state are 'outsourced' to the private sector. As generally understood, if we refer to the Indian context, neoliberalism describes the situation where the state is no longer the dominant actor in social and economic contexts that it was in its post-colonial developmentalist incarnation (see, for example, Gupta 1998). In the early 1990s, as the title of an article suggests, 'the [Indian] state changed its mind' (Sengupta 2008) and launched upon 'the active process of creating space for private capital articulated through a market society' (Roy 2020: 219). I have, as I explain later, chosen to explore the specificity of the relationship between markets and social life through a framework that accounts for a situation of a 'reconceptualised state project' but also accounts for *local* social and economic histories that cannot be explained under the rubric of 'neoliberalism'. The following example that touches upon a masculinist understanding of urban space in India will be helpful.

During the 1990s, Devika (2009) suggests, there was an increasingly strident debate in the state of Kerala that indexed 'augmented public fears about sexual transgression' (Devika 2009: 33) by women. Hence, 'visions of dystopia in public discussion in Kerala in the 1990s' was 'painted heavily with the horrors of "sexuality unleashed"' (Devika 2009: 33). Significantly, young women who had been subject to sexual crimes were often portrayed not as victims, but those whose 'worldliness' – particularly related to their presence in urban public spaces – was to blame for the crimes they suffered. A court judgment on the so-called Vithura case of 2000 involving the serial rape of a teenage girl noted that she was a '"lascivious strumpet" who, as the days passed by ... became more and more coquettish and voluptuous by availing the services of beauty parlours' (Sreekumar 2001, quoted in Devika 2009: 33). As Devika points out, the 'fixation with the sexualisation of female bodies is ... telling of how misogyny forms a sizable part of elitist cultural panic' (2009: 34). Women in public spaces not conforming to masculine rules of 'modesty' are frequently the source of a great deal of masculine (and patriarchal) anxiety regarding the apparent decline of social values. As the discussion of Chapters 3 and 4 explains, discourses of masculinity engage with the idea of the 'independent' woman – those who seek to occupy public spaces in equal measure to men – through ideas that represents them as desirable but also threatening subjects of the city. Invocations of 'neoliberalism' cannot explain how, in such circumstances, women in cities might both exercise 'autonomy' – as participants in consumerist activity, for example – and demonstrate deference to custom through 'appropriate' consuming behaviour.

The book suggests that it is inadequate to invoke 'neoliberalism' – as it is so frequently done – as an explanatory framework that can account for the complexity of lifeways under regionally specific forms of capitalism. I argue that there is a need to better understand the relationship between its regionally specific forms and the social life it encounters in each location. It is in this context that I introduce two terms, 'post-nationalism' and 'moral consumption' (Srivastava 2015), to make sense of relationships between older structures that produce gender norms, rapidly transforming urban milieus, and the newer ways of being that are produced at the juncture of 'gender' and the 'city'. These terms will find play in different parts of the book and also act as unifying concepts for the disparate contexts of analysis.

Post-nationalism

The sense in which I invoke the term 'post-nationalism' is different from some other recent deployments that have similar etymological grounding. In terms of the present discussion, the term 'post-national' does *not* mean to imply that the nation-state is insignificant as a context of analysis, or that we now live in a 'post-patriotic' age where the most significant units of analysis are certain 'postnational social formations' (Appadurai 1993: 411) – such as non-governmental organisations (NGOs) – that putatively problematise nationalist and statist perspectives. Further, my deployment is also different from another sense in which it has been used. Here, it is posited as 'a distinct ethico-political horizon and a position of critique' and a concept 'that can be instantiated by suspending the idea of the nation as a prior theoretical-political horizon, and thinking through its impossibility, even while located uncomfortably within its bounds' (De Alwis et al. 2009: 35). Post-nationalism, as I will deploy the term, is the articulation of the nationalist emotion with the robust desires engendered through new practices of consumerism and their associated cultures of privatisation and individuation (see also Gooptu 2013).

As suggested earlier, I wish to invoke 'post-nationalism' as a context of analysis in preference to 'neoliberalism' (Flew 2014; D. Harvey 2005; Ong 2006; Rose 1990), which might be interpreted as describing the same set of social and economic circumstances. The key point I wish to make is that neoliberalism 'is unable to account for the specific *national* histories that transform into postnational ones' (Srivastava 2017: 99, original emphasis) and that there is no 'universal neoliberal moment' (Srivastava 2017: 99) that allows for a 'global' view. As Terry Flew (2014) points out,

> [the] debate about neoliberalism as *one of a number of competing ideas about the organization of capitalist economies and societies* has been largely overwhelmed by those arguments that present neoliberalism as the ascendant ideology of global capitalism, so that the world is seen as being, or becoming, more and more neoliberal in its institutional structure and policy choices. (Flew 2014: 55, emphasis added)

My use of 'post-nationalism' seeks to avoid the 'too-easy application of models of capitalism and neoliberalism that obscure the variety of local experience', as Mains (2007: 660) suggests in his discussion of Ethiopian young men and their experiences of time and space. This is not to suggest that there is no empirical evidence pointing to the set of economic, administrative and cultural policies, activities and aspirations now identified as 'neoliberal'. It has been powerfully demonstrated that, in different parts of the world, there is now a common language through which human progress is spoken of – in terms of 'self-management', 'self-discipline' and 'enterprise' (Gooptu 2013;

Rose 1990); 'flexibility' (Freeman 2014); and 'reflexibility' and 'optimization' (Ong 2006). Such prescriptions regarding how the state and citizens might 'move ahead' and 'maximise' collective and individual welfare address a variety of contexts. A vast and productive body of scholarly literature has analysed how neoliberal thought spans across education, personal relationships, urban governance, infrastructure development, health policy and (perhaps most importantly) relationships between the nation-state and its citizens.

There has, however, been far less focus on how the subjects of neoliberal policies and exhortations *engage* with them. This requires closer – ethnographic – attention to specific historical and cultural conditions within which new forms of economic and cultural processes unfold. Otherwise, there is the risk that we simply 'read off', say, the Indian situation from analyses built upon the North American or the European one. The reverse would, quite rightly, be considered preposterous.

The significance of the local and the historical as crucial to understanding the *varied* trajectories of capitalism is powerfully underlined by Carla Freeman (2014) in her ethnographic approach to neoliberalism in Barbados. While underling the global currency of certain terms – 'affective labour', for example – that are used to describe neoliberal economic and cultural processes, Freeman asks important questions regarding their meaning within specific contexts. This is more than an anthropological fetish; rather, it goes to the heart of an understanding of a global condition in situated ways:

> What is the difference between the requirement of affective labor demanded by one's corporate employer, as in Hochschild's [1983 study of] flight attendants, the demands as set by the clients of one's service occupation, as in the case of many of the Barbadian entrepreneurs, and the demands they set for themselves? How does the history of the plantation and the dominance of a tourism economy lend a particular set of meanings to such emotional labors in the current service economy? (Freeman 2014: 136)

Building upon Michel Foucault's notion of 'biopolitics', Aihwa Ong suggests that '[n]eoliberalism is merely the most recent development of such techniques that govern human life, that is, a governmentality that relies on market knowledge' (Ong 2006: 13). However, though neoliberal discourses might foreground the need 'to respond quickly and with agility to the ever changing conditions and requirements of market trajectories' (Ong 2006: 125), the nature of the responses cannot be predicted without a biography of their spaces. In this way, as with Freeman and others (Mains 2007; Baviskar and Ray 2011), I seek to explore localised engagements with 'market trajectories' that, I will suggest in the book, are usefully captured through the term 'post-nationalism'. Rather than 'simply "localize" an understanding of neoliberalism' (Freeman 2014: 35), I use the post-national framework to explore the actual – rather than idealised – forms of relationships between markets and social processes. This requires an understanding of the ways in which people make a home within the market, rather than seeking to flee from it to an imagined home.

In this book, post-nationalism describes the nuances of relationships between local and global processes, including those of class, caste, religious identities, gender, the state and consumer cultures. My discussion focuses on the ways in which experiences of 'masculinity' and the 'city' are intertwined and produced through registers of meaning that cannot be reduced to either the 'local' or the 'global'; both at the level of abstract discourses and the quotidian experience of being men in the city, how local histories and preoccupations engage with transnational 'flows' (Appadurai 1996) have a great deal to tell us about gender in the city. The discussion also emphasises the significance of analysing the manner in which 'the national' plays a significant – but changing – role in the making of Indian social life. And, finally, the book suggests that it is important to understand contemporary cultures of the Indian city through a conjoint understanding of those of masculinity because the city in India has *always* been imagined as a masculine space. And that, in this way, anthropological and sociological engagements with urban life in India – and what it tells about Indian society in general – are incomplete without a focus on cultures of masculinity. Subsequent chapters will reflect upon relationships between the city, masculinity, the state and the market in different contexts. At this juncture, however, it is useful to illustrate the local – post-national – nature of certain global processes through a brief exploration of the contemporary politics of urban spaces in Delhi.[6]

In 1999, soon after being elected to office, Delhi's erstwhile chief minister, Sheila Dikshit, 'called for an active participation of Residents Welfare Associations (RWAs) in governance' (Ojha 1999). The rationale for this was the apparent 'failure' of 'civic agencies' to carry out their normal tasks. The chief minister's secretary noted that the call to actively involve RWAs in urban governance heralded a new era, marking as it did 'the first step towards a responsive management of the city' (Ojha 1999). Positing a 'moral' distinction between the state and the 'community,' the secretary further noted that such a 'failure' of 'civic agencies' meant that 'it's really time for the community to be given direct control of managing the affairs of the city' (Ojha 1999). The government subsequently decided to 'empower' RWAs to 'take certain decisions on their own' (Ojha 1999). It was proposed that RWAs be given control over the management of resources such as parks, community halls, parking places, sanitation facilities and local roads. A more direct relationship between the state and RWAs was also mooted through the idea of joint surveys of encroached land – that is, land that had been 'illegally' occupied, usually by slum-dwellers – with the possibility that all illegal structures would 'then be demolished in a non-discriminatory manner' (Ojha 1999). Finally, it was proposed that RWAs be allowed to impose fines on government agencies that failed to carry out their assigned tasks.

In 2005, the Delhi state government announced that it would raise electricity tariffs by 10 per cent. A body known as the Delhi Residents' Welfare Association Joint Front (RWAJF) was formed in the same year to protest against the measure. The Front consisted of 195 separate member RWAs from around the city. The increase in power rates for domestic consumers was the second one since the state-owned electricity body was 'unbundled' in June 2002 as part of power-sector reforms. As a result, three privately owned companies secured contracts for electricity distribution (Sethi 2009). There was vigorous protest over the price raise and, in addition to the RWAJF, NGOs such as People's Action and another group known as Campaign Against Power Tariff Hike (CAPTH) joined the collective effort. Individual RWAs asked their members to refuse payment of the extra amount, while the RWAJF lobbied the government and organised city-wide protests. The protests gained broad coverage in both print and electronic media and, echoing Gandhian anti-colonial strategies, the organisers were reported to have deployed 'the ideas of "civil disobedience" and "people's power"' (Sethi 2009: 5). Indeed, the parallels drawn between the Gandhian anti-colonial moment and the present times were even more explicit, with the convener of the RWAJF referring to the protests as 'non-violent *Satyagraha*' (Sirari 2006: 5). The term *satyagrah*, made up of the words *satya* (truth) and *agrah* (insistence), was used by Mahatma Gandhi to refer to non-violent resistance in his struggle against colonial rule. Eventually, the Delhi government backed down, and the price raise was shelved. According to Sanjay Kaul, the president of the People's Action NGO, the protest's success heralded the making of a 'middle-class revolution' (Sethi 2009).

The circulation of ideas of civil disobedience, *satyagrah*, and revolution, as well as the consolidation of the notion of a 'people' contesting the state, occur in a context that might be called post-national. In this specific context, the moral frisson of terms such as *satyagrah* and 'revolution', a significant cultural context engendered through anti-colonial sentiment and action, no longer holds. Indeed, in an era of post-Nehruvian economic liberalisation characterised by consumerist modernity (Fernandes 2006; Mazzarella 2003; Osella and Osella 2009), the ethico-moral universe of the anti-colonial struggle is no longer part of popular public discourse. Within this new context, earlier emphases on 'nation-building', the ethics of saving and delayed gratification for the national good – indispensable ideological accompaniments to civil disobedience and *satyagrah* – do not find any resonance (see, for example, Mazzarella 2003).

National and post-national moments are, of course, also linked to specific forms of identity. As I discuss later through the example of a masculine type I refer to as the Five-Year Plan hero, both masculine national identities and ideas of urban life in the period immediately following the end of colonial rule were influenced by cultural and economic logics specific to the period. The current period is characterised by cultural and economic flows of a different order, and these require different conceptual tools of analysis. However, and as I have noted earlier, the term 'post-national' does *not*, in my usage, mean to imply that the nation-state is insignificant as a context of analysis. Rather, it refers to the new ways in which the nation-state relates to citizens, the contexts within which it relates to *different* fractions of citizens – particularly the middle classes – and the manner in which it relates to capital.

Finally, in this context, one of the most significant ways in which the post-national moment resonates within the politics of urban space concerns the repositioning of the language of anti-colonial nationalism from the national sphere to the suburban one. This, in turn, also indexes the move from the idea of the 'national' family to the nuclear (gated) one and the translation of the notion of nationalist solidarity to (middle) class solidarity. Indeed, the most significant ways in which apartments in gated communities are advertised is through the trope of the nuclear family heralding a new kind of national identity (see, for example, Brosius 2012: chs. 1–2 and Srivastava 2012). This also has specific consequences for how women are imagined in an urban context, for the shift in gaze is from the national *family* to the new nuclear *family*. There is, in other words, no symbolic space for imagining a woman out of the context of the family, including ideas of non-reproductive sexuality; the un-attached woman's being 'does not meet normative standards of feminine beauty, reproductivity, and heterosexuality [and hence] becomes excluded not only from marriage but also from social recognition' (Lamb 2018: 65). The politics of masculinity in the time of post-nationalism is one that enfolds meanings of gender that draw upon notions of 'Indian values' as well as global processes.

Moral Consumption

This section outlines the second of the two concepts I utilise as background to the discussion of the book, namely moral consumption. At different points in the book, I will suggest that discourses of 'proper' masculinity (Chapter 3) and 'femininity' (Chapter 6) are couched in the language of 'appropriate' consumption that allows for participation in urban worlds, 'protection' from putative threats to masculinity and the 'inappropriate' behaviour by women. Moral consumption refers to a context 'where … active participation in consumerism is accompanied by an anxiety about it and its relationship to "Indianness"' (Srivastava 2011: 381). It also, as I explain later, indexes a situation where consumerist activity is accompanied by discourses on the possibility of exercising control over consumption activity. This is different from viewing consumerism as a threat to established lifeways, which, as some scholars suggest, is a significant reaction to consumerism in India (van Wessel 2004). Rather, I suggest that recent contexts of consumerism indicate that the long-standing cultural discourses of the sacrificing and nurturing mother that actively proscribe 'indulgent' consumption (see, for example, Donner 2011) can be encompassed *within* acts of consumerism by women. Let me provide two examples to illustrate this point. First, women visitors to the Disneyfied (and hyper-consumerist) Akshardham temple complex in Delhi can move seamlessly between playing consumers and devoutly religious persons precisely because the same space provides opportunities for both consumerism and religiosity (Brosius 2012; Srivastava 2011). That is to say, the (masculine) anxiety over female consumption is assuaged through a process of moral consumption whereby women take part in hyper-consumerism *and are also* able to withdraw to the realms of religiosity.

And, though each realm is interpenetrative, each is imagined as separate. Hence,

> [t]he making of a moral middle class, one that has control over the processes of consumption, and hence modernity, is, in fact, located in the processes of … consumption itself. For it is only through consumption that one can demonstrate *mastery* over it. So, one consumes a wide variety of products of contemporary capitalism – IMAX cinema, the Disneyfied boat ride, Akshardham baseball caps – in combination with 'spiritual' goods such as religion and nationalism. What differentiates the moral middle class from others is its *capacity* to take part in these *diverse* forms of consumption, whereas a more 'de-racinated' (or 'Westernized') middle class might only be able to consume the products of capitalism. (Srivastava 2011: 381)

The relationship between the new and the old middle classes is, of course, of relevance to the politics of gender in contemporary India but is also of more general significance. It is, for example, at the heart of contemporary discourses of Hindutva that is couched in the language of anti-elitism. This speaks in the name of an 'ordinary' middle-class citizen who has been denied 'his [*sic*]' rights due to 'appeasement' of, say, religious minorities and the poor (Srivastava 2020).

My second example of moral consumption draws upon the rise of gated residential enclaves in India. There is a long-standing discourse of public-ness in India within which the place of women is a fraught one. The woman in public is seen to have abandoned her natural task of being the guardian of tradition, one task connected to the domestic sphere. Within gated communities, however – where the 'street' is not the street, and, for precisely that reason, is a site of intense middle-class activity – 'public' women can be both the guardian of tradition *and* take part in sexualised presentations of the self. So, while on the occasion of the Hindu festival of Karva Chauth, women dressed in traditional (and elaborate) Indian clothing pray for their husband's welfare, they can also be found pacing the condominium grounds on their exercise rounds dressed in skin-hugging clothing. And, unlike the constraints placed on women at public celebrations of Holi (the festival of splashing coloured water), at one gated community where I carried out fieldwork, Holi celebrations were sponsored by an alcohol multinational and men *and* women danced together to Bollywood songs on an open-air stage. Consumerism here is the grounds for the making of a moral middle class.

That is, through practising moral consumption, women are seen to be not determined by modernity but are able to take part in it and 'return home' to tradition when required. Post-national consumerism provides the *grounds* for the making of moral consumption: for one must take a vigorous part in consumerism to be able to display one's ability to withdraw from it. The relationship between post-nationalism, moral consumption and the new urban spaces of gated communities also speaks to the long history of anxiety about the public woman through the question: how can the public woman belong both to the world and the home? As the various chapters of the book will point out, 'secure' domestic spaces serve to define the ways in which men might range over the city.

Masculinities and Colonialism

The ways in which cultures of masculinity and those of the city relate to each other has a history that must be accounted for an understanding of the contours of the present. In all cultures, including the European, a wide variety of conceptions of masculinity existed before the advent of the modern era. Many forms of expression – body appearance, gestures, voice, and so on – were seen to be part of maleness. In fact, some theorists argue for a strong connection between modernity and currently dominant forms of masculinity. It has been suggested that the binarism and essentialism of modern thought that characterised diverse fields of activity also had a strong influence upon ideas of gender identity. This was manifested in a 'separation of reason from nature [which] works to divide men from their emotions and feelings which become threatening to [their] identities as men.... [Men are exhorted to] disdain emotions and feelings as signs of weakness and so as potentially compromising [their] sense of male identity' (Seidler 1994: x–xi).

Increasingly, in terms of the European Enlightenment discourse, this came to be expressed in terms of a split between being 'scientific' and 'rational' and being 'unscientific' and 'irrational'. And further, it was accompanied by the idea that the only 'real' things were those that could be measured and quantified. Indeed, for influential thinkers such as Francis Bacon, science itself came to be seen as a new masculine philosophy (Seidler 1994: 6). Modernist social theory has been greatly influenced by developments in the seventeenth and eighteenth centuries in terms of ideas of 'reason', 'science', 'emotions', quantification, and so on. As we will see in Chapter 2, a significant strand in Indian nationalism was to cleave to this line of thought through positing the city itself as a place of reason and science and hence a masculine space.

While social theory and historical analysis based upon western contexts provide a useful background, this is inadequate for an understanding of gendered complexities in other parts of the world. We might, here, begin with the colonial context. The colonial era was particularly important in the career of modern masculinity. Colonialism consolidated 'hegemonic' masculinity, which combined the valorisation of science, 'feminisation' of non-European people and the idea of masculinity as an irreducible essence. In many ways, then, colonialism became an expression of the masculine ideal which had been developing in Europe through the seventeenth and eighteenth centuries. Critical studies of colonialism also suggest that it is impossible to understand contemporary *European* male identity without also taking account of the colonial encounter. However, we should not understand from this that, for example, colonial powers, such as the British in India, 'invented' certain types of masculine cultures and introduced them into the culture of the colonies; and that certain ideas that came to be associated with masculinity – such as being 'war-like' – simply did not exist before colonialism. As Rosalind O'Hanlon has argued, 'martial masculinity' (O'Hanlon 1997: 17) *was* an important aspect of pre-colonial life, one which the colonisers built upon and incorporated into the discourses of colonial masculinity.

Nevertheless, it is important to understand the *intensification* of certain forms of discourses regarding masculinity that occurred during the colonial period and their continued circulation during our own time, inflected, no doubt, through the politics of the present. The term 'colonial masculinity' expresses the importance of the relationship between two social contexts, namely colonialism and masculinity. Colonial masculinity does not simply refer to the ways in which colonial processes produced certain ideas about natives; rather, this term also suggests that colonialism influenced the identities of both the colonised and the colonisers. It is in this sense that it was suggested earlier that the making of European male identities during the nineteenth century cannot be understood in isolation from the events and processes of the colonial era. One scholar speaks of the relationship between European identity and the colonial sphere by asking us to 'rethink European cultural genealogies across the board and to question whether the key symbols of modern western societies – liberalism, nationalism, state welfare, citizenship, culture, and "Europeanness" itself – were not clarified among Europe's colonial exiles and by those colonized classes caught in their pedagogic net in Asia' (Stoler 1995: 16).

Chapter 2 reflects upon the 'pedagogic net' as it unfolded in the Indian context. It explores how local versions of global colonial discourses on masculinity came into play in the making of post-colonial Indian identities. The background to the chapter – that explores nationalist ideas on Indian masculinity and the city as the site of its elaboration – is linked to the prominent discourse that circulated around the education of the English elite. The English public school was crucial in the development of what has been referred to as 'muscular Christianity' and 'moral manliness' (Mangan 1896) through which colonialism came to be identified both as a divine calling and as a rite of passage for 'real' men. The ideal of 'moral' manhood (Mangan 1986: 147) took on the nature of an imperative that defined the essence of elite British male-hood and explained the glittering successes of the imperial enterprise. A race filled with moral and physical certitude, instilled on the playing fields of the English public school, now sallied forth to sow the effete, tropical winds with the manly seeds of a more robust environment. In its Indian incarnation, the politics of class, caste and urban elite identity transformed this discourse into one of the post-colonial masculine-urbanism. It is important to remember, however (and as we will also see in the following chapter), that Indians did not simply *reproduce* ways of thinking that originated in England; the English public-school emphasis on corporeal manliness was transformed into a 'scientific' one, where the city became the site of rational thought as well as a rite of passage and a 'robust' post-colonial Indian identity was sought to be nurtured within its confines.

Within the colonial sphere, the obverse of the 'masculinisation' of Englishness was the 'feminisation' of the natives, where the latter term refers to the attribution of 'women-like' traits to men in the context of the lower value placed on female gender identity. Hence, whether in Asia or in other parts of the colonised world, there emerged a remarkably consistent discourse on the native male's incapacity for self-government and informed decision-making due to his inherent 'effeminacy' (see, for example, Sinha 1997).[7]

Colonial discourses of masculinity did not, however, completely obliterate older and more ambiguous contexts of gender norms (see, for example, Hansen 2004 on the 'homoerotic gaze' and transvestite performers in Gujarati, Parsi and Marathi theatre). However, the colonial characterisation of the 'effeminate' native was one that particularly rankled certain sections of the native intelligentsia. Historians have pointed out that the 'self-image of effeteness' (Roselli 1980) came to be widely accepted among nineteenth-century Indian (Hindu) intelligentsia, and many came to believe that their 'emasculation' was, among other things, due to the long history of Muslim rule that had reduced Hindus to the status of a subject population. Attempts at 'rectification' were many and varied. One response was connected to the acceptance of the association between science and masculinity, as I explore in Chapter 2, and consisted in promoting the spread of western science. The other, as Chapter 5 explores, consisted in the making of a masculinised *Hindu* identity. What is distinctive about the discussion of Chapter 5 is its focus on the ways in which a new Hindu identity is sought to be constructed not through a withdrawal from the world and a return to an 'essential' core; rather, that it consists in multiple entanglements with the cultures of the city.

From Colonial Scientific Masculinity to the Post-colonial Five-Year Plan Hero: A New Man of the City

Colonial-era nationalist and post-colonial preoccupations – marked by an association between science, masculinity and the city – gave birth to a particular imagination of the 'new' man of the city. To better grasp the complexity of post-colonial gender politics – especially in the context of masculine subjectivity – it is particularly important to engage with the cultural discourse of science and rationality in the life of the modernising nation-state beyond the initial years after independence in 1947. The project of the transformation of the 'native' to the 'citizen' was a gendered one, and science and 'reason' played a particularly important role in defining the contours of modern identity in India. The national heroes of post-colonial modernity were, typically, men such as P. C. Mahalanobis (1893–1972), an active Brahmo Samaji,[8] keen researcher of anthropometry, founder of the Indian Statistical Institute and a leading influence upon the formulation of the second Five-Year Plan (Rudra 1996; see also Chatterjee 1993b: ch. 10; Nikhil Menon 2022 for a discussion of planning in India).

It is the context of twentieth-century development theory, as expressed through the post-independence Soviet-inspired planning regime and concurrently articulated in Hindi films of the 1950s and 1960s, that provides the next rung of my discussion.[9] In another work on the career of India's most famous 'playback' singer, Lata Mangeshkar, I have noted the emergence during the immediate post-independence period of a masculine type

I referred to as the Five-Year Plan hero (Srivastava 2006). I suggested that Lata's 'little-girl' voice should be counterpoised not just to any postcolonial masculinity but to quite a specific one, that of the Five-Year Plan hero. The iconic presence of the Five-Year Plan hero gained its legitimacy through the idea that he stood both for government intervention and for delayed gratification through the reinvestment of savings for the 'national' good.

The Five-Year Plan hero of Indian films was – unambiguously – a man of the city and represented a particular formulation of Indian masculinity where manliness came to be attached not to bodily representations or aggressive behaviour but, rather, to being 'scientific' and 'rational'. This was the idea of a middle-class 'epistemological' or science-based masculinity as it emerged from sites such as the Doon School (Chapter 2).[10] One of the ways in which this came to be represented on screen was through the operation of very specific spatial strategies, where roads and highways and metropolitan spaces came to be the 'natural' habitat of the Five-Year Plan hero. So, for example, in many Hindi films in the 1950s and 1960s, the bitumen road was a significant space of encounter between the hero and the heroine, the backdrop to crucial song sequences, and a place that provided musical interludes for the display of the Five-Year Plan hero's technological aptitude as he adeptly handled that epitome of modernist desire – the motor car. Indeed, roads and highways in these films carried such an aura of a planned modernity – all those aspirations of 'progressing' in both literal and figurative senses – that the woman at the steering wheel and women on bicycles riding along the open highway become one of the most powerfully evocative representations of the 'modern' Indian womanhood; 'these' women come to embody a manual dexterity that marked them as visibly different.

The recurring association between the road/highway and the Five-Year Plan hero serves to emphasise another point: that of the 'natural' milieu of the Five-Year Plan hero – the metropolis.[11] We get some idea of the metropolis as a structuring trope through a series of post-independence Hindi films. So, 'in films such as *Shri 420* (1955, Raj Kapoor), *New Delhi* (1956, Mohan Segal), *Sujata* (1959, Bimal Roy) and *Anuradha* (1960, Hrishikesh Mukherjee), the struggle over meaning and being in a post-colonial society takes place in a context where the metropolis is always a wilful presence' (Srivastava 1998: 165). Here, as in other films, the metropolis is, by turns, a site of decadence and extravagance, luring 'innocent' men into its web, a progressive influence upon 'backward' intellects, and the promise of a contractual civil society that would undermine the atavism of kin and caste affiliations, ostensibly typified by the cinematic village. These themes – particularly the one related to the city as a threat to masculinity – reappear, as we will see in Chapters 3 and 4, with great force in the contemporary period.

Spatial strategies are particularly important representational tools in these, and other similar, films where, as I have noted in another discussion, 'the aura of the metropolis manifests itself through a new language of cinematic space, [and] where striation and secularisation become important expressive principles' (Srivastava 1998: 165). So, the opening shots of *New Delhi* establish the sense of the post-colonial modernity the hero hopes to find in the milieu of the city. It is a modernity that expresses itself through the measured grid of roads, traffic lights and footpaths; and the camera, the hero and the audience look out at these landmarks from a car being driven along major thoroughfares along which are dotted office buildings and other memorials to the nation-state. In *New Delhi/*New Delhi, economic planning and city planning come together 'at a juncture where state intervention and a geometrical sensibility of modernity produce a peculiarly post-colonial nationalist aesthetics' (Srivastava 1998: 166).

Aditionally, an important strand in the 1950s and 1960s films was the profession of the hero: quite often he was an engineer (building roads or dams), a doctor, a scientist or a bureaucrat. In significant instances, the filmic presence of the hero was not as a muscular 'type' and could now easily be characterised as 'effeminate'. However, this aspect of the heterosexual hero could coexist quite comfortably with a nationalist ideology that identified post-independence manliness as linked to the 'new' knowledges of science which, it was held, would transform the 'irrational' native into the modern citizen. In the field of popular culture, then, the immediate post-independence period was particularly important in terms of representations of what could be called the aesthetic of planning and development.

In some instances, the aura of the filmic city was presented as the capacity of the male body to infiltrate those national spaces – rural ones, for example – that may still be under the sway of 'primitive' influences. Here, the metropolitan male body hurtled along national highways and train tracks, en route to the cinematic village; its object of social transformation to be achieved through the transformation of 'backward' personalities; its presence became metropolitan virtues incarnate and the chief therapy for regressive tendencies that needed improvement. The hero was both an instrument of change and its personification. His metropolitan male body *was* the nation.

In the context of popular culture, the time of the Five-Year Plan hero had run its course by the late 1960s. Of course, even during the height of his popularity, the economically and sexually frugal saviour of the nation – who also saved on its behalf – had been shadowed by the vigorous urbanity of the on-screen personality of actor Shammi Kapoor (1931–2011). However, the most decisive blow to the Five-Year Plan hero's identity as a culturally meaningful icon was delivered by the complex screen presence of the Bollywood superstar Amitabh Bachchan (b. 1942). The grounds for the articulation of the masculinity portrayed by Bachchan were, however, prepared in a number of ways throughout the late 1960s and into the 1970s. So, for example, credit is due to the antics of the vehemently exuberant Jeetendra (b. 1942) and the slow but steady filmic journey of Dharmendra (b. 1935) from the 'softness' of *Bandini* (1963, dir. Bimal Roy) to the muscular jocularity of *Sholay* (1975, dir. Ramesh Sippy). Of course, an important context in popular culture representations of masculinity during this period was the very real shift in the context of class consciousness, with the 'lower classes' finding an important niche both as characters and as audiences (on this see Mishra 2002).

The Demise of the Five-Year Plan Hero: Small-town Men in the City

It has been variously noted that Amitabh Bachchan's success lies in the anti-state, 'angry-young man' presence of his on-screen persona (Prasad 1998). This is no doubt true. I would also like to suggest, however, that Amitabh Bachchan's characters also brought to the screen some very significant aspects that have to do with relationships between 'provincial masculinity', the metropolis and the consuming and expressive capacities of the previously unrepresented small-town men. In particular, this relates to skin colour, language, homoeroticism and an *incipient* relationship with commodities. Anecdotally speaking, in various discussions about the appeal of Amitabh Bachchan with men in cities such as Patna and Lucknow, I have yet to come across a single instance of where their responses were articulated in terms of his anti-statism. In non-metropolitan areas (and indeed in larger cities), the state, simultaneously as it is loathed, is also an object of great desire. There are the everyday complaints about its arbitrariness and high-handedness (Gupta 2012), but alongside these is an almost sensuous craving to be recognised, touched, fondled and assimilated by it. The loving detail with which newspapers – particularly in smaller towns – report the 'movements' of the district magistrate, the superintendent of police, the housing board chairman, the cane commissioner, the revenue commissioner, the station house officer and a variety of other officials reflect the situation of constraint and desire with respect to the state.

The two significant features that have tended to be overlooked in explanations of Bachchan's popularity have to do with his skin colour and his language. Bachchan was perhaps the first of the dark-skinned heroes on the Hindi cinema screen. Even in *Teesri Kasam* (1966, dir. Basu Bhattacharya), the role of a Bihari (most likely lower caste) villager was played by a very unlikely, fair-skinned Raj Kapoor. Through the late 1970s and 1980s, the Bachchan persona foregrounded the provincial-male-body-in-the-city. It was one that was easily recognisable by the skin colour and the distinctive Hindi spoken in the city of Allahabad (now renamed Prayagraj). The latter aspect became such an indispensable part of the Bachchan persona that in, say, *Namak Halal* (1982, dir. Prakash Mehra), though Bachchan's on-screen character (Arjun) starts off being a village yokel from Haryana (going by his accent), as the film progresses, the Haryanvi 'Jat' accent gives way to an Allahabadi lilt. So, both through his colouration and his language, the on-screen Bachchan marks an important move away from the Five-Year Plan hero. What I wish to suggest is that a significant aspect of the Bachchan phenomenon concerns the representation of provincial masculinity in a metropolitan milieu. And, further, the provincial man comes to be associated with various forms of action, commerce and individualism. Hence, the Bachchan hero moves – physically – through a world of container terminals, five-star hotels, wedding cakes, fancy shoes, international brand alcohol, dance halls, casinos, airports and other sites and objects of industrial production *and* consumption. The Bachchan hero is the first-generation consumer, having recently broken the shackles of the savings regime of the Five-Year Plan political economy. He is as much anti-statist in taking the law into his own hands as announcing the beginnings of a consumerist agenda. His significance lies in the fact that his actions represent the loss of faith in the intentions and capacities of the Five-Year Plan state, as well as the establishment of the provincial male as a potential participant in consumerism.

Bachchan's on-screen persona also represents the incipient forms of post-nationalism and moral consumption. Through Bachchan's body, metropolitan and provincial spaces become intertwined: provincial masculinity haunts metropolitan spaces, seeking to share in its fortune, interrogating its lifeways and taking up residence in its *jhuggi-jhopri* (shanty) localities. I explore this context in Chapter 3, which takes up for discussion urban 'sex clinics' and the 'footpath pornography' they are associated with. The clinics are visited by poor men in search of 'strength', 'vigour' and 'performance', and the booklets are significant texts in terms of providing models of subaltern urban masculine identity and behaviour.

Conclusion: Masculinities and Modernities

This chapter has sought to provide a selective account of the variety of relationships between myriad contexts of urbanity, modernity and masculinities. The chapters that follow pick up on some of the strands outlined in the earlier discussion. In particular, I focus upon sites that allow for explorations across registers of science as a discourse of the self, urban life and gender identity and the refashioning of the 'tradition–modernity' dialectic – rather than its dissolution – in a time of consumerist efflorescence. Concurrently, the discussion will move across different socio-economic registers to locate cultures of masculinity within multiple cultural and political economies.

Ideologies, as Henri Lefebvre (1991) was to point out, need spaces to be institutionalised and become visible. Educational institutions are crucial spaces for the making of gender identities, and Chapter 2 begins the task of exploring connections between ideologies and spaces through focusing upon discourses of science and middle-class masculinity as it unfolded at a significant site of educational modernity in India, namely the Doon School, a famous boys' boarding school in the north Indian city of Dehradun. Apart from outlining the relationship between nationalism, masculinity and the city, this chapter has another objective. It provides the background for differentiating 'nationalism' from 'post-nationalism'. That is, it lays the groundwork for thinking about forms of nationalist discourses and the constantly evolving nature of ideas of national identity and masculinist discourses across times, spaces and social contexts.

Chapter 3 begins the move towards exploring facets of post-nationalism and moral consumption as aspects of urban masculinities. It focuses on subaltern men of the city and urban 'sex clinics' – advertised as sites of traditional medicine – visited by them. I suggest in the chapter that the sex clinics of Delhi and Mumbai are significant sites of knowledge and debate regarding working-class masculine identities. The chapter also analyses the publications I term 'footpath pornography'. If sex clinics are sites of practical advice on masculinity-in-the-city, the footpath booklets contain masculine imaginaries that construct fantasy worlds of life in the city. The chapter explores the ways in which masculine identities are sought to be made within the crucible of consumer cultures, and the desire and fear of the 'modern' woman.

Chapter 4 continues the exploration of post-nationalism and the city by focusing on another kind of popular literature that enjoys great popularity in the urban milieu. It extends the investigation into the location of masculine forms – and their elaboration – within new cultural and political economies that, notwithstanding their 'newness', sustain traditional structures of power and dominance. The chapter investigates the masculine and sexual cultures of contemporary Hindi-language 'detective' novels by focusing on the writings of one of India's biggest-selling authors, Ved Prakash Sharma. The chapter suggests that the sexual motif in the novels sits alongside an unstated discourse of 'Indian traditions' – that of *brahmacharya* (celibacy) and 'the stable Indian family'. The novels, the chapter argues, reinstate and sustain the meaning of masculinity-in-the-city through a constant relay of choices between the world of globalised consumerist modernity and 'traditional' morality.

Chapter 5 builds upon the discussion on the spaces of masculinity through an investigation of the entanglement of two distinct ideologies, namely religion and masculinities, across different urban locations. The chapter focuses upon a group of young men belonging to the Bajrang Dal, an organisation of the Hindu right, to explore their lives as urban subjects whose actions unfold across several registers, of which 'Hindu nationalism' is just one. The discussion embarks upon an ethnography of 'fragmentation' and 'splitting', presenting these as significant processes in the making of masculine identities. It suggests that these concepts foreground the ways in which new consumer cultures play a role in the making of masculine power and the notion of an 'all-consuming man'.

Contemporary cultures of consumerism create new spaces and tools – malls, metro stations, apps – that enfold all genders. However, as different parts of the book seek to demonstrate, they also lead to masculine anxieties about consuming-women. For, when consumption becomes a public activity and the resources and technologies of consumption become accessible to women, the threat to a historically male domain becomes very palpable. Chapter 6 explores the discourse of masculinity that seeks a solution to a very significant urban conundrum: how can the contemporary Indian city be both a site of vigorous cultures of consumerism and also control and direct women's participation in it? That is, what are the methods through which women might take part in 'appropriate' forms of consumerism, be present in the public sphere but not lay claim to it in a similar manner to men? Through a discussion of recent measures that seek to promote 'women's safety', the chapter suggests that this is sought to be achieved through imagining the city as a 'technotopia' – whereby technology is seen as a panacea for complex social problems – and, coupled with the idea of 'moral consumption', produces a masculinist urban imaginary.

The final chapter concludes the discussion of the book by taking up many of the themes discussed in the earlier chapters and applying them to recent significant changes that have marked Indian political and social life. It takes up for analysis the discourses of masculinity that gathered around the persona of Prime Minister Narendra Modi. Media discourses – both independent journalism and advertisements – during the 2014 general election in India articulated a gendered focus on a significant aspect of Narendra Modi's public representation relating to his forceful masculinity. His election campaign – as well as the popular discourse that surrounded his pre-prime-ministerial persona – significantly focused upon his 'manly' leadership style: efficient, dynamic, potent and capable of removing all policy roadblocks through the sheer force of personality. The chapter suggests that 'Modi-masculinity' is a reformulation of older versions of Indian masculinist discourse in a time of consumerist modernity and that it stands at the juncture of new consumerist aspirations, the politics of 'Indian traditions' and gender, and the refashioning of masculine identities. The chapter argues that Prime Minister Modi represents a new urban type, bringing together, as it does, both the anxieties and solutions that mark life in the rapidly changing Indian city. It also reiterates the significance of the frameworks of post-nationalism and moral consumption for an understanding of contemporary relationships between masculinity, city and forms of capital.

In sum, the book utilises the overarching framework of post-nationalism to provide an empirically grounded and theoretically informed account of the gendered city in a non-western context. It approaches the topic through close attention to how the most significant aspects of contemporary Indian life – the family, educational processes, sexuality, ideas of 'tradition' and modernity', consumerism, religiosity, rural–urban migration and the 'strong' man as a political trope – are intertwined with the cultures of urbanism and masculinity.

Notes

1. While at many places in this chapter, as well as throughout the book, I will use the term 'masculinity', it is important to remember that it is *masculinities* that form the focus of this book. The many ways of being (and becoming) men lie at the heart of masculinity studies. To speak of multiple identities is, in effect, to problematise the idea of a norm.
2. The following discussion has been adapted from Srivastava (2018).
3. 'Extract from the Abstract of the Proceedings of the Council of the Governor General of India, assembled for the purpose of making Laws and Regulations under the provisions of the Act of Parliament 24 & 25 Vic., cap. 67, dated 3rd October 1870', Home Department Files, National Archives of India, New Delhi (hereafter NAI), No. 1744, 27 September 1870 (emphasis added). See also Nigam (1995).
4. As Pradhan (2017) points out, for first time since census operations began in 1872, data from the most recent census (2011) show that the growth in the urban population is higher than the rural.
5. Keeping in mind that most official data point out that most rape cases happen within domestic spaces and the perpetrator is usually known to the victim.
6. The following discussion is adapted from Srivastava (2015).
7. While some natives were feminised, others were represented as 'martial races' – the Sikhs and the Gurkhas, for example (Omissi 1991) – and hence worthy of respect, even though they could not be regarded as equals of the British since they did not possess sufficient *intellectual* prowess.
8. See Srivastava (1998) for a discussion of the connections between the Brahmo Samaj and 'modern' Indian identity as promulgated through educational institutions such as the Doon School.
9. Masculinity has had a varied career in Hindi films; for some other examples, see S. Chakravarty (1993), especially chapter 6, and Kakar (1990). It should also be added that the singing voices that most typified the Five-Year Plan hero were those provided by Mohammad Rafi and the

'earlier' Kishor Kumar. And that the dominance of Lata's voice was part of the same process that established the styles popularised by Rafi and Kishor Kumar as the norms for male singers.

10. As Mubarki (2018) suggests, the model of manhood I point to was not the only one and cinematic depictions of a 'plebian public sphere and subaltern masculinity' offered 'competing visions of masculinity in early post-colonial India' (Mubarki 2018: 3). However, my concern here is with the relationship between masculinity, modernity and the city and I build my discussion around a strand of popular culture that is most relevant to it.

11. The following discussion has been adapted from Srivastava (1998: 165–167).

2

Nationalism, Masculinity and the City

Introduction

This chapter explores the imagination of the city as a site of elite masculine identity at the turn of the twentieth century. The broader aim of the chapter, and the key reason why it inaugurates the book, is to suggest that, notwithstanding the overwhelming focus on the village as a site of a nationalist fashioning of 'authentic' India, there was also an important strand of modern Indian thinking that saw the city as a site of post-colonial futures. Further, the present discussion is a necessary background to a fuller discussion of the notion of post-nationalism – outlined in the previous chapter – that forms the key conceptual framework that sutures the discussion of the book. To move beyond a 'national' framework of analysis, it is important to first deal with it. This chapter explores the different ways – materially and symbolically – in which city-ness constituted a significant aspect of the nationalist imaginary and the making of class identities in the early twentieth century. The discussion moves between historical analysis and ethnographic vignettes to explore metropolitanism both as a system of thought and a structure of feeling.

The focus of the discussion is the Doon School, an elite residential school for boys in the north Indian city of Dehradun in the state of Uttarakhand. The moving spirit behind the School, founded in 1935, was Satish Ranjan Das, Law Member of the Viceroy's Executive Council, sometime treasurer of the Boy Scouts of Bengal and the Lodge of Good Fellowship, and a prominent member of the reformist Brahmo Samaj that originated in Bengal. The School has been a historically significant site for the production of elite discourses on modernity and citizenship. It was to be the site where, as Das wrote to one of his sons in 1927, 'the problem of the nationality of Indians' (Singh 1985: 11) would find its resolution and a place where they would learn to be citizens and come to grips with the demands of modernity.

This chapter is concerned with thinking about the School as a significant site for the construction of narrative of the metropolis – and modernity – through its discourse that made urban life stand for 'civilised' post-colonial existence. The establishment of the Doon School marked the articulation of a redemptive tactic of post-coloniality: it was imagined as an institution where 'natives' would be converted into citizens. Here, the citizens-in-the-making of the coming nation-state were to be suspended in the ether of a new age, that is, the imperatives of the techno-scientific attitude that was been to be hallmark of modernity. The site chosen for the school was itself a homage to the 'scientific attitude', for the campus was formerly the Forest Research Institute, one of the several 'Institutes' and 'Surveys' – and clock-towers at important crossroads – that proclaimed the presence of a 'rational' Occident in the 'irrational' Orient. It was to this Occident that the Indian sponsors of the School wished to align themselves. It was the spirit of this Occident that engaged the attentions of an indigenous class that was already a part of the utilitarian and rational world of early twentieth-century capitalism.

Although a considerable part of the financial backing of the School was provided by feudal aristocracy (Singh 1985), most of its earliest students came from 'professional' families, primarily sons of a nascent middle class consisting of doctors, engineers, bureaucrats and members of the legal profession. These were men of the city and their image of the nation was inextricably enmeshed in pageants of urban life; the metropolis was where dreams of modernity were fulfilled. The city, in their minds, was not merely a conglomeration of specific spatial practices – 'which embraces production and reproduction (Lefebvre 1991: 32–33), that is, physical and material flows – but also a configuration of 'social inventions ... that seek to generate new meanings of possibilities for social practices' (D. Harvey 1989: 261). It was the template for a post-colonial future.

The Province and the Metropolitan Imaginary

The discourse regarding the metropolis that emerged at the Doon School was part of a wider dialogue on Indianness prevalent during the early part of the twentieth century. Within this narrative, the metropolis, its concrete presence apart, was also a settlement of the mind. It was an imagined configuration of desires and comforts, hopes and projections. This process of imagining the city was also bound to what might be called the fetishism of the metropolis, one where the metropolis 'has been transformed ... into a sign' (Appadurai 1990: 16). It was, further, based upon an abstract idea of the metropolis that effaced its objective reality, the relations of power and exploitation that characterise the actual city, taking on a life of its own. The fetishism of the post-colonial metropolis was the process of the transformation of the city of lived experience to that of a commodity that could be part of the elite post-colonial imagination. The metropolis as the site of Indian modernity became, in this way, 'a very queer thing, abounding in metaphysical subtleties and theological niceties ... [taking on] an enigmatical character' (Marx 1978: 76).

The valorisation of the metropolitan milieu in India was, then, coeval with the formation of an early national consciousness. For a significant section of nationalists, such as those associated with the Doon School, it was not just an abstract Indian nation that was to be imagined (Anderson 1986), but one with a very specific *metropolitan* identity. This was to be a national community whose inhabited spaces would be animated by the spirit of a rupture between the 'backward' and the 'progressive', its inhabitants alive to the necessity of new spatial and temporal regimes. This metropolitan model of national identity faced contestation – the Gandhian emphasis on the village, for example. However, ironically, it also drew sustenance from this contestation and eventually triumphed at the very moment that its opposition – the provincial or the non-metropolitan model – provided the most cogent picture of other possibilities. The reason for this lay in the objectifying and essentialising arguments employed by the critics of the metropolitan model of an Indian post-colonial future. In presenting the case for an alternative model of national life – encompassing, inter alia, the education system, a national language, and the methods of the creation and distribution of private and public wealth – thinkers such as Gandhi also constructed certain typologies of non-metropolitan life that were easy to caricature.

In turn, the metropolitan project at the Doon School unfolded through an engagement with these typologies as *static* categories, a characterisation made possible by the manner in which votaries of the 'non-metropolitans' such as Gandhi formulated their own arguments. Specifically, it was the establishment of a series of binary oppositions between the milieu of the metropolis and that of the non-metropolis – the symbolic opposition between the mill and *khadi* cloth, for example – that set the stage for the modern nation-state's assault on the 'primitivism' within it. The point is this: the proponents of the alternative point of view, those who sought to contest the 'modernist' world view of the state, presented their case in such terms as to reduce their actors to passive caricatures. They presented their protagonists and their life-worlds as changeless, their actions to be judged according to a predetermined and static morality and world view. The view of the 'non-metropolis' as a zone of morals and goodness was an objectification that undermined its own position.

In a different context, sociologist Andrew Metcalfe speaks of the 'logic [that] underlies the work of all theorists who *analyse* society as they might analyse an organism or thing' (Metcalfe 1989: 13, original emphasis). This line of analysis proceeds, he suggests, as if 'workers are merely the bearers of a proletarian essence' (1988: 13) and that history can simply be 'read off' in a mechanical manner from these essential qualities. The proponents of non-metropolitan India similarly objectified the rural-provincial figure who was meant to provide the alternative model of the post-colonial citizen. Thus, the latter, imbued with a static morality and made part of a fixed, absolute world view, came to be constructed as a caricature of the ideal citizen rather than as an individual negotiating life between the bounds of structures and the imperatives of agency; in significant ways, Gandhi provided the text for the objectification of the 'other' India. For him, the *khadi* programme was the blueprint for national regeneration: material, moral as well as spiritual. The spinning wheel would provide not merely the mechanics of personal prosperity to pauperised villagers, but also stood for the fabrication of a symbolic web knitting the entire Indian population into the seamless fabric of a moral community. The discussions on the importance of *khadi* became a platform for comparisons of the metropolitan ethos with that of the non-metropolitan one.

The All-India Spinners' Association, Gandhi suggested, could be instrumental in providing employment to those villagers who, in the absence of gainful employment in their immediate localities, were forced to migrate to cities. He noted that villagers worked in the cities under 'immoral' conditions and returned to their villages 'bringing with them corruption, drunkenness and disease' (Gandhi 1928: 109). The villager is here no more than a passive object who becomes infected with the contagion of the metropolis, a contagion which exists as an essence apart from the social and political life – the exposed injuries of class and capital and the hidden exploitations of caste – in which the inhabitants of the metropolis are embroiled. The corollary of this view was, of course, that the non-metropolis has its own essence, its own spirit.

In the wake of the adoption of the *khadi* 'spirit', Gandhi noted, village artisans will find local employment and find themselves 'reinstated in their ancient dignity. as is already happening wherever the spinning wheel has gained a footing' (Gandhi 1928: 109). Gandhi was not, of course, the sole contributor to the objectifying metropolis versus non-metropolis discourse. His colleague and fellow nationalist, C. Rajagopalachari, asserted that 'the peasants of India ... are gentle, industrious and good folk', and that their enforced migration to the cities had turned 'such people' into 'victims of vice' with debilitating effects on the 'national programme' (Gandhi 1928: 756).

In this defence of the non-metropolis, the actual lives (and aspirations) of those who occupied such spaces was effaced and they became merely objects that were constantly acted upon. Their defence by Gandhi and Rajagopalachari became the defence of a timeless essence. In turn, within discourses of modernity at sites such as the Doon School, they were made into strategic caricatures upon the surface of a montage of the 'pre-modern', which it becomes the urgent task of modernity to transform. The sympathisers of the non-metropolis can be seen, in this way, to be complicit in the political and cultural processes of manufacturing precisely the kind of urban modernity that the sponsors of the metropolis saw as the necessary corollary to the task of constructing a nation.

Objectivism, Pierre Bourdieu suggests, subjects practice to a 'fundamental and pernicious alteration', and through 'withdrawing from [the action] in order to observe it from above and from a distance, [it] constitutes practical activity as an object *of observation and analysis, a representation*' (Bourdieu 1977: 2, original emphasis). In the Indian situation, the contested terrain of national identity – metropolitan versus non-metropolitan, modern versus the pre-modern – was, then, queered in favour of the metropolitan-modern by those very groups who sought to present an alternative to the dicta of modernity. The championing of the *khadi* programme, a potentially fundamental critique of the organisation of civil society and the pauperisation of large sections of the non-metropolitan population, was elaborated through an essentialist moral schema that reduced its constituents to a state of passive observers, the noble primitives.

One of the ways in which we might think of the relationship between men such as Gandhi and Rajagopalachari and the non-metropolis they sought to represent and defend is through reference to another kind that has only recently come under scrutiny. I refer to the ways in which anthropologists have chosen to represent relationships between themselves and 'their' villages. Gupta and Ferguson note that 'representations of space in the social sciences are remarkably dependent on images of break, rupture, and disjunction' (Gupta and Ferguson 1992: 6). The social sciences, they suggest, posit 'the distinctiveness of societies, nations and cultures upon a seemingly unproblematic division of space, on the fact that they occupy naturally discontinuous spaces' (Gupta and Ferguson 1992: 6). The lack of a problematisation within anthropology of a 'spatialised understanding of cultural difference', they further argue, has, notwithstanding efforts to the contrary, led to a subtle nativisation of 'the other'; the latter has come to be straitjacketed through its confinement 'in a separate frame of analysis' (Gupta and Ferguson 1992: 14).

The 'unproblematic division of space' assumed in Gandhi's and Rajagopalachari's discussions of the village and the city denied the interconnected nature of the two and, along with it, the possibility of questioning the 'radical separation between the two that [made] the opposition possible in the first place' (Gupta and Ferguson 1992: 14). The case for the non-metropolis, as presented in Gandhi's dialogue against the city, elided a more fundamental critique of the sensibility of space that characterised debates on national identity; what it sidestepped was the issue of 'exploring the process of *production* of difference in a world of culturally, socially, and economically interconnected and interdependent spaces' (Gupta and Ferguson 1992: 14, original emphasis).

In other words, a radical critique of 'separateness' in the Indian case would have concerned itself not with villagers as a people 'native to the village', 'but as a historically constituted and de-propertied category systematically relegated to the [village]' (Gupta and Ferguson 1992: 16). Human social experience, as Raymond Williams (1975) suggests, cannot simply be broken down into distinct 'singular forms' such as 'town and country'; it consists, on the contrary, of many kinds of 'intermediate' and new kinds of social and physical organisation (Williams 1975). The metropolitan idea elaborated in several diverse ways within elite nationalist discourses – with the Doon School being a key site – was defined through a history of objectification of non-metropolitan populations. Paradoxically, those opposed to the pernicious aspects of the Indian modernist project contributed to it as much as those who championed it. The idea of the city, in this context, was one that derived from relationships between colonialism and anti-colonialists, notions of authentic and inauthentic Indias and through reducing social problems – of poverty, class and caste, for example – to spatial etiquette.

Post-Coloniality and the Production of Desirable Spaces

The idea of the city that emerged in narratives of Indian modernity expressed the desire to erase the nation's imagined 'primitive' spaces, namely villages, as well as the pre-modern temporality they were seen to embody. The metropolis was an image of the nation as a category of thought. B. G. Verghese was a student at the Doon School from 1936 to 1944 and a distinguished journalist who served as the editor of the *Hindustan Times* and the *Indian Express*. In the mid-1960s, Verghese criss-crossed the country, writing of his travels in a series of newspaper articles. A quintessentially utilitarian modern journey, Verghese's wanderings – from this factory to that laboratory – were in the nature of a progress report on the post-colonial nation-state. He aspired 'to report on economic development and social change after almost 15 years of planning' (Verghese 1965: vii). Along the way, the traveller 'rediscovered an immensely exciting country pulsating with life and vigour, a country in which great things are happening and one full of abundant promise' (Verghese 1965: vii).

The underlying and consistent tendency towards 'progress' that Verghese discovers submerged under the capriciousness of surface events emerges from a survey and valorisation of a very specific landscape. 'The assignment', he noted, 'took me to farms, factories, mines, dams, power stations, research establishments, *zila parishads* and co-operative offices, industrial estates, technical institutions, housing developments ... defence establishments, large and small industry, and co-operative enterprises' (Verghese 1965: x). In this enumeration of the topography of 'nation-building', the overwhelming presence of the metropolis is too obvious to belabour. Further, the spirit of metropolitan life, Verghese suggests, can be put to the service of transforming non-metropolitan impediments to modernity into the foot-soldiers of a technocratic regime. The 'tribals' of Orissa, he argues, can easily be 'de-tribalised' through 'large residential schools with mechanical workshops' that will enable them 'to participate fully in the industrial civilisation developing around them' (Verghese 1965: 110–111).

The analytical importance of the post-colonial metropolis lies both in its role as a motif for a modern nation-building project and as an abstraction from the actual city of inequalities and contestations. As Chandoke (1991) points out,

> [the] coming together of two complex worlds interacting in major ways in a division of labour yet distanced and differentiated from one another [in which] the urban poor subsidise the city in terms of services, the provision of casual labour and yet are slated to live out their lives outside the enclosure of the formal city' is the uncomfortable reality of the metropolis. (Chandoke 1991: 287)

However, in the dialogue of the nation, which is the focus of this chapter, it is the *sentiment* of the metropolis, its metaphysical aspect, that predominates.

To return to Lefebvre (1991), we might say that in the discourse of the post-colonial nation-state, the spatial *practice* of the metropolis ('which embraces production and reproduction') was overwritten with that of *representational* spaces. The latter form the canvas for the murals of the nation-state in which imagination becomes substantially free from the constraints of experience. As far as nationalist narratives were concerned, the 'inconvenience' of analyses which also engage with a materialist sense of the metropolis is that 'they take on specific meanings and these meanings are put into motion and spaces used in a particular way through the agency of class, gender, or other social practices' (D. Harvey 1989: 264). A consciousness of the metropolis expressed in the lexicon of the material and physical flows that order its existence, and the antagonisms of class, gender and ethnicity that characterise its social fabric, threatened the integrity of the desired image of post-colonial nationhood.

The valorisation of the sentiment of the metropolis – celebrations of 'progress' and 'civilisation' – has not, of course, been confined to the post-colonial context such as the Indian one. In other, non-colonial contexts, the city becomes the battleground and the descriptive trope for a different set of meanings and images. For Charles Baudelaire, for example, the modern ethos that shapes the metropolis is not experienced as a social project – the transformation of the primitive subject into the modern one – but, rather, as strictly personal consciousness. The crowd that occupies the spaces of Baudelaire's metropolis consists of abstract figures, and not the exemplars of an idealised citizen. The 'metropolitan masses' that surged through Baudelaire's pages have no specific identity: 'They do not stand for classes or any sort of collective; rather they are nothing but the amorphous crowds of passers-by, the people in the street (Benjamin 1992: 161–162). Such non-utilitarian pleasures were scorned by India's nationalist 'nation-builders' for whom the metropolis was an episteme.

Contractual Spaces of the Little Republic

Perhaps one of the most articulate examples of the conflation of the metropolitan sentiment with the ideal of the post-colonial citizen comes to us from the autobiography of the turn-of-the-century Bengali nationalist Bipin Chandra Pal. His journey from the provincial backwaters of his hometown of Sylhet to Calcutta (now Kolkata) in order to pursue a tertiary education in one of the premier colleges of the colonial metropolis was also for him a journey to the realm of a new world view. Pal departed Sylhet towards the end of December 1874 to join Calcutta's Presidency College on a government scholarship. His recollections of city life, noted in his autobiography written some fifty years later after his own transformation into the archetypal metropolitan, neatly summarise the perspective that found favour in the milieu of the Doon School.

Upon arrival in Calcutta, the relatively prosperous Pal joined the Sylhet 'mess', one of several such establishments organised along regional lines that catered to the eating requirements of (male) students from outside the city. The messes also functioned as centres of social activity where prospective doctors, lawyers, civil servants and others – the native intelligentsia – made each other's acquaintance and, quite often, formed life-long friendships. Unsurprisingly, membership was exclusively from the higher castes. It was at the Sylhet mess, Pal says, that he had his first 'taste' of city life, one he interpreted as the difference between the stark atomism of metropolitan existence versus the community ethic of the non-metropolis. Whereas in his father's house everybody, 'whether master or servant, had the same kind of food', at his mess – 'for the first time' – he saw that my neighbour had fried eggs which were not served to me. Another gentleman had ghee with his dal, which he did not share with anybody else; and someone had curd which was not given to others. (Pal 1973: 156)

Located at the intersection of fragmentary existence and non-traditional aspirations, the student messes of Calcutta were metropolitan inventions par excellence. It is the sentiment of the metropolis as the anticipation of the post-colonial nation-state that is expressed in Pal's portrayal of their functioning:

The student messes in Calcutta [he writes], in my college days, 56 years ago, were like small republics and were managed on strictly democratic lines. Everything was decided by the voice of the majority of the members of the mess.

... almost in everything that concerned the common life of the mess, the members had a supreme voice. If a seat was vacant applications for it came before the whole 'House', and no one was admitted into the mess unless he was known to or certified by responsible people to be a decent and respectable fellow.... Disputes between one member and another were settled by a 'court' of the whole 'House'; and we sat night after night, I remember, in examining these cases; and never was the decision of this 'Court' questioned or disobeyed by any member. We made from time to time laws and regulations for the proper administration of our little republics.... (Pal 1973: 157–158)

That the author means to present the 'little republic' as a microcosm of the life of the city itself – as distinct from the ethos of the provincial places of origin of its members – is more explicit in his discussion of the 'compromise' over food between 'the so called orthodox and the Brahmo and other heterodox members of our republic'. The 'republic', Pal says, passed a rule by unanimous vote 'that no members should bring any food to the house which outraged the feelings of Hindu orthodoxy' (Pal 1973: 159). Pal's fond remembrances of the student messes of his youth were directly linked to his conception of the hopes and desires a modernising society may place in the milieu of the metropolis; the student mess was a metropolitan artefact in the sense that it mirrored the larger milieu of which it was a geographical and cultural subset.

In the city, Pal meets individuals actively involved in the process of transforming the *Gemeinschaft* rigidities of traditional native existence into the *Gesellschaft* or individualised imperatives of a new age. There is, for example, Babu Pyari Charan Sircar – active in the cause of widow remarriage among upper-caste Hindus – who is described as 'the man who had the greatest influence over forming my mind and character' (Pal 1973: 178). The influence of the metropolitan milieu became crucial in charting a different life-course. It transformed the intimacy of his mother's death into his own personal passage to a public realm. There is a piquant sense in which the gathering sentiments of the metropolis in the young Calcutta student come to signify the substitution of the biological mother with a new maternal ideal. The corporeal ideal – the mother, bound in tradition – was replaced by an abstract entity, the city, aligned to 'progress' and the future. The episode concerns a breach between Pal and his father over the former's rejection of Hindu orthodoxy in the context of his mother's death. For nearly a year after her death, Pal reports that he dutifully performed the *shradh* (remembrance) ceremony in strict conformity with Hindu tradition. However, the force of metropolitan influences determined a different course of action and,

> [t]owards the close of the year, and before the day of the first anniversary of my mother's death came, I had openly rebelled against the old faith and society, and thus gave it [the *shradh* ceremony] up. That was the first cause of open rupture between father and son. (Pal 1973: 179)

In the early decades of the twentieth century, the metropolis as the redemptive scene of modernity – marking the rupture with a 'primitive' past and the eager union with a progressive future – was also the theme of a series of post-independence publications entitled the Bombay Citizenship Series; the nomenclatural embrace between citizenship and a city is worth noting. The narrative of the metropolis employed in the book slips in and out of a discourse of nationhood with relative ease. We are presented with a meta-vision of the national future determined by the civil society of the metropolis: a homogeneous history to be made by the secure classes of the city in the absence of proper judgement and suitable faculties on the part of the 'provincial' populations.

Here, the nation–city identification takes the perennially evocative route through borrowing the vocabulary of nationalism itself, within which the nation transforms into a mother. Bombay is described as the 'mother city' (Bulsara 1948: vii); the city is the template whose manner of life and culture is put forward as the exemplar of nationhood. The province, in turn, is the site that requires a new inscription of identity to emulate the ways of the 'mother'. However, the civilisational destiny of the metropolis – as a template for a national future – is constrained by the physical presence of obstinate sentiments within its boundaries:

> ... merely removing or cleaning up dustbins, refuse sheds and dirt carts from the city will not keep it clean, so long as the people, who create the conditions of filth, remain *in the same primitive mental condition.* Our trouble is not merely physical or external. It is *psychological, social and internal.* We suffer from a preponderance of illiterate populations, which we recruit year by year from our numerous villages. Its mind is still largely rural. It is almost completely undisciplined.... [W]e have to instil in this population a sense of civic consciousness, which demands a mind trained to the restraint of co-operative living. Their illiteracy and profusion of dialects is a hindrance in the path-of quick progress. (Bulsara 1948: 19–20, original emphasis)

To return to the discussion of Doon School, from the earliest days of its existence, its students, especially those who had travelled overseas with their parents, learned to absorb metropolitan sentiments as second nature. One of these was an eighteen-year-old recent graduate of the School who accompanied his diplomat father to the United States in 1942 and recounted the experiences of his journey in an open letter to his alma mater published in the *Doon School Weekly* magazine. The letter is in the form of an itinerary of colonial desire tracing the journey via many secondary ports of call, en route to the 'true' metropolis. It unfolds as the concrete manifestation of several imaginary excursions made earlier. The passage to the true metropolis was littered with provincial outposts of the global economy, and this traveller, for one, noted their presence with the acuity of a pilgrim bound to the centre of a sacred civilisation:

> [After Cape Town] ... The next stop was Trinidad. I was particularly looking out for the various landmarks which had been made familiar to me by Mr Gibson's strenuous efforts to instil some geography into our arable heads.... I cannot say that I particularly liked Trinidad. It is a dreary place with a lot of rain, tropical vegetation and a whole lot of rum-swilling planters: the most inefficient and oppressive Negro waiters who breathe onions and garlic down your neck, but rather meek and polite Indian taxi

drivers (there are quite a number of Indians there). I was certainly glad to get away. (*Doon School Weekly* 4 April 1942)

There were, it would seem, undesirable provincials and primitives everywhere. However, the moment of encounter with the exemplar proves in every way to be a fulfilment of the abundant promise of the wait:

> We docked at Hoboken, New Jersey.... I have some vague, but nevertheless vivid mental pictures of London and Paris, but New York is in a class by itself. A majestic monument to man's engineering genius. I cannot ever hope to put down in this letter even a small description of New York, or give an idea of the emotions which I felt when I saw this city. (*Doon School Weekly* 1–4 April 1942)

The idea of the School as the microcosm of metropolitan existence – linked to a global city-ness – was reiterated through imagining it as a community of contract, much as Bipin Chandra Pal had described his experience of colonial Calcutta. The 'progressive' ethos of the city was to be replicated through ideas such as the *absence* of prohibitions on who may or may not join the community – for such prohibitions were regarded as pre-modern – and heterogeneity of the school's population. The depiction of the metropolis as the space of individualised existence unfettered by the oppressive demands of custom and tradition which characterise the province has been a significant strand in global imaginings of city life. The 'essentially intellectualistic character of the mental life of the metropolis', Georg Simmel was to note, is in contrast to 'that of the small town which rests more on feelings and emotional relationships' (Simmel 1971: 325). It is precisely this movement away from imagined primitivism that the Doon School wished to convey by depicting itself as a community of *contract* rather than *prescribed* association. 'We pride ourselves', a school publication pointed out, 'in the fact that two boys can sleep in adjacent beds for six years and be friends without even finding out each other's background' (*Chandbagh I: A Doon School Miscellany* 1954). The School as the embodiment of the 'progressive' anonymity of metropolitan space is nowhere made more explicit than here.

The idea that the milieu of the School would approximate that of the city – the community of contract and coincidence – was also present in the *Constitution of the Indian Public Schools Society* (IPSS 1936 [1986]), the organisation which administers the Doon School. Among the objectives of the Society listed in its Constitution was the founding of 'Schools in India ... without distinction of race or creed or caste or social status' (Indian Public Schools Society 1986 [1936]). However, if the metropolis was to serve as the prototype of the post-colonial national community, then the heterogeneity, which is a characteristic feature of modern existence, must also be tempered by the needs of cooperative existence. Another School publication contains the following passage: 'Boys from all parts of the country, from all castes and religions mix together and lose their regional and religious identity because the School deliberately plays down these differences by a common uniform the same food/the same facilities'.[1] It was true that the School attracted students from different parts of the country and from different castes. However, as might be expected, the difference among castes was that between one upper caste and another. The heterogeneity of the School's population, which aligned it to the image of the city, was of a uniform kind. This social uniformity was necessary, much as the authors of the Bombay Citizenship Series believed it to be, for constituting an ordered, cooperative, civil society, namely the ideal metropolis.

The ostensible reproduction of the conditions of modern urban life within the School's boundaries – the multiplicities of cultural, social and economic backgrounds – also has its corollary in the field of the political, that is, the representation of the School's milieu as a training ground for the future citizens in the theory and practice of democratic existence. The student council, for example, became an important part of the representational pastiche through which the School sought to secure its place in the grand narrative of post-colonial nationalism. Chaired by the headmaster, the council is the 'apex student body of the School' (S. B. Singh 1985: 62) and meets every month to 'consider all matters which affect the discipline, manners and amenities of life at School' (S. B. Singh 1985: 62). The minutes of the council meetings are published in the *School Weekly* and student members 'represent' different grades as well as different areas of school activity.

The sentiment of civic life at the School was, however, intended to be a *differentiating* device: it sought to establish both the future of the nation-state and the identities of those most qualified to be at its helm. Others – 'tribals', 'provincials' and women (as I discuss later) – provided the peripheral backdrop to the essential procedures and groups of the nation:

[The School Council] ... has a written constitution [and] ... endorses each year the award of School colours for good citizenship.

The working of the School Council and the freedom allowed to the [Doon School] Weekly are, in a sense, training for the wider world, when the boys are expected to be knowledgeable, responsible and active citizens of a democratic country. (*Doon School Book* 1948: 62–63)

The city-state milieu of the School cast its redemptive spell on many a pilgrim on the road to modernity. Karan Singh, son of Maharaja Hari Singh of the erstwhile princely state of Jammu and Kashmir, and later a minister in the Indira Gandhi government, was a student at the Doon School from 1942 to 1946. In his autobiography, the School is presented as the sacred ground of a secular rite of passage and the site of the birth of the modern *man*. Singh speaks of his father's decision to send him to Doon, rather than one of the many 'Chief's Colleges' established by the British for the Indian feudal aristocracy, as 'imaginative and forward looking' (K. Singh 1982: 24). His years at Doon made it possible for him, he further notes, 'to make the crucial transition from feudal to democratic life' (K. Singh 1982: 24).

Heirs Apparent, Minions of Destiny and Vertical Invaders

The School, imagined as the space of metropolitan modernity was, it need hardly be overstressed, intended as a project to produce metropolitan men, the citizens of the future nation. However, though it is the students who were objects of transformation, certain kinds of teachers within the School also provided important indications regarding the nature of 'metropolitan' trajectories. Their personal and professional biographies provide important clues to the *actually existing* politics of metropolitanism and the social processes that define it. It is also, in a sense, a biography of the cultures of class in the post-colonial nation-state.

Historically, the School has always had two 'types' of teachers: those who consciously chose to teach there, and others who found themselves there due to circumstances beyond their control, primarily that they may not have found other sources of employment that provided similar benefits. It is the latter group that constitutes one of the fragments of otherness against which the official ethos of the School both defined and differentiated itself in an explicit manner. I will first deal with the former group, which was part of the metropolitan milieu of the School.[2] AB was a teacher at the School from 1984 to 1991. Before joining, he had been an executive with the Indian subsidiary of a prominent international publishing house in Calcutta. An MA in history from the prestigious St Stephen's College in Delhi, he also studied at Oxford University. The avenues of social and economic mobility open to an individual such as AB in Indian society would seem to be almost infinite; and yet he made a conscious choice to opt for a career as a schoolteacher, which – given the low regard in which the school teaching profession is held in India – might seem like a surprising choice. Krishna Kumar notes,

> With the advance of the colonial system of education, the school curriculum became totally disassociated from the Indian child's everyday reality and milieu.... Moreover, the teacher had no say in the selection of knowledge represented in the school curriculum. His low salary and status ensured that he would not exercise any professional autonomy or even have a professional identity. (Kumar 1991: 14)

The post-independence situation in India represents a variation of the same theme.[3]

So why does someone like AB, socially and economically a part of the metropolitan system in India – the 'right' type of education and contacts – willingly opt for the life of a schoolteacher? The reason lies in the informal 'reservations' system of post-colonial metropolitanism, one that defined the relation between class and cultural capital in the colonial and early post-colonial system of 'distinctions' (Bourdieu 1984). Through this, if we take the School as the microcosm of a system, the best jobs at important public schools, such as the headmastership, have circulated among a small group – the culturally metropolitan – on recommendations from others of similar background who have preceded them. The headship of a prominent public school – the maturation of investments in metropolitan cultural capital – carries with it the benefits of both an immediate and concrete nature and the more abstract social capital, the system of connections it generates.

The headmaster of a school such as Doon enjoys a lifestyle that parallels that of a very senior public servant or corporate executive: an expansive bungalow with extensive and beautifully manicured grounds, caretakers for their upkeep, a car, an entertainment allowance, travel allowance and several other perquisites that make for a life of considerable comfort. These are, of course, in addition to the facility of free education at the school for the headmaster's children. In his professional life, the incumbent makes the acquaintance of a wide cross-section of parents who are often some of the most influential people in the country – politicians, senior bureaucrats, corporate chiefs, industrialists, officers of the defence forces, university vice chancellors[4] and eminent journalists, to name just a few. We may usefully speak here of a lithe web of social capital, 'the aggregate of the actual or potential resources which are linked to possession of a durable network of more or less institutionalised relationships of mutual acquaintance and recognition ... which provides each of its members with the backing of the collectively owned capital' (Bourdieu 1986: 248–249).

That the greatest responsibility for the maintenance and advancement of an institution that defined post-colonial citizenship in terms of a metropolitan identity should be seen to devolve upon those identified as 'metropolitan' is not, perhaps, surprising. After just seven years as a schoolmaster, AB left the Doon School to take up the headmastership of another well-known public school. By any yardstick, he had made exceptional progress through the ranks to the new position he held. Many teachers at the School resented this, but also recognised that 'people like AB are destined to progress rapidly'.

Of course, not all those of AB's background necessarily go on to headships of other public schools. The point, however, is that they form a distinct substratum of School society. They are regarded by others – those of 'provincial' backgrounds whom I will discuss later – as enjoying the privileges of those charged with the responsibility of representing the ethos of the School. They are 'hegemonic organic intellectuals' in Gramsci's terms (O'Neill and Wayne 2017), charged with the duty and authority of propagating a cultural programme of a national self. The most powerful signifier of the privilege that this metropolitanism bestows upon its acolytes, as far as the 'non-metropolitans' at the School are concerned, comes in the form of a dispensation: the relative ability to determine one's own destiny.

KS was also a teacher at the School and his journey from a small town in south India to the Doon School is also the narrative of the cultural economy of the post-colonial nation-state in India. It was a pithy rendition of the multitude of several such journeys undertaken by all those of KS's peripheral cultural circumstance to the social nuclei of the nation-state. A 'gold-medallist' in undergraduate studies from his home-town university, his reasons for accepting a position at Doon constitute reflections on the cultural and economic constraints faced by the group of teachers at Doon I have earlier referred to as the 'non-metropolitans'; and, during our conversations, they were offered to me in tones of both resignation and anger occasioned by perceptions of their constrained circumstances.

In 1979, KS's father, a junior official in the state bureaucracy, retired from his job and, in the following year, died of a heart attack. This forced KS into a profession that, as he put it, 'was certainly not my first choice'. But the compulsions of economic need form only a part of the story of how men such as KS come to be at Doon: there is also the determining force of cultural capital which constitutes that insurmountable difference between the metropolis and the province. For the majority of the teachers at the School, teaching was not a 'first choice'. Almost all members of this group came from an educational and cultural milieu that had experienced systematic devaluation in the metropolitan 'nation-building' agenda of the post-colonial nation-state. They had studied in schools where the medium of instruction had either been Hindi or one of the vernacular languages and graduated to universities that occupied a similarly enervated space of linguistic backwardness (LaDousa 2014).

Given the school's historical world view, from its earliest days, the non-metropolitans at the School had no choice but to mimic metropolitan lifeways. It was always a matter of cultural survival. The 'mimic-men' role (Bhabha 1984), which is the lot of the non-metropolitan teachers at Doon, is both prescribed – for metropolitanism needs its other to authenticate itself[5] – and adopted as a strategy of negotiating their position at the School. In private conversations, many of these teachers made it clear that in this way they masked their 'real' beings. Where the non-metropolitan is forced to mimic the metropolitan, to measure up to the definition of the 'ideal' and live a double existence, mimicry is the manifestation of the purgatory of identity; 'we have to act like someone else', as KS once said to me, adding that the only way for him to be his 'real self' was to go back to his home-town and 'get a job there'.

But for most of the teachers of KS's background, the dreams and plans of returning to a place where they are not the constant objects of a normalising gaze (Foucault 1979) – the 'hometown' – turn out to be illusory. 'The final return', John Berger says of the yearnings of the 'provincial' migrant worker in metropolitan Europe, 'is mythic. It gives meaning to what might otherwise be meaningless. It is larger than life. It is the stuff of longing and prayers. But it is also mythic in the sense that, as imagined, it never happens. There is no final return' (Berger and Mohr 2010: 220). For, despite the strong expressions of outrage at the perceived ignominy of their life at the School – 'disrespect' from students and 'metropolitan' colleagues, poor prospects of 'moving up', lack of any voice in the running of the school – very few actually 'return'. In the helpless embrace of a double bind – 'wanting and not wanting a relation' (Metcalfe 1988: 197) – they barter their ignominious present for a more hopeful future.

This future is that of their children, who are entitled to free education at the School. Through this education, the latter are able to join the circuit of the metropolitan cultural capital whose lack in their parents has condemned them to their present, strongly perceived, ignominy; Doon School education is beyond the means of men such as KS and teaching at the School is the only practical way of acquiring the cultural and social capital of the metropolis for their children. For this reason, the majority of the teachers who have a clear perception of their own invisibility and marginality as autonomous agents at the School do not, in fact, leave once they have, say, qualified for a pension. The concern with ensuring their children a foothold in the cultural world of the metropolis was constantly reiterated in my conversations with some of the older teachers at the School. The metropolis as a system of thought and a structure of feeling – of class and cultural capital – comes together at this juncture.[6]

To use a phrase John Berger (1965) employs to describe Picasso – the European provincial who conquered Paris – these children are the 'vertical invaders' who arrive at the cultural metropolis through the 'trap-door' of the School. Each, however, remains 'conscious of being a vertical invader, always [subjecting] what he has seen around him to a comparison with what he brought with him from his own country, from the past' (Berger 1965: 41); their affections for the School, unlike their metropolitan counterparts, are guarded, and they speak of it as a staging point, rather than as 'home'. And for the ontological leap from the culture of the province to that of the metropolis, their parents must pay through bartering their 'real' selves.

Gendered Localities

I will conclude by returning to the image of the School as a microcosmic representation of the metropolitan milieu and to my earlier discussion of the connection between the metropolitan sentiment and those of civil society. I have argued in this chapter that the citizenship project at the Doon School is one whose philosophical underpinnings lie in an ethos of 'metropolitanism' that reflected a particular (and significant) strand within the cultural politics of the late colonialism and, subsequently, the post-colonial nation-state. And further, that those who were seen to belong to a different milieu became the other of this project. Metropolitanism, in this way, was a site of distinctions, rather than the city imagined as a site of new freedoms.

The 'contractual' foundation of metropolitan existence, Georg Simmel was to say, stands in direct contrast to the milieu of the 'small town and rural existence ... rooted in the steady equilibrium of unbroken custom' (1971: 325). The most salient characteristics of the metropolitan ethos are 'punctuality, calculability, and exactness, which are required by the complications and extensiveness of metropolitan life' (Simmel 1971: 328). 'Cities', Simmel further noted, 'are above all the seat of the most advanced economic division of labour. It [the city] is a unit ... which is receptive to a highly diversified plurality of achievements' (1971: 325). The idea of the contract provides the means through which the diverse elements of the metropolis are seen to relate to each other, free from the 'trivialities and prejudices which bind the small-town person' (Simmel 1971: 325).

The School as a contractual settlement was also central to its self-image. However, as an official history pointed out, it had to find its feet in an environment where there were

> a variety of institutions ... which reflected the social environment in which they existed. There were Hindu *tols* and Muslim *madarasas*, both of which imparted learning in their respective religious traditions. There were [also] the newer Christian mission schools.... The System established at these and other institutions did not seek to educate their students for the challenges of the future. Instead, they maintained the status quo, instilling in their students all the taboos and conventions of a rigidly structured society. (Singh 1985: 9)

This, then, is 'the mental life' (Simmel 1971) of the non-metropolis, resting 'on feelings and emotional relationships. These latter are rooted in the unconscious levels of the mind and develop most readily in the steady equilibrium oft unbroken custom' (Simmel 1971: 325). 'Lasting impressions', Simmel says, 'the slightness in their differences, the habituated regularity of their course and contrasts between them' characterise the life of the non-metropolis. The Doon School, on the other hand, was represented as being marked by the unmistakable signs of metropolitan life: the intrinsic 'punctuality, calculability, and exactness' (Simmel 1971: 328) of its daily routine; diversity of population; wilful arbitrariness in the selection of this population; and lack of barriers to entry. As the official account of the School put it, the school contains 'children of all castes, creeds, religion and colour, without distinction' (Singh 1985: 19).

The 'stories of the origins of civil society', it has been pointed out, can be found 'in the classical social contract theories of the seventeenth and eighteenth centuries' (Pateman 1989: 33). It is in this sense that the Doon School might be seen to have presented its 'contractual' metropolitan ethos as constituting a vital ingredient of post-colonial civil society. And it is precisely here that we must recall the silences 'about the part of the story that reveals that the social contract is a fraternal pact that constitutes civil society as a patriarchal or masculine order' (Pateman 1989: 33). While the metropolitan model championed at the School was founded on the rejection of the paternal forms of non-metropolitan existence, it was also part of the process of absorbing and 'simultaneously [transforming] conjugal, masculine patriarchal right' (Pateman 1989: 37). The logic of masculinity at the School lay, however, not so much in the emphasis on physical activity (on this see Alter 2011) but, rather, in the metropolitan spirit that saturated the spirit of the School, which simultaneously and unequivocally defined the citizen as a male subject. In this way, the sentiments of the metropolis translated the idea of Indian civil society as a gendered locality.

The passage to the city – here, the School – was also the process of effecting a necessary break from the Indian home. Parents who had accompanied their children to the school on its opening day in 1935 had been 'warned in advance' to 'hand over' their wards to School authorities in the morning and to 'keep away from them till the evening' (*Doon School Book* 1948: 3) when they would be invited for 'tea' on the school campus. And when the guardians joined their newly enrolled wards for afternoon tea, the latter would already be part of another world. For 'their measurements had been received in advance' (*Doon School Book* 1948: 3–4) and 'in the afternoon when the parents arrived, they found their boys all playing games in their school-clothes' (*Doon School Book* 1948: 3–4).

The resolution of the problem of the nationality of Indians (to paraphrase Chatterjee 1993a) was to be achieved, then, through handing over future citizens to the care of men (or fathers) and away from the pernicious environment whose chief guardians (in this line of thought) are women. Men would look after the well-being of the civil-society-to-come through their own institutions, which in turn would reflect civil society itself; school children would pass from being natives to citizens.

It is here that the multiple strands of this chapter converge. Manifestations of masculinity at the School were not – as I have noted earlier – expressed through techniques of the corporeal self; rather, they were elaborated through alignments with new knowledges (science) and new forms of community, to wit, the community of contract. It is these that articulated the imaginings of a specific national community through the vocabulary of difference. This specific form of post-coloniality inscribed its territory against its various others: so, not for it the masculinity of brute strength, for that belonged to the realm of one of its primitive pasts, for example, the feudal nobility that sent its children to schools such as the Mayo College at Ajmer (see Srivastava 1998) or 'tribal' populations that required 'detribalisation'. The realm of *this* post-coloniality lay in the flux of pragmatic actions and 'scientific' thoughts, contractual existence and the 'equality principle', for these signify a masculinity that sets it against the identities of the 'natives within'. This process of differentiation – of outlining a metropolitan masculinity marked by the conspicuous absence of the body from the scene of robustness – was, at this juncture of national life, also the articulation of an insistent dialogue on the functioning of capital. It outlined both the 'requirements' of life under the regime of capital and the fate of those who are seen to fall outside its ken.

Conclusion

The history of metropolitanism that I have just outlined – utilising a specific site of Indian modernity as an entry point to a mode of thinking – is, of course, a history of desire. This narrative educated and conditioned several generations of post-colonial elites, those who went to be important decision-makers and producers of the cultural discourses of Indian modernity. The city was the metaphorical grounds upon which there played out a politics of class, caste and gender. However, as we will see in subsequent chapters of the book, the founding myths of civility, masculinity and metropolitanism have now fragmented across a number of different registers, each offering a unique view of the life of the city and social relations within it. The politics of masculine identities with the city as its *mise en scène* has been, as I also show, a significant aspect of lives lived in more modest circumstances than that discussed in this chapter. That is to say, the topic offers us a fruitful entry into social processes across a range of social and economic circumstances.

In the next chapter, it is to the streets and footpaths – symbolic sites of 'other' lives – that I turn. I do not, however, mean to suggest that these are sites of lifeways that have nothing to do with the kinds of issues discussed in this chapter – the form of the nation and family, the nature of class, for example – rather that they refract these ideas in different ways, forcing us to confront the entangled nature (Srivastava 2015) of the life of cities and the politics of identities *across* different temporal and socio-economic contexts. The discussion that follows is, then, an attempt to track the ideologies and practices of metropolitanism as it moves beyond – but also articulates with – the nationalist tropes discussed in the chapter, to the post-national contexts that mark the present.

Notes

1. Document entitled *Innovative Leadership Provided by the Doon School*, published by the Doon School, no date.
2. The ethnographic discussion is adapted from Srivastava (1998).
3. See, for example, Report of the Education Commission (1964–66) of 1966.
4. For example, one position on the School's Governing Council is reserved for an 'educator', usually the vice chancellor of a prominent university.
5. 'As a subject of a difference that is almost the same, but not quite', as Bhabha puts it (Bhabha 1984: 126).
6. In terms of caste, it is rare to find teachers in such schools that are not from the upper castes.

3

Dislocated Masculinities and the Unofficial City

Introduction

The elite metropolitanism identified in the previous chapter was intended to be part of a redemptive strategy of elite nationalism. City life was to be the template for civilised values and an antidote for curing a variety of social and cultural ills. Within this discourse, however, there was no attempt to explore what makes a city what it is; its asymmetries and the ways in which those who occupy its margins negotiate uneven social and economic terrains did not interest the advocates of elite metropolitanism. What was being imagined was urban life without the experiences of urban living.

Urban modernity in India is, however, the product of contests between formalised visions of an idealised urban civility and tangible lifeways enmeshed in the informality of governance, residence, livelihoods and life choices. Elite visions of the city – and national life as city life – invariably become mired in the quotidian and improvised (Simone 2019) politics of 'the street and the ward level as critical spaces in which the poor barter for access' (Weinstein, Sami and Shatkin 2014: 40) to resources for material well-being as well as a life of the imagination. I turn in this chapter to streets and footpaths and a variety of other spaces of informality to bring to view those relationships between the city and masculinity that tell us something about both subalternity and desires for worlds beyond it. The chapter also initiates a discussion on the post-national condition. This overarching framework ties together explorations of urban spaces as crucibles of masculine desires, aspirations and anxieties as the latter engage with multiple social and economic structures such as class, caste, religious belief and the politics of domesticity.

This chapter focuses on urban cultures of masculinity and sexuality that provide insights into the anxieties of masculine immigrant life in the metropolis. Its subjects are the precarious subjects of the city who, in early 2020, expressed their precarity through desperate attempts to leave the city in the wake of the COVID-19 epidemic; they are in the city though their claims as full residents are rarely recognised. They are both essential to its economy and marginal to its culture. The COVID pandemic graphically underlined connections between precarious livelihoods, the striving for belonging and the masculinity that is in the city but not of it and is an appropriate place to begin the discussion of this chapter.

Invocations of the term 'informality' are accompanied by a sense of its liminality: that it is a staging post on the way to 'formality'. So, informal work is meant to lead to its formal counterpart, and informal housing is the unfortunate stage that awaits a better future. This is an understandable perspective as 'informality' – notwithstanding connotations of spontaneity and conviviality – is also a state of socio-economic marginalisation. That is certainly the most striking aspect of scholarly discussion on aspects of urban informality (see, for example, Shatkin 2014; Bandyopadhyay 2016). However, with respect to Indian cities at least, the key aspect is how to think about the *persistence* of informality as a seemingly permanent aspect of urban life. Urban informality is inextricably linked to the informality of labour, and this is a historical norm (Breman 1996).

Informality of work – that does not guarantee security of tenure – is a significant context for the enforced mobility of a large section of the population that criss-crosses the country in search for livelihood (women mainly move after marriage). The 2011 Census indicated that the number of internal migrants is around 450 million. Circular migration – between villages and cities – is a well-established aspect of the informality of life and work that characterises the lives of a very large section of the Indian population (Samaddar 2020). Around 30 per cent of the urban male workforce is of migrant origin (Rajan and Bhagat 2021).

Soon after 24 March 2020, as the Indian government declared a national lockdown to prevent the spread of the COVID infection – with just four hours' notice – the country was witness to scenes reminiscent of the mass movement of panicked populations in the wake of the Partition in 1947. Women, men and children of all ages rushed to find whatever means available to flee their city homes and return to their rural locations. Millions crowded train and bus stations, and others walked on foot across hundreds of kilometres in dystopic scenes of desperation, confusion and expulsion. Realising that the cities that they worked in would prove to be a hostile environment once their livelihoods were lost, the migrant workforce decided to return to places where they might receive a modicum of support from kin and other networks. Migrant working-class masculinity is located at the bottom of the urban socio-economic hierarchy, and the COVID episode was not just an economic calamity; it also struck at the heart of men's self-perception as protectors and providers of 'their' women and families.

This chapter explores the place in the city of those who lined the streets and highways in the first half of 2020 in tragic queues of an internal diaspora. I focus upon relationships between their marginal social and economic status as urban dwellers, the anxieties of threatened masculinity and how they seek to deal with them. Masculinity and marginality serve as a window to an understanding of their place in the city and the city as a place of desire, anxiety and aspirations for its most marginalised populations. I explore these aspects through a discussion of the 'sex clinics' of Delhi and Mumbai. The clinics are my entry points towards an exploration of how subaltern men negotiate urban processes to make sense of their marginality and, perhaps, transcend it. The tying-together of subaltern masculinity and sexuality is not, however, intended to present poor men as inherently more sexualised than, say, middle-class ones. Rather that, moving beyond regarding the urban poor primarily as economic beings, this chapter explores their engagements with the city as complex social subjects. Intimacy – sexuality – is the poignant scene of this engagement.

Users of rail and bus transport have long been familiar with clinic advertisements scrawled in large letters at entrance points to urban areas and on various walls within cities, at bus depots and along railway tracks. 'Sex and Vitality Clinics', as they are sometimes also known, are a significant urban phenomenon with a large clientele of men from lower socio-economic categories. The clinics offer a variety of services to their clients, including 'cures' for sexually transmitted diseases, impotence and premature ejaculation, ways of enhancing sexual 'performance' and the promise of male progeny. Clinic operators deploy medical and scientific terminology in conjunction with 'traditional' notions of masculinity, sexuality and sexual well-being to attract their clientele. Perhaps the best known of all the sex clinics in north India is the Khandani Shafakhana, and the starch-turbaned image of its founder, Hakim Hari Kishan Lal, that beams down majestically from a plethora of billboards in Delhi is a familiar part of the city's visual landscape. The hakim (from Arabic: 'physician') is no longer alive, and the clinic is now operated by his sons, though the image of the patriarch (Figure 3.1) is still seen as crucial for defining the clinic's public presence. I will return to this image of masculinity later in the chapter in order to position it within the political and cultural economies of the city in India.

Figure 3.1   Hakim Hari Kishan Lal

Source: Author.

The larger context of the public presence of the sex clinics is the arena of a host of non-western healing systems, such as Ayurveda and the Unani (Perso-Arabic) system. Hence, in addition to the relatively low cost of 'treatment' offered by the clinics, their historical legitimacy also derives from a surviving popular memory of traditional healing systems. Sex clinics are usually located near three kinds of places: major transport nodes such as railway stations and inter-state bus depots; newly established outlying 'colonies' of the metropolis which may contain a mixture of slum dwellings, light industrial units and new and old *pucca* (permanent) housing; and older and established commercial localities, such as Chandni Chowk in central Delhi, an area that is also home to industrial and semi-industrial labour forces from small towns and villages. Their location maps the spaces where the city's migrant underclass enters its borders, secures dismal residence and contracts uncertain employment.

In this chapter, I treat sex clinics as informal sites of communication, knowledge and 'treatment' for populations that belong to the informal economic and cultural worlds of the unofficial or improvised city that sprawls beyond the confines of city master plans. These communication sites both interrogate and conform to dominant modes such as the formal medical system, specialist journals and government advice. Most significantly, they allow for an exploration of urban lives in the realms of 'political society' that exists beyond the domains of the 'civil' one (Chatterjee 2004). The clinics are one of the several sites of the articulation of masculinity, gender relations, class, the national and commodity cultures of modernity and the tensions of urban life for the poor. It is these aspects – with the city as the *mise en scène* – that the chapter explores.

The chapter will also explore *this* public life of the city through a set of publications that are part of the cultural, economic and *pedagogic* worlds of the sex clinics. They too offer a view of the anxieties and aspirations of subaltern masculinity and allow us to flesh out the narratives of marginal men in the city that emerge from the sex clinics' material. I refer here to the vast body of Hindi language 'footpath' pornography that is sold in places that are contiguous to areas where sex clinics are located. Sex clinics and footpath pornography constitute a subterranean world of debate and discussion, ostensibly about the intimate lives of men, but also about masculinity and the city. Together, they constitute an arena of secret but public modernity and silent though thick circulation of knowledge. Authors – made legendary through longevity and public visibility – such as Mast Ram and Kamini Devi, and titles such as *Sexy, Sexy, Sexy, Mujhe Log Bole* (Sexy, Sexy, Sexy, People Call Me), *Sulagati Chahat, Machalte Arman* (Burning Desire, Uncontrollable Wishes) and *Kaam Samasyane* (Sex Problems) have for long been an important part of Indian urban culture. To invoke a term deployed by city governments to describe informal settlements, the clinics and the booklets constitute an 'unauthorised regularised' forum, and the unauthorised regularised discussions that gather around them tell us a great deal about contemporary urban subaltern subjectivities. In the following discussion, I will move between the sex clinics and the footpath pornography material. Apart from sharing clientele, some clinics also publish 'advice' manuals and other literature that share the footpath space occupied by the pornographic literature.

The chapter explores contemporary masculine sexual cultures as a way of understanding the consolidation of what might be called provincial cultures within the metropolis through processes of rural–urban migration, the most visible manifestations of which are the *jhuggi-jhopri* (shanty) settlements and the 'Unauthorised Regularised Colonies' of Indian cities. This also constitutes a way of coming to grips with relationships between various cultures of capitalism *within* national boundaries as an aspect of globalisation. This is a significant aspect of city-making in post-colonial societies. Indian cities are fundamentally characterised by the juxtaposition of 'metropolitan' and 'provincial' cultures that have a particular relationship with respect to each other as well as to the wider changes we now characterise as 'globalisation'. The present discussion is, then, an ethnography of the human topography of the city carved out by informal bureaucracies, haphazard economics, erratic knowledge regimes and their savants, dislocated gender positions, and hybrid commodity cultures – a territory that is both similar to the 'McDonaldised' commoditisation described by Ritzer (1993), and yet also different in terms of its informality.

It is within these contexts of post-nationalism and moral consumption – changing relations between the state and private capital on the one hand and the rise of consumer cultures on the other – that we find new questions about what it might mean to be the modern urban male subject who lives in the city but is marginal to its circuits of power and well-being. These questions derive from life-worlds that are complex configurations of commodity desires, masculine anxiety, and a new urban spatial sensibility that is formed by – but is not reducible to – global flows.

The discussion that proceeds through an investigation of the making of urban sentiments and emotions does not, however, assume that there exists an unbroken and undisturbed world of emotions that have been passed down to Indians through an ancestral cultural bequest. The chapter does not seek to investigate, for example, 'ancient' emotional templates or define contemporary ways of sensing the world (Kakar 1990; Lynch 1990; Trawick 1990). Rather, it demonstrates that urban sentiments are built out of contemporary commodity cultures, globalisation, media flows (Appadurai 1993), masculine norms and those of family life and the peculiar ways in which these combine in spaces of the city. That is, it investigates the processes of post-nationalism and moral consumption.

No doubt cultural difference – and the different history of cultures – provides us with radically different conceptualisations of emotions, but these differences cannot be understood as the simple heritage of something called 'Hindu culture'; rather, they must be conceptualised as the constant (re)conceptualisation of 'Hindu culture' itself by Hindus (and others) in the broader context of the forces of modernity. So, 'Indian notions of family and what mother's love in it means' (Lynch 1990: 24) need to be situated in contexts of rural–urban migration, popular literature, over half a decade of advertisements for Farex baby food and Johnson's baby powder in magazines such as *Dharmyug* (now ceased publication), as well as Indian films, advice columns and the media. What counts, then, as emotion in the Indian context is itself historical and contingent, rather than unchanging and attached in a monolithic manner to a given template. It is, therefore, subject to the major processes of different eras. The life of the city – and that within it – *defines* ways of feeling within it. For its underclasses, the city is a site of both the struggle to make it a home and aspirations that weave narratives of belonging. It is from within this crucible that urban subjectivity emerges.

Footpath City

The relationship between a particular kind of commodity culture, urban anxieties and 'traditional' remedies forms the entry point to this discussion. This is a space created by the processes of economic liberalisation inaugurated in the 1990s (Sengupta 2008), Bollywood versions of small-town-masculinity-come-to-the-city (see Chapter 1), and the entrepreneurial 'mainstreaming' of traditional remedies in the service of a 'traditional modernity'. The type of masculinity discussed in this chapter – slotted at the bottom of the city's socio-economic hierarchies – is no longer constrained by the language and emotions of anti-colonial nationalism. It is also not aligned to the imagined subject of post-independence slogans such as 'Jai Jawan, Jai Kisan' (Hail the Farmer, Hail the Soldier). *This* city-man encounters the precarity of the city's entrepreneurial milieu and scrambles to make a life in a context where new relationships between the state and private capital have substantially changed the former's attitudes regarding its pastoral duties towards the poor. In this milieu, he negotiates a post-national world of changing economic circumstance but largely unchanged personal social beliefs. The post-national city might expect greater entrepreneurialism as a strategy of survival, but the subaltern man is not yet converted to a 'pure' entrepreneurial type. While he moves among the world of apparently free-floating goods and commodities, he remains, I suggest, tied to older ideas regarding men, women, kinship, honour and family. In the post-national city, these social elements – that were earlier deployed in the service of 'nation-building' – now circulate as marketised ingredients that might be pressed into the service of new selves.

I have no formal studies to draw upon and must rely upon my own observations to suggest that the Hindi-language footpath pornography under discussion has a huge market all over north India. The quite poor production values – including missing pages, blurred images and inexplicable endings to climactic narratives – make the booklets cheap to acquire. Being an intrinsic part of the accoutrements of urban footpaths, customers can, literally, obtain these on the run or opt for leisurely perusal while killing time waiting, say, for the next bus. Cover photographs often portray either European women or some version of westernised images of Indian women in various poses of desire/seduction or 'availability'. Both the authorship and readership of these booklets would primarily appear to be male, though it is difficult to be certain about this. However, given their *public life* as commodities – subject to a myriad casual and passing inspections – it can safely be said that at least most of the purchasers are men. The booklets are usually published by city-based, small-scale presses such as the Bansal Press in Seelampur in north-east Delhi. Seelampur took its current form in the wake of the national emergency (1975–1977) when many residents were given plots of land in return for agreeing to the demolition of their 'slum' homes and being sterilised under an infamous programme overseen by Indira Gandhi's younger son, Sanjay (Sarkar 2008). The area is home to a significant working-class Muslim population, and in December 2019 it witnessed large-scale violent protests against the government's Citizenship Amendment Act (CAA) that is seen as discriminatory towards Muslims. The booklets are produced in localities where many of their readers – who are also potential clients of sex clinics – live.

The booklets combine a wide range of functions: as a bridge between 'tradition' and 'modernity', windows to the world of contemporary commodity culture, the complex sites of fantasy culture of modernity, and propaganda vehicles for a 'modern' nuclear family. A wide variety of 'goods' are advertised throughout the publications (though most often at the end), and the list below provides some indication of the nature of the advertisements.

1. The founder editor of the daily *Taj Times* and Basant Prakashan says in an advertisement that some men robbed him of his car after threatening to kill him and his wife at a particular location in Agra. And that he is willing to provide a reward of 25,000 rupees for information leading to their apprehension.

2. A firm from Gaya (in Bihar) advertises for a ring that is

> capable of giving its wearer complete control over any man or woman; can ensure success in business, legal matters, in exams, a good job, marriage according to personal wish, protection against bad spirits, successes in lotteries and gambling, freedom from debt, the ability to see buried treasure in dreams, bad *grah* (luck) will improve, power of memory will improve, recover lost goods, health will improve. Tantrik ring Rs 51; A tantrik ring made according to your horoscope Rs 151; A special strong silver ring for those who have faced disappointment in all aspects of life Rs 251.

Further, the advertisement points out, 'All letters are treated as confidential, so please do not hide anything from us, and provide all details. Our address: Lalita Ashram, (BA/9) PO Lai Bigha, Gaya.'

3. An advertisement for Ayurvedic treatment offers cures for '*safed daag* [white spots], sexual diseases and piles; Vaidhya Shri Jwala Prashad (registered), Post Office Katri Sarai, Gaya. Note: if you want to visit, please write and receive instructions on getting here'.

4. 'Lion Zorro automatic folding revolver, no licence required; Gupta Trading Co., 4995 Rehman street, Chandani Chowk. For security, theatre, picnics, etc.; emits a loud bang along with smoke and sparks.'

5. 'Asli Bara Harmonium, a book written by an expert, contains many new types of songs, *raginis, ghazal, thumri, dadra, quawalli,* film songs, etc., taught through a numbering system so that even those without any knowledge can learn. Rs 50 excluding cost of postage.'

6. 'New *sabun-tel shiksha* course: make different types of oils and soap and sell for profit. Market purchased oil often smells of kerosene and is harmful. Be rid of all that.'

7. 'Colourful photo album: Despite possessing physical beauty, millions around the world are unhappy, many pictures of smiling women; contains many things worth knowing both before and after marriage.'

8. '325 secrets to great wealth. Learn to establish industries which require little capital but generate great profit, such as detergent powder, paint varnish, *dhoop batti* [incense], textiles, pharmacy, electrical goods, auto-parts, phenyle, *tinopal* [a whitening agent], vim washing powder, *neel* [whitening agent], etc., the secrets of manufacturing, how to get loans, etc.'

9. 'Sure ways of increasing height; based on many successful experiments in America and Europe.'

10. 'Sex course with naked pictures: published for the first time in India; 600 colour photos; successful *suhaag-raat* [first night of the wedding], lack of children, *swapandosh* [nocturnal emission]; how to have enjoyable sex, etc.'

11. 'Judo karate course: based on Japanese techniques (Rs 50)....' Ashoka Prakashan, Chandani Chowk.

12. 'A necklace with 108 beads: takes away all your troubles cast spells, pass exams, riddance from debts and diseases, success in business, lotteries and gambling. We will refund all costs if not satisfied'.

13. 'Now in India a new age 35mm camera.'

14. 'Learn to speak English in 50 days.'

Commodities, as anthropologists have long realised, 'represent a subject on which anthropology may have something to offer to its neighbouring disciplines, as well as one about which it has a good deal to learn from them' (Appadurai 1997: 5) It is this aspect of 'learning from commodities' that requires attention in the present context. What is the connection between masculine and sexual culture and these bewildering variety of advertisements that vie for the reader's attention? What is the relationship between the consumer and the objects and processes for sale? How do we understand the 'moral economy that stands behind the objective economy of visible transactions' (Kopytoff 1997: 65)?

An important context for the inventory of advertisements listed earlier is that this is a market – by the standards of mainstream capitalism – for slightly soiled goods of urban life: amulets for miraculous cures and bewitchment and necklaces that cast spells upon one's enemies. In one sense, this is card-trick capitalism, where the 'devil and commodity fetishism' (Taussig 1980) come together. However, in another important way, it may contain the potential to problematise the notion of 'commodity fetishism in as much as the commodities *are* also the subjects since the project of becoming human is inextricably bound with certain perceived aspects of commodities. That is, if we are to conceive of things as having a 'social life' (Appadurai 1997), it is important to reflect upon the subjectivity of 'objects'. So, one might say that in this context, the commodity does *not* become 'a very queer thing, abounding in metaphysical subtleties and theological niceties ... [taking on] an enigmatical character' (Marx 1978: 96). Instead, it gains its character concurrently with the character that humans seek to secure. As Kopytoff points out:

> ... even things that unambiguously carry an exchange value – formally speaking, therefore, commodities – do absorb the other kind of worth, one that is non-monetary and goes beyond exchange worth. We may take this to be the missing, non-economic side of what Marx called commodity fetishism. (Kopytoff 1997: 83)

The relevant point for my discussion is the one Kopytoff makes regarding the drive towards the 'singularisation' of commodities, the other side of the commoditisation imperative. He suggests that commodities may acquire their 'social power' (Marx's notion of their 'fetishisation') '*after* they are produced, and this by way of an autonomous cognitive and cultural process of singularization' (Kopytoff 1997: 83). This suggests an active relationship between things and humans, produced and reproduced by cultural and historical circumstances. Hence the magical cures, the Lion Zorro automatic revolver, the colourful picture album, the film acting guides and the Judo-Karate course – not all of them commodities in the classic exchange-value sense – are both objects and processes of culture, rather than merely occupying the status of fetishes, *once and for all* defined by the existence of an exchange-value system. In the context of this discussion, this means that different commodities are singularised and given 'additional' individual valuations in the face of their homogenised nature. That is, their lives unfold through the contexts we summarise under the rubrics of, say, 'tradition', 'modernity', 'the province', 'the metropolis', 'class' and 'commodity culture'.

The market that searches for customers in the pages of the pornography booklets described earlier is the transactional space of the *intra-national* diasporic subject, for whom the promises of capitalism – liberalisation, and so on – always seem out of reach. It is a subject on the margins of capitalism and yet one that seeks to engage with it and bring it under control by casting its strategies of engagement as widely as possible.For it is through the capacity for un-differentiated consumption – that ranges across magical and 'real' goods – that the urban subaltern male expresses his masculinity. In Chapter 6, I will return to the topic of masculinity-in-the-city as the desire to be the 'all-consuming' man. The *post-national* city, always out of reach, generates desires for masculine control through acts of *consuming* in-the-nation, rather than, as was the case of the elite Five-Year Plan hero, *saving* for it.

Cautionary Tales of Masculine Survival

The 'success' that is being imagined in the commerce of greater height, magic potions to pacify one's enemies, miraculous rings for overwhelming power, a course for successful *suhaag-raat,* 'a new age 35mm camera', and learning to speak English 'in 50 days' within the shared space of sex stories says something about the contiguity of the narratives of consumption and masculine sexual culture. It is a context that provides us with rich material for analysing the parallel arenas of discussion and debate that exist on the margins of the formal city.

There are significant points of overlap between consumption and sexual culture that assist in understanding the making of urban subaltern masculinity and the role of sex clinics. The city is both a place of aspirations and also anxiety. For, while it offers the possibilities of those other worlds that the village may not, these are, at least in principle, open to both men *and* women. This is a source of masculine anxiety; while the consuming man expresses a sense of control through the consumption of myriad goods, the consuming *woman* is a problematic figure as far as his masculinity is concerned. She expresses desires for *herself.* In the discourse that circulates around sex clinics, there is both advice and also cautionary tales regarding the urban dangers to masculinity. I return to footpath pornography for a representative example of the cautionary tales they carry regarding the dangers to subaltern masculinity from the city and its women.

The Consuming Woman and the Dangers of the City

While the narratives of the footpath pornography booklets are firmly based within urban spaces, there is a significant sense in which they are concurrently located in the realm of *spaceless* narratives of desire and anxieties. Both in terms of readership and places of production, the footpath material is aligned to contexts of great uncertainty and dislocation, and that it indexes a situation of enforced rootlessness for the urban underclasses. Hence, the visual fragments of footpath pornography are marked by a lack of spatial specification, or, to put it another way, their narratives are strewn across a number of spaces, so as to make for an 'aesthetics of dislocation' where

> roughly sketched semi-nude couples in apparent moods of ecstasy stand to attention in a mélange of bleeding hues, 'westernised' women strike suggestive poses within colorfully vacant backdrops, and 'disco' dancers career motionlessly against barely lit backgrounds. [This is the context of an urban lifeworld where] ... spaces are rapidly transforming, often
> hostile, bewilderingly unfamiliar, out of reach, and, depending upon how often one is 'cleared out' out of urban slums and shanty towns, literally shifting beneath one's feet. (Srivastava 2007: 185–186)

Dislocated desire is a fragment of the erotic narratives of subaltern urban modernity, where the experience of modernity is one of a series of ruptures. The booklets speak of these ruptures, and their sensual narratives are built out of them. The second context that relates this narrative has to do with the women of the booklets. A wide variety of women jostle for (primarily male) attention both in visual and narrative forms. Typically (and as noted earlier), visual representations consist of European women or 'westernised' Indian women. There is a continuity here with Indian cinema and the persona of the vamp, the most famous of whom was Helen (b. 1938), the Anglo-Indian actor who was famous for her 'western' dance numbers (see, for example, Pinto 2006). 'Helen' was the site of the displacement of male desire: a western (or westernised Indian) woman who could be the receptacle of fleeting desires (the 'girlfriend') rather than the anchor of a more permanent relationship (such as the wife).

'Helen-ness' finds play in the booklets through a number of ways, and the following story from the *Raat Ki Rani Digest* (Queen of the Night Digest; 'Raat Ki Rani' is also the name of a fragrant flower that blooms after dark) by Mast Ram ('The Merry One') provides a good flavour. The story is called 'Pyar Ka Bhoot' (The Obsession of Love) and concerns an affair between Tejinder and Shirley. Tejinder is a wealthy young Sikh businessman whose electronics business has been built entirely through dint of hard work. Building upon colonial and post-colonial lineages of Sikh identity (see Omissi 1991 and Das 1995, respectively), Tejinder is presented as the epitome of virile Indian masculinity. 'Shirley George', on the other hand, is a Christian from the state of Kerala and lives by herself in an apartment in a posh South Delhi locality. Quite frequently in the story, 'Shirley' is written as 'Shir-lay': unfamiliarity with women who carry the name Shirley also tells us something about the worlds of the men who are the readers (and authors) of the booklets.

Shirley carries the signs of an Indian modernity that is both seductive *and* requires caution: she is single, a Christian (hence 'foreign' in the popular imagination), lives alone and rides pillion on motorcycles (not side-saddle where legs can be kept together) with unrelated males. Shirley is also fond of whiskey and 'western' items of food, such as omelettes. Shirley/Shirlay and Tejinder launch upon a passionate affair that involves long car rides, frequent stays at five-star hotels (at Tejinder's expense), a great deal of whiskey and passionate sex that is characteristic of the modern women as frequently represented in the booklets. The couple decides to visit Switzerland for a holiday. While there, Shirley launches upon a shopping spree, incurring a massive debt. She asks Tejinder for 'five thousand dollars' that, she says, is needed to 'help' her father. Tejinder expresses his inability to pay, and Shirley refuses to see him any longer. One day, Tejinder finds her drinking in the lobby of a five-star hotel in the company of an 'army captain'. He asks about her declarations of undying love for him. She tells him to 'get lost' and adds that she could never be 'slave' to one man. Soon after, Shirley files a 'false case' of rape and abduction against Tejinder. Despite his protestations of innocence, he is sent to jail. His 'obsession of love', the story concludes, finally dissipates.

'Pyar Ka Bhoot' is a cautionary tale about the seductions and dangers of the 'deep' modernity of women such as Shirley (and Helen); these are women of the city. However, in an age of hyper-consumerism, the desire for the active and consumerist woman, such as Shirley, is also a desire to take part more intensively in the cultures of consumerism that the city offers. Shirley's deep modernity is the site of an intense erotic charge as well as a threat, and the 'problem' translates into one of how to consume modern sexuality and yet remain in control of one's masculinity: How to have but not have the modern woman? How to live in the city and ward off the dangers to one's masculinity?

There is – advice emanating from urban sex clinics suggests – a possible solution to the questions posed here. 'There is a wrong impression among certain young men', a booklet produced by the Khandani Shafakhana sex clinic points out, 'that all time erection, repeated erection or over excitement for intercourse are the signs of complete and perfect man-hood but in fact this condition soon turns into impotency' (Kishan Lal n.d.: 27). The discourse of deferral is, here, ensconced within the larger narrative of consumption culture. That is, 'proper' sexuality can be purchased in the marketplace – the clinic – and that it is an aspect of the 'good' life that the city can provide. However, this is also the interface between the cultures of globalisation and the attempt to define the local: an unstable equilibrium where commodity culture is good, but only if reshaped according to a different – traditional – consumption pattern than that in the west and promoted by the forces of globalisation. So, women are recognised as possessing the desire for 'excitement'. However, Hakim Hari Kishan Lal warns that

> young men should be careful on their first wedding night. They often think it is essential to inter course [sic] on the first night to prove their manhood. Due to their ignorance they fail to excite their brides on the first night. (Kishan Lal n.d.: 27)

A proper, *Indian*, course of *moral consumption* is best advised for a 'happy married life', and the possible pitfalls of the city can best be tamed through navigating a life in the city that is of it (being a consumer) but also requires constant wariness of the dangers to manhood. The greatest danger is encountered through the women of the city who do not practise moral consumption and exceed the bounds of Indian traditions. I will return to the idea of 'proper' consumption in Chapter 6 to further explore the tensions between masculinity and the consuming woman; if the city is the site of consumerist activity – traditionally a male domain – in which women now also take part, masculinist ideology deals with this apparent encroachment upon its entitlement through moral consumption. It consists of a strategy of engaging with a fraught context where consumerism is desired but also sought to be moulded according to tenets that seek to maintain masculine control.

The sex-clinic milieu is one where 'traditional' ways of predicting the future – through the commoditisation of charms and *mantras* – engage with a future that is imagined to be part of 'rational' laws of supply and demand. One of the traditions invoked is through a particularly well-known public image, that of Hakim Hari Kishan Lal, that beams down from countless billboards in Delhi (Figure 3.1). In an age of the free market, the muscular film hero, cultures of bodybuilding (Baas 2020) and westernised headgear (the baseball cap, for example), the Hakim's image is even more striking for the imagined markets it may be directed at. For here is a feudal landlord-like, moustachioed, double-chinned and starch-turbaned figure that appears to borrow its representational codes from an entirely different era; it is an image of masculinity that would appear to be curiously out of sync with contemporary ideas of metropolitan male identity. What then is the appeal of this image? The masculine code represented here has a very particular appeal for the urban male migrant. It is the appeal of *restoration*, and the promise of re-location at a time of dislocatory anxiety. In their experience, such men are confronted with an environment where their authority (as men) is frequently threatened by a metropolitan environment that stymies the kinds of actions a man might take to assert his 'natural' patriarchal rights.

In the post-national city, men of little means are condemned to both aspire to the new life that commodity cultures promise and seek control over those aspects that threaten 'emasculation'. This involves an infinite series of engagements with consumption as moral consumption. An aspect of the Hakim's therapy is, then, the possibility of the maintenance of 'Indian traditions' in threatening environments, and the appeal of maintaining one's *khandan* (lineage) through the advocacy of moral consumption. It is the promise of agency over both the world and the home. As we will see in Chapter 7, when this promise is translated into ideas of 'manly' political leadership, it has potent consequences.

The *hakim*'s image performs, then, an important task – it assuages male anxieties. The swirl of commodities that speak to the sense of modern subjecthood – the circumstances I have outlined in earlier paragraphs – is an unstable, but also desirable, aspect of urban life. It is both a promise and a threat. To be a man in the city is to be able to exercise choice – through consumption – but also direct and control consumption in ways that mitigate the ever-present danger to masculinity that participation in urban consumerism entails; moral consumption is a way of being in the city on one's own terms.

This chapter and those that come after it outline contexts that mark a move away from the Five-Year Plan hero model of masculinity discussed in Chapter 1. This male figure is also the prototype that animated the discourse of sites such as the Doon School. The Five-Year Plan hero stood both for government intervention and for delayed gratification through the reinvestment of savings for the 'national good'. Though a man of the metropolis, he was not, however, a consumer and, rather than spending on 'frivolous' goods, he saved for the national good. The Five-Year Plan hero finds almost no resonance in the non-middle-class contexts described in this chapter. This is echoed, for example, through the sex-clinic discourse on male masturbation: several of their publications routinely pointed to its 'harmful' effects, whilst the majority of the operators I spoke to said that they did not condemn it in their discussions with their clients, and usually regarded it as a harmless pastime that was surrounded by many myths. The post-colonial history of the discourse on 'semen-conservation' is also an aspect of the overall narrative of frugality and saving. It is also about the duty of men to contribute to 'nation-building'. This perspective, while popular during the early years of the Indian nation-state, hardly has much play in the contemporary era of consumerist modernity; the sex clinics and their clients exemplify this transformation in the national mood. In any case, delayed gratification for the national good may hold little attraction for those whose gratifications seemed to be perpetually delayed. Instead of scientific masculinity (Chapter 2), we are now in the era of a corporeal one where the male body is the shining surface of the commodity (Baas 2020) and, unlike the 'intellectual' Five Year Plan hero, the qualities of the male commodity are much more immediately expressible. It is in this sense that we might speak of a new commodity culture. This is also, of course, the shift from the national city to the post-national one.

Conclusion: Ramesh Vishwakarma – Carpenter, Believer in Spirits, Sex-Clinic Client

The marginalisation of traditional systems of healing and experience from 'respectful' therapy and validated knowledge and the role of the former in the life of the immigrant to the city is the most direct context through which this chapter has explored subaltern urban masculinities. Despite the existence of government-funded universities and hospitals, medical systems such as Ayurveda suffer low prestige in terms of the status of their practitioners, even though they have a very wide clientele and Ayurveda is widely regarded as home remedy. Almost all sex-clinic operators are either qualified Ayurvedic doctors or represent themselves as relying upon Ayurvedic or Unani medicine. For example, the following discussion occurs in Hakim Hari Kishan Lal's booklet on the treatment of impotency:

> [S]ome medicine for the rich production of semen and thickening the semen should be used. For this purpose, some of the Indian Herbes [*sic*] such as Asgarandh (Withania Somnifera), Kouch (seeds of Coucharge), Vidari Kand, Talmakhana (Hygrophila Spenosa) and Musli in due proportion are of unique efficiency. (Kishan Lal n.d.: 19)

The official suspicions that keep watch over non-allopathic systems of medicine need to be juxtaposed to the material and cultural conditions of life for the marginal populations of the metropolis. This is the milieu of the sex clinics and the conversations they engender about both masculinity and the city. The uncertainties of metropolitan life with its official promises – and everyday disavowals – of a better future and an urban space of contractual existence are most saliently articulated through the competition between official and unofficial knowledge regimes. I will conclude the discussion of this chapter with an ethnographic vignette drawn from fieldwork in a sex clinic in that most iconic of migrant cities, Mumbai. This further illustrates the nature of the unofficial city and the post-national one. As precarious Mumbai hillsides provide tenuous slum-shelter to an increasingly large number of migrants from states such as Uttar Pradesh, they also serve as the grounds upon which the apparent formality of the city is contested by the stridency of a displaced people. The post-national city is also the scattered locale of knowing and being that not so much authorises the law-and-order legends of modernity as places them in confrontation with 'other' knowledge through the agency of the migrant who forever dreams of a return to the province.

I was introduced to twenty-one-year-old Ramesh Vishwakarma by the owner of Kaya Kalp sex clinic, Dr Arun Kumar. We met at the clinic's Borivali premises in north Mumbai. Kaya Kalp is the most widely advertised and perhaps the most successful of the city's larger sex clinics. Its hoardings and posters can be found on almost all of Mumbai's suburban railway stations, as

Figure 3.2   Kaya Kalp office and logo (inset)

Source: Ahonaa Roy.

well as inside many train carriages. The red, yellow and green graphic with its key motif of a lion and a silhouetted naked woman in a standing posture is one of the most pervasive parts of Mumbai's visual landscape. The tag line reads 'Strength, Health, Beauty'.

Dr Kumar, the son of a dentist, trained as an Ayurvedic doctor from the Satya Sai Murlidhar Ayurvedic College, Moga, Punjab. The Borivali clinic has morning sessions, whereas another branch in the suburb of Dadar opens at 3 p.m. On most days, Dr Kumar works from around 9 in the morning to 10:30 at night, with a break of about two hours in between. At all times during my visits, the sitting rooms at both clinics were full to overflowing. The Dadar clinic had a separate, air-conditioned room to gather the overflow from the regular waiting area, and this too was invariably crowded with patients.

The clinic premises in Dadar are on the second floor of a commercial block next to the railway station. The clinic sign is also visible from a flyover next to the building. On the first floor are situated the offices of Gemini Arts and Om Graphics (companies making wedding cards), Nutan Beauty Collection (a jewellery shop), the Deccan Merchants Co-operative Bank and the Dadar Commercial Institute (a secretarial training institute). On the second floor, the clinic shares space with the Chitalia Infotech Academy and the Bhartiya Kala Sangeet Mandir (a music school). The small lanes that surround the Kaya Kalp building contain a variety of shops selling electrical goods, cheap clothing and plastic shopping bags printed with (unauthorised) versions of internationally and locally recognisable designs. The footpaths are crowded with stalls selling fruits and vegetables, fruit juices and soft drinks.

Itinerant hawkers wander the streets with their wares of handkerchiefs, travel bags, belts, ties and a multitude of other goods of uncertain quality. At night, the entire area converts to an open-air market for different kinds of herbs, vegetables and plant matter used in religious ceremonies. The periods of lull in activity in the area appear to be quite brief, perhaps for a few hours during late night and very early morning. It is at this juncture – where the promises of formal capitalism are modified through the *personal* economies of small-scale commerce, space, intimacy and migrant dreams of going back 'home' – that the sex clinics are located as metropolitan sites of therapy par excellence. Ramesh Vishwakarma has lived in Mumbai for about two years, leaving behind a young wife and the rest of his joint family in a village in the district of Azamgarh in Uttar Pradesh.

At our first meeting at the Kaya Kalp premises, he is relaxed and keen to seek answers for his 'problems' of the lack of a sustained erection and any children. He thinks I am a medical doctor, or at least someone with specialist training in 'sexual matters'. I explain that I am an anthropologist. He looks disappointed but agrees to continue the conversation. We speak briefly, mainly to build rapport. I ask him if we could meet again, to which he readily agrees, and we next meet in a small teashop near the suburban Andheri railway station in the western part of the city. This time he is accompanied by an 'uncle', a man of perhaps forty, and our conversation is more wide ranging. Ramesh tells me that after he has saved up enough money, he would like to return to Azamgarh, that he stays in the informal locality of Kranti Nagar with some people from 'home', and that, like many others from his region, he frequently consults occult practitioners such as *tantriks* and *ojhas* for a variety of complaints. Of course, there is a ghost world, both Ramesh and his uncle tell me over *samosas* and tea; the city is full of malevolent spirits and those that deny people like them a decent life despite their unrelenting labour. The milieux of the formal political economy of the city with its circuits of social capital (Bourdieu 1986) – or those of criminality with its own systems of distribution and redistribution of resources — are inaccessible for men (and women) of Ramesh's background. It is in this context that there emerges the sphere of the unofficial – ghost? – city, and an alternative landscape of knowledge and experiences, to which the metropolis of the official master plans and tourist brochures is merely an adjunct.

In this unofficial city, we find the project of the 'Ayurvedic body': a proliferation of advertisements by pharmaceutical companies ('From Zero to Hero with Safe, Ayurvedic PLUS capsules') and sex-clinic operators that promise to overcome nutritional constraints through recourse to the therapy of tradition. Most clients of the sex-clinics milieu lack the means to a healthy body available to better-off Indians, including adequate nutrition, a clean environment and functioning medical facilities. So here, a marginalised medical system provides succour to the life strategies of marginal populations. Perhaps the most important of these is the one where the body is sought to exceed the limits imposed upon it by the political economy of the formal city. In such cases, the physical body may suffer the pangs of hunger, but hunger is sought to be overcome through the social process of the remedies offered by the sex clinics. These remedies consist of 'advice' on leading a fulfilling family life, how to avoid contracting sexually transmitted diseases, eating proper food and maintaining masculinity.

In an urban environment that is the cause of a great deal of mental and physical debilitation, the sex-clinic discourses significantly focus on youthfulness and the remedies it can provide. 'Youth', as Hakim Hari Kishan Lal points out, 'is the most vital period of life of any human being. At this stage only [*sic*], a man comes to know about the real happiness of life' (Kishan Lal n.d.: 2). Here, there is a shift from the scriptural notions of Indian (Hindu) existence, where youthfulness is not necessarily valorised over old age, a shift linked to the emerging culture of consumption and contemporary capitalism. The narrative of lost youth stands, we might say, for the dangers of losing one's masculinity in the city. It is a common strand within all the different booklets published by sex clinics in Delhi and Mumbai. It is usefully positioned in the context of the political economy of hunger and poverty when youth and 'masculine vigour' are, for most of the sex-clinic clientele, fleeting experiences.

Youth also figures in the context of 'unnatural means' of satisfying desire, namely masturbation and homosexuality: Due to excessive masturbation, it is pointed out, 'by the time of marriage, young males are totally incapable to enjoy [sic] marital bliss' (Kishan Lal n.d.: 2). The latter is linked to 'complete control over momentary pleasures' and preservation of semen 'which is a valuable treasure of life' (Kishan Lal n.d.: 2) Here, the discourse of consumption – to which youthfulness belongs – is combined with that of the deferral of pleasure, so that pleasure becomes available at a later point within a sanctioned – moral – framework. Enjoyment–consumption– saving–deferral–proper enjoyment constitutes here the discourse of modernity. The front cover of the booklet Safal Jiwan (Happy/Successful Life), published by Delhi's Ashok Clinic, consists of a colour drawing of an 'ideal' modem family: Facing the camera, there is a young father with his son on his shoulders and his pretty wife standing slightly behind him. They are in a garden; the nuclear family, happiness, through consumption, but also through its deferral. Once again, moral consumption.

For Ramesh Vishwakarma, a safal jiwan is a constant state of deferral. The anxieties of subaltern masculinity – caught between the city's hostile political and cultural economies and the fearful desire for it – tell us something about the fragility of actually existing identities. However, though safal jiwan promised through sex-clinic discourse might – as the enforced COVID-related flight from cities illustrates – be illusory, the trope of domestic conjugality continues to act as a powerful template for masculine identity. In the swirl of urban modernity, masculinity finds its anchor in the certainty of familial norms and behaviours. The next chapter elaborates upon this aspect through a focus on the world of Hindi-language detective novels – whose readership is very similar to that of footpath pornography – and the ways in which urban masculine cultures they speak to grow out of the relationship between the home and the world.

4

Thrilling Affects

Sexuality, Masculinity, the City and 'Indian Traditions' in the Contemporary Hindi 'Detective' Novel

Introduction

In Chapter 3, I suggested that the urban informality that characterises the lives of immigrants to the city produces an anxious masculinity that seeks to salvage a sense of the self through strategies of hybrid consumerism. The informality of work, residence, options for well-being, among others, engenders erratic relationships with the world of goods: magical potions and those for sexual potency co-mingle with the 'Lion Zorro automatic folding revolver' as men of limited means seek to recuperate masculinity through the putative power of consumption; to consume a multiplicity of goods and services is to seek dominion over different realms in the hope of gaining a measure of control over an environment where hardly anything appears to be controllable. The strategies of subaltern masculinity are distinct. This chapter continues the discussion of the previous one, building upon one of its themes, that of the desire for a *safal jiwan* – a 'happy married life' – and the ways in which cultures of subaltern masculinity attach to that of a 'traditional' family. In the pell-mell of consumerist modernity and its seductions of the world, where does the home and the family fit in? This chapter explores the ways in which ideas of family life anchor masculine identity simultaneously as men seek to be of the world. How to take part in the affairs of the world and yet keep at bay the instability that it might introduce – possibly diluting manhood – has been an important theme in Indian life (Chatterjee 1993a). This discussion expands upon this theme at the level of the city. This also prepares the ground for the material of Chapter 7, which will return to this aspect through an exploration of the public appeal of Prime Minister Narendra Modi.

As in the previous chapter, I proceed from the understanding that masculinity and sexuality are intertwined topics. And further that, in order to talk about their relationship in the present times, we need to move beyond the stereotypical understanding of 'Indian sexuality' that is frequently framed by perspectives that assume a fixed cultural template. Within this, it is common to suggest a direct link between contemporary Indian sexual cultures and 'classical Indian love texts' such as Vatsayayana's *Kama Sutra* and Kalyanamalla's *Ananga Ranga* (Roy 2000). Quotidian sexual cultures in India have been formed, however, in the crucible of a variety of nationalist politics and transnational flows, assertions of non-heterosexual identities, global sexual-health programmes, debates around 'sex work', the effects of new consumer cultures, changing patterns of work and leisure among young women, and the effects of different media flows (see, for example, John and Nair 1998; Mazzarella 2001; Pigg and Pike 2004; Reddy 2004; Srivastava 2007). That is, a substantial portion of sexual cultures in the non-western world is made from hybrid transactions (Pigg 2005) that defy easy categorisation as 'authentically non-western' (cf. Foucault 1990). This hybridity, as Chapter 3 demonstrated, is also characteristic of the post-national city. The previous chapter focused upon sex clinics and footpath pornography to move away from the 'classical' focus on the making of intimate lives in India, thereby positioning the city as a significant *mise en scène*. The discussion of this chapter – on the sexual and masculine cultures of Hindi language 'pulp' detective fiction – seeks to reinforce that perspective by further exploring the overlapping and unstable contexts of cultural, social and economic flows. The chapter focuses on the writings of Ved Prakash Sharma (1955–2017), chosen for both the prolific nature of his output and their continuing popularity since his death. A measure of Sharma's popularity lies in the fact that new books continue to be published under his name. These are now penned by 'guest writers', including his son, Shagun Sharma.

In many parts of the non-western world, crime fiction – also referred to as 'detective fiction' and 'thrillers' – has a complex and shifting relation to processes of modernity and 'modernisation'. So, for example, while the post-Ottoman Turkish state and its intelligentsia 'attached great importance to translation [of western "classics"] within the Westernization project' (Tahir-Gürçağlar 2008: 138), the Turkish editor of a 1940 anthology of 'translated European literature in Turkey' noted that 'he had neither the urge nor the opportunity to include an exhaustive list of "detective and adventure" novels' (Tahir-Gürçağlar 2008: 138). And, in a 1961 Chinese dictionary, the definition of detective fiction was provided as 'a kind of popular fiction that was ... low-grade, arousing base passions for sex and violence' (Kinkley 2000: 2). The various projects of modern 'moral', educational and social 'improvement' that have characterised societies as divergent as Turkey, China and India are important contexts for the production, reception and critique of crime fiction. Moreover, their nature as morality tales is linked to the fact that they have 'provided reading material to a section of a society changing worlds' (Tahir-Gürçağlar 2008: 139). This aspect is particularly true of the contemporary Hindi detective fiction. In particular, the changing world is that of the city, and actions within these works are also instructions to men about managing change.

The detective novel in India was 'introduced first when translated from English into Bengali and then from Bengali into other Indian languages at the end of the nineteenth century' (Orsini 2004: 436). And while it is unclear if the widely acknowledged precursor of the detective genre, Edgar Allen Poe's *The Murder in the Rue Morgue* (published 1841), was ever translated into Hindi, others, such as G.W. Reynold's best-selling *Mysteries of the Court of London*, were (Orsini 2004: 447). This history of translations is a shared one among the several non-western countries where the genre found new readership. In some cases, it also meant new forms of creative borrowing. In Turkey, for example, translations spilt over into 'pseudotranslations', a term that refers to 'texts which have been presented as translations with no corresponding source text in other languages ever having existed' (Tahir-Gürçağlar 2008: 134).

A vital element of the collective history of detective fiction in the non-western world concerns the manner in which it borrowed from 'internal' cultural sources. Hence, Chinese, Turkish and Indian detective fiction not only introduced new concerns, locales and characters with respect to 'crime' and criminal activity but also incorporated long-standing *local* beliefs relating to custom and law, and traditions of 'folk' entertainment into the narrative. Jeffrey Kinkley points out that 'ghosts and anomalies appear even in modern Chinese detective stories' (Kinkley 2000: 114–115) and that 'traditional aspects of jurisprudence' are also embedded within the stories. So, for example, a 'fixation on the name of offenses' (Kinkley 2000: 133), 'justification of legal procedures for their "utility" rather than their "justice"' (Kinkley 2000: 134), the treatment of 'mere accusation' (when a 'crime' was brought 'to the attention of the authorities') (Kinkley 2000: 134) and the figure of the 'truly exceptional person' (Kinkley 2000: 135) who enforces the rule of law are, Kinkley suggests, remnants of older ('Imperial') aspects of jurisprudence. Similarly, Tahir-Gürçağlar points out that '[i]n the case of the Turkish Sherlock Holmes ... the model of these pseudotranslations can be traced back to another tradition, namely the rewrites of folk stories' (Tahir-Gürçağlar 2008: 148).

The Indian case is no less striking for the relationship between the modern – 'popular' – literary form and older narrative traditions. In north India, detective novels were referred to as 'jasusi upanyas' (spy novels) and '[t]he use of the term *jasus* points back to the history of state and private spying and investigative operations established by the Mughal and post-Mughal regimes and modified by the British' (Orsini 2004: 448). Further, Orsini notes that '[i]n [Perso-Urdu] romances and dastan narratives, every king, good or bad, had spies or jasus who collected information and were sent out to discover the enemy's plans' (2004: 448). I provide this brief history of the imbrication of different worlds within the novels in order to present Ved Prakash Sharma's works as a site where a variety of 'Indian traditions' beyond literary ones structure and give meaning to urban masculine cultures.

The most significant aspect, as far as the present discussion is concerned, relates to the city as the invariable site of detective-modernity: villains and vamps, cars and ill-lit streets, spy-rings and cabals, hotels, nightclubs and bars mark the city as not just a background but the formative site of action, behaviour, identities and destinies. *The city makes the plot what it is.* Further, as in the case of Chinese detective stories, 'exceptional' male personages play a significant role and wield extra-judicial powers. These keep the city under masculine control, exercising authority both over urban spaces and women. This chapter is particularly concerned with the ways in which these concerns, simultaneously as they are positioned as aspects of Indian transnational modernity, are circumscribed by enduring local concerns with concepts such as 'masculine honour', feminine propriety and the centrality of the family within 'modern' life. As characters and plots move in and out of a variety of urban landscapes, sexuality is the invariable *mise en scène*. It is the fulcrum around which social and individual crises take shape and are resolved, the site of both human flaws and strengths, and the trigger that propels human destinies along different paths. Sexuality is simultaneously 'un-Indian' and yet fundamental to the making of contemporary Indianness. And, while the booklets focus upon both male and female sexuality, the greater significance attaches to the manner in which sexuality forms the irreducible grounds of the making of urban masculine identities.

'Whatever its status or readability, Indian *English* pulp [fiction]', Tabish Khair suggests, 'is an interesting marker of significant cultural and economic changes in India' (2008: 71, emphasis added).[1] The Hindi detective novel is also an important sub-genre of pulp fiction in the language and shares many aspects of its moral and cultural universe. The history of Hindi pulp fiction is also a history of desire pitted against the strictures of the nation-state. Charu Gupta points out that one strand of the nationalist movement during the late nineteenth century aimed at 'linguistic standardization' (2002a: 197) of Hindi as well as the 'purification' of Hindi literature. In Gupta's felicitous phrase, once ideas of romance, sexuality and eroticism came to be viewed as transgressive of nationalist ideals, '[a]esthetics became an exercise in ethics' (2002a: 197). Notwithstanding such 'reformist' zeal, 'ashlil (obscene)' (Gupta 2002a: 197) publications formed a significant part of the print cultures of colonial north India (see also Gupta 2002b). 'By the early twentieth century', Gupta points out, 'wide-ranging pulp and popular literature – semi-pornographic sex manuals and romances in colloquial Hindi, … flooded the market' (2002a: 198). As we will see in this chapter, ethical behaviour – particularly in the shape of moral consumption in a 'dangerous', post-national city – acts as a significant structuring principle in the detective novels.

Placed alongside the impressive body of scholarship on mass-appeal literary genres in the west, India-related scholarship that addresses non-English language popular writings constitute a far more meagre offering (see, for example, Venkatachalapathy 1997 on Tamil popular fiction; and Chandra 2008, McLain 2009 and Srinivas 2010 on 'religious comics'). Given the large body of such material published in different Indian languages, this is indeed a strange lacuna. The scholarship dealing with English-language material are similarly thin on the ground (see Tyagi Singh and Uberoi 2005 on romance fiction in 'women's' magazines, and Dwyer 2000 on the writings of the novelist Shobha Dé). If we further consider the Hindi detective novel sub-genre, there are – as far as I have been able to discover – no academic works that take up its *post-colonial* incarnations.[2] And yet these novels might be said to have almost as wide a following as Bollywood cinema. Their leadership certainly overlaps with it and Ved Prakash Sharma is one of its biggest names of the Hindi detective genre. If the 1927 Hindi novel *Chaklet* by Pandey Bechan Sharma (translated into English [2009] by Ruth Vanita) 'brought into public view emergent urban male attachments and alternate sexualities, posing a danger to civilization' (Gupta 2002a: 201), then Sharma's novels speak of a twenty-first-century world of urban encounters where (hetero-)

sexuality and civilization are entwined contexts: to be modern is to be able to express one's sexuality, and sexuality is at the root of human happiness, foibles and failures. Further, the 'city' and 'sexuality' constitute complementary settings as well as grounds for the processes of Indian modernity. I will explore these themes by focusing upon two of Sharma's novels, namely *Vijay Ke Saat Phere* (Vijay's Wedding Rituals, 2010a; Figure 4.1) and *Naukari Dot Com* (Career Dot Com, 2010b). Though the sexual theme present within

Figure 4.1   Cover illustration of *Vijay Ke Saat Phere*

Source: Author.

these novels repeats in a number of his other works, taken together, the two novels serve particularly well as explorations of the salience of sexuality as an organizing principle of, and social commentary on, Indian modernity and masculinity. Further, *Naukari Dot Com* was published immediately after *Vijay Ke Saat Phere*, an aspect that – as we will see in later sections – allows me to make an additional point about sexual activity within Sharma's works.

Family Ties in Time of Sexuality

If a key characteristic of 'pulp' fiction consists in its 'mass' nature (Khair 2008), then the Hindi detective novel is pulp fiction par excellence and it is not uncommon for writers to claim to have written *several hundred* books.[3] It is also, as a mass-produced commodity, an object of, and about, the city. However, whereas many other leading lights of the genre began their literary careers as translators of the works of western writers (such as Ian Fleming's James Bond series), Ved Prakash Sharma's popularity is based entirely on his own works. Sharma was born in the village of Bihara, located within the district of Bulandshahar in north-western Uttar Pradesh. He claimed to have written his first book at the age of fifteen.[4] By 2011, he had published around 160 novels. While in the earlier part of his career, he was associated with a number of publishing houses (particularly Delhi's Manohar Pocket Books), he later founded his own company, Tulsi Paper Books [*sic*].

The novels are cheap to purchase, varying from 30 to 50 rupees (English ones generally range from 150 rupees upwards). Their cover price and sites of sale – footpath bookstalls, railway stations and bus depots – suggest that their most significant market is among men of relatively modest means. At many urban footpaths, they share space with the footpath pornography material.[5] The language of the novels is a mixture of 'street-Hindi', Bollywood dialogue, a smattering of English words that have become a common part of urban patois, and Sanskritised 'high' Hindi when irony or mockery is called for. The following translated excerpts from *Naukari Dot Com* illustrate these linguistic styles in turn, their purpose being to both make for easy reading and establish the stories as 'everyday' literature:

A) Woman to Police Inspector: Thankfully, when my car fell into it the crater was filled with water. Otherwise by now I would have been on my way to Heavensville [Ishwarpuri]. (p. 35)

B) Police Inspector to sidekick of underworld don: You are free to follow your own course in life, but here is one thing you must never do. Not ever.

Sidekick: What's that?

Policeman: Never trust a Policeman (English dialogue written in Devanagari script; p. 13)

C) Young woman to Police inspector: 'As you like Inspector Johnny!' (p. 32)

D) Policeman to underworld don, in Sanskrtised Hindi: 'Mere aho bhagya jo swamiji mujhe aisa samajhte hain' [It is my great fortune that my lord should think so highly of me]. (p. 12) (Sharma 2010b)

Certain aspects mark Sharma's publishing enterprise as a distinct genre of the great variety of urban print cultures that scholars have begun to analyse (see, for example, Jain 2007 on 'calendar art' and Ramaswamy 2010 on 'mapping Mother India'). Each forthcoming novel is publicised through an announcement on the back cover of Sharma's latest work (Figure 4.1). Hence, at any time, readers are aware that the next novel is, perhaps, no more than a month away. In this way, the schedule of publication mimics the furious pace of the action between the covers as well as the life of the city. Second, there is the manner in which the narrative content of the novels – significantly organised around a variety of sexual meanings – is distanced from the self-presentation of the author as well as the mode of marketing the books. The distancing is achieved through two kinds of relationships that Sharma establishes with his readers. The relationships are symptomatic of the ways in which his writings position the sexual sphere as both *deus ex machina* and a warning; in the post-national city, a site of both aspirations and seductions, masculinity is always under threat from the wiles of dangerous women, and the novels have their own versions of a Tejinder who both desires Shirley and must also exercise constant vigilance and stay firm in his masculinity (Chapter 3).

All of Sharma's novels open with a letter to the reader. The letters follow a familiar pattern and are in the nature of a familial contract – in the manner of a father figure speaking to his wards – that serves to position the sexual material of the *rest of the book* at a distance from the kinship established relationship between the writer and his readers. There are different ways in which this is sought to be achieved. First, in the letters, Sharma talks about his family life, correspondence with 'fans', reasons for the delay (if any) in publication, and battles with 'exploitative' publishing houses and 'jealous' competitors. The excerpt below is from a letter in *Naukari Dot Com*. It is part of a long-running narrative thread that introduces each novel as the product of familial effort and family ties that the reader is invited to join:

> My Dear Readers,
>
> [...]
>
> I present before you my new novel – 'Naukari Dot Com'. I want, firstly, to talk about the new 'getup' of the novel ... you will see changes in the size ... paper ... and print. The number of pages is around the same as before ... [but] the price has only been increased by ten rupees.
>
> [...]
>
> This achievement is entirely [my son] Shagun's. He is the one who looks after the affairs of Tulsi Paper Books. Shagun is young and enthusiastic and has a great desire to do something new in his lifetime. Perhaps that's why we have been having a long debate about this [the new 'getup' and the increase in the cover price].
>
> He said to me, 'Papa, we don't keep up with the new ways of the world, we will be left behind. We must change according to the times.'
>
> [...]
>
> The result is before you.
>
> I don't know whether you will support me or Shagun in this 'battle', but I will certainly request you that if the younger generation wants to do something different, then we must both support and encourage it. (Sharma 2010b: 5–6)

The familial is presented to the reader in other ways as well:

> In the end, I would also like to tell you something important: even before 'Naukari Dot Com' was published, my son, Shagun, has published his novel 'Gidhdrishti' [The Vulture's Gaze]. You must read it.... (Sharma 2010b: 6)

The circle of familiarity and family-ness is completed in a postscript at the conclusion of *Naukari Dot Com* where Sharma asks that readers contact him either through email or 'sms' on the 'mobile number provided below' (Sharma 2010b: 284).

The second strategy of relating is one that presents as a conversation about 'threats' to Indian society and 'traditional' family. Hence, Sharma's letter to his readers in *Vijay Ke Saat Phere* notes that his next novel (*Naukari Dot Com*) is about a group of young people who became 'addicted' to the internet and 'sex websites' and that it explores 'this frightening world of the internet and where it is taking us' (Sharma 2010a: 8).

When published, *Naukari Dot Com* did not (as we will see later) have any resemblance to the plotline presented by Sharma in his earlier 'announcement'; he simply used the same title to present a completely different story to what had been promised. What is of significance, however, is that the announcement provided a context for reiterating the nature of the relationship between Sharma and his readers. Hence, simultaneously as his novels position the centrality of the sexual theme within their narrative, Sharma takes on the role of a concerned elder male of the family, warning against the 'dangers' to society posed by 'youngsters' led astray by the new forms of sexual seductions. The reader is, once again, enfolded in a kin-like conversation. Beyond the marketing exercise ('buy my son's book'), however, what is the significance of the side-by-side positioning of the familial and the neighbourly, and depictions of an urban milieu where corrupt bureaucracies, violent police, rampant underworld activity and global criminal networks are brought into a relation through sexual acts? It can be located, I suggest, within a more general tendency through which sexuality is represented in mainstream Hindi material such as novels and magazines that circulate within domestic and other familial environments. In another discussion on mass circulation of Hindi 'women's magazines' such as *Grhasobha* (The Splendour of the Home) and *Meri Saheli* (My Girlfriend) (Srivastava 2007), I have explored the social meaning of explicit discussions on sex and eroticism within their pages. The magazines carry – for the Indian context, at least – remarkably explicit articles on sex and sexuality alongside those on more familiar topics such as cooking, home decoration and religion. Such discussions ('Virginity of the soul is superior to that of the body', *Meri Saheli* November 2001), I have suggested, are part of the context of 'retractable modernity' (Srivastava 2007: 311). The interweaving of different kinds of materials imagines an Indian woman who, in these 'modern' times, can be expected to have an interest in 'foreign' topics such as sexuality and the commodity cultures that surround it. However, the female reader being imagined is *also* 'authentically' Indian inasmuch as she is also able to relate to 'traditional' female interests and expectations: she is, unlike the 'westernised' Indian woman, able to engage with the demands of modernity, but also 'pull back' and return to 'tradition' when required. In this way, she takes part in moral consumption, maintaining an appropriate relationship with masculinity.

This perspective can be expanded to include the imagined *male* readership of Sharma's novels, where the familial and the extra-familial – here as non-procreative sex – are juxtaposed to both discussions about sex and simultaneously characterise those taking part in it as having the capacity to transcend sexual 'miasma' and return to 'traditional' Indian values. Further, Sharma's novels are not so much concerned with erotic descriptions – there is remarkably little of it, notwithstanding the important role of sexual acts in his works – as (hetero-)sex itself. This marks an important distinction between the Indian detective novel and its classic western counterpart. So, for example, in Raymond Chandler's writings '[w]hat sex there is takes place off stage, suggesting that Chandler is more concerned with the process of desire than its consummation' (Plain 2001: 61). In Sharma's novels, on the other hand, *consummation* is the site of the making and unmaking of human destinies, and what leads to it is of minor importance. The manner in which masculine sexual culture is presented in the books is significantly linked, I suggest, to their role as guidebooks to life in the city.

I now turn to the two novels mentioned earlier, *Vijay Ke Saat Phere* and *Naukari Dot Com* which immediately followed it. The following discussion investigates a context where 'depictions of violence, cynicism and the urban malaise' (Plain 2001: 61) sit alongside the 'sexual' as contiguous themes, but where the latter is also a site for the reiteration of 'Indian' identities – masculine ones in particular – and 'traditions'.

Vijay Ke Saat Phere: Celibacy, Masculinity and Sexuality in a Time of Globalisation

The plots of Sharma's novels are masterworks of convolution. Action and characters range across *mohalla*s (neighbourhoods); Indian cities and international metropolises; police stations and secret hideouts of criminal gangs; exclusive localities and slums; by-lanes and major highways; call centres and courthouses; airports and railway stations; night clubs and coffee houses; and shopping malls and corner shops. Further, these places are peopled by 'terrorist rings', police officers, bureaucrats, politicians, small-time crooks as well as leaders of international gangs; judges and lawyers; devious foreigners and patriotic Indians; criminal masterminds and their eager pupils; stoic fathers and worried mothers; beguiling temptresses and sisterly women without guile; street-smart men and fast-talking women; and, of course, detectives and spies. Crucial events transpire across several different time periods and geographies, resulting in the unlikeliest of encounters, relationships, global and local enmeshments, and dénouement. Storylines proceed by connecting a series of overlapping lives, with sexual relations playing a significant role in establishing key relations, which, in turn, are also contexts of anger, humiliation, desire for revenge and infinite suffering and torment through miscalculations with regard to sexual encounters. Among all this, it is the nature of urban life that is the *mise en scène* for the unfolding sexual dramas of life, death, national pride, and masculine honour and entitlement.

Vijay Ke Saat Phere (henceforth *Vijay*) is based in Delhi, and Vijay, the eponymous protagonist of the novel, is the son of a senior police officer, Inspector General Thakur Nirbhay Singh. Unknown to the latter, Vijay is a celebrated and very senior member of the 'Indian Secret Service'.[6] The plot turns upon the actions of Vijay, the young and attractive Menaka, Vijay's sister Sonu, her husband, Keshav Pandit, Vijay's devoted junior colleague, Vikas, and Alfansey, a London-based internationally renowned criminal and master of disguises.[7]

Before proceeding to an outline of the novel, it is pertinent to point to the use of *in medias res* technique in all of Sharma's novels. This, as Orsini (2004) points out, was a common feature of the early Hindi detective novel. So, Devakinandan Khatri's *Virendravir* (1895) 'begins in *medias res*, information is only gradually released, and the narrative agent is either part of the story or claims a partial perspective' (Orsini 2004: 453). Orsini usefully suggests that the technique introduced Indian readers to a different manner of relating to fiction, eventually preparing the grounds for the modern novel. 'What we have then', she says, 'is a new genre, with a new contract between the author and readers' (Orsini 2004: 454). In the present discussion, I extend the idea of a 'new contract between the author and readers' in another direction. The approach – *Vijay* opens with an episode that occurs in the 'middle' of the story and other episodes are similarly 'out of order' – is, I suggest, intended to simulate the disorienting urban world inhabited by Sharma's characters, a disorientation and disorderliness caused by 'incorrect' sex. The disorientation – where men take part in the constantly shifting tableau of people and events but must also maintain constant vigilance against dangers to masculinity – is not dissimilar to the 'cautionary' narratives of the footpath pornographic material. The 'contract' between the author and his readers is one where the former leads the latter towards recognition of his true – 'Indian' – self through the haze of 'urban malaise' (Plain 2001: 61) and transnational uncertainties. The *in medias res* technique is both in the nature of a cautionary method and also as the background against which the reader must recognize 'his' 'true' self.

Vijay opens with a 'seduction' scene, with Menaka as the seductress. Menaka is the Canada-born niece of Puran Singh, an old and trusted retainer of Vijay's. She has been sent to India to find a husband in the 'home' country. Vijay and Menaka meet at a party organised by Puran Singh. Vijay feels attracted to Menaka but acts boorishly so that she might feel repelled by him (the reason for which will become clear later). Vijay's parents, however, are interested in Menaka as a match for their son. Soon after, Menaka is kidnapped by a *goonda* (local thug) who sends a ransom note to Vijay's policeman father, suggesting that his son is part of a crime syndicate. Vijay proceeds to free Menaka, while his father also rushes to the scene and arrests him for criminal activities. However, following a mysterious call from the 'Home Department' (from Vijay's boss), Vijay is released. The latter suspects that an old adversary, Keshav Pandit, is behind the kidnapping. In the meanwhile, Menaka, impressed by Vijay's rescue attempt, falls in love with him.

Keshav Pandit – married to Vijay's sister Sonu – seeks revenge upon his brother-in-law for destroying his criminal empire. Pandit has vowed to strike at the heart of what is most precious to Vijay: his vow of *brahmcharya* or celibacy. This relates to the seduction scene with which the book opened. Keshav Pandit is aware of Menaka's feelings towards Vijay and enlists Sonu as an accomplice. At one of their meetings 'at McDonalds in the Rajnagar Mall', Sonu taunts Menaka that, given Vijay's vow of celibacy, she would never be able to marry him. Menaka undertakes to prove her wrong.

Menaka tells Vijay that she is in love with him and that he cannot stop her 'from putting his *sindoor* [vermillion] into her [hair] parting [sign of marriage for Hindu women]' (Sharma 2010a: 48). Vijay spurns her advances.

Menaka turns to Sonu for help, who supplies her with a drug called Cabricorn, which, she informs Menaka, 'generates excitement in men, filling them with intolerable heat ... that only dissipates after sexual union' (Sharma 2010a: 49). However, Sonu then asks, 'what if he doesn't agree to be yours with his heart', and 'what if he doesn't agree to marry you?' (Sharma 2010a: 50). Menaka replies that it does not matter as she considers him her husband 'man aur tan se' ('with my mind and body'). Then, Sonu offers her a ring that she says will help in making Vijay fall in love with her, as had happened between her and her husband, Keshav Pandit: 'this [Sonu says, echoing a familiar theme in a great deal of literature accessed by subaltern men, see Chapter 3] is a *chamatkari* [magical] ring' (Sharma 2010a: 50). Menaka puts the ring on her finger and, at the first opportunity, spikes Vijay's drink with Cabricorn. This is the prelude to the seduction scene with which the novel opens. The most significant aspect of the opening sections of the book is the implication that Cabricorn took effect, and that Menaka's attempt at seduction was successful.

Menaka tells Vijay that what has transpired between them is 'what happens between a man and his wife' (Sharma 2010a: 13) and that now it is only a matter of 'saat phere' (the wedding rituals). All this while, Keshav Pandit has been listening in to the conversation between Menaka and Vijay, for the 'magical' ring that his wife had gifted Menaka is actually a transmitter device. Pandit laughs derisively, for Vijay's public image is of an unwavering patriot whose only 'bride' is the nation and his masculine force is reserved for the 'national good'. This is the reason why he rebuffed all of Menaka's advances. Keshav Pandit now confronts Vijay and threatens him with legal action if he does not marry Menaka, implying that he would face the ignominy of the accusation of rape. The global world of crime syndicates is abuzz with the news that Vijay is to be married; it is unthinkable that Vijay has broken his vow of 'national' chastity. The city, with its wily ways, has undone Vijay's 'pure' virility.

The scene of action now moves to London, where Alfansey, a criminal mind of great renown, is engaged by the UK-based crime syndicate Cobra Organization to travel to India to find out the 'real' reason behind this extraordinary news.[8] The novel moves towards a dénouement through an extraordinary series of twists and turns (lasting some 300 pages) that includes the following episodes: Menaka is kidnapped and murdered by Vikas (Vijay's assistant); Keshav Pandit seeks to prove that Vijay had a hand behind the murder as he did not want to marry Menaka; and a live camera feed on national television that informs the audience that Vijay had sex with Menaka and then had her killed. The concluding sections of the book are devoted to events surrounding Alfansey's exhortations to Vikas to murder Menaka as 'punishment' for having made Vijay break his vow. Finally, we learn that it is, in fact, Alfansey, disguised as Vikas, who has murdered Menaka. But what of Vijay's unbreakable vow of celibacy – the crux of Vijay's steadfast masculinity in a 'corrupting' urban environment – that is at the centre of the hydra-headed plot? The seduction scene at the start of the book was not what it seemed: despite the Cabricorn, Vijay exercised extraordinary self-control. He also convinced Menaka that she must not be an accomplice in the plot to break the 'life-long vow of brahmcharya' (Sharma 2010a: 143). Menaka is full of admiration for Vijay's steadfast devotion to a 'noble' cause. The two agree to pretend that 'something' has happened between them in order that Vijay might bring Keshav Pandit and others to justice.

I have provided a detailed outline of *Vijay* to demonstrate the crucial nature of the sexual act – rather than 'the process of desire' (Plain 2001: 61) – as a pivot for the narrative, plot and dénouement. Let us begin with *brahmcharya* (celibacy), masculinity and the nation. These terms have a conjoined past, as well as a continuing life in the globalised present. The Hindu idea of *brahmcharya*, as Joseph Alter (2005) points out, has an important place in the modern Indian history of 'bodily reform'. Hence, '[Mahatma] Gandhi's mass appeal was partly effected on a visceral level at which many Hindu men were able to fully appreciate the logic of celibacy as a means of psychological security, self-improvement, and national reform' (Alter 2005: 310). Alter goes on to suggest that 'a male concern with celibacy is couched in terms of a discourse about truth, and that truth translates directly into the moral politics of nationalism' (2005: 311); and that the celibate body 'evokes a divine and heroic mystique of epic proportions' (Alter 2005: 311). In post-colonial discourses of *brahmcharya*, it is frequently pitted against 'westernisation', with the coda that the masculinity that emerges from 'self-control' is superior to that aligned to sexual virility and 'potency' (Alter 2005: 315–316).

As the outline of *Vijay* demonstrates, sex – or the sexual act – defines the key turning points in the plot: Keshav Pandit seeks revenge upon Vijay through the dismantling of his vow of celibacy and Menaka is keen on the plan *not* because she is merely interested in a sexual relationship with Vijay for itself, but because she believes that this would lead to marriage. Additionally,

Alfansey exhorts Vikas to 'punish' Menaka for the apparent harm she has done to Vijay – and to 'Indian' (or, rather, Hindu) traditions – by leading him to break the vow. Finally, as readers make their way along by-lanes, streets, roads, highways, criminal dens, shopping malls and airports marked with the sexual imprint, they learn that Vijay's celibate status remains intact. What is crucial, however, is that the novel positions *brahmcharya* – representing Indian-ness – within overwhelmingly 'westernised' lifeways that the city represents and, simultaneously, assigns it a crucial cultural role within that context. That is, while Vijay's appeal as the celibate hero no doubt draws from historical (and religious) conceptions of celibacy, the latter is positioned within a complex world, one where both renunciation (bodily and of material goods) and desire *coexist*.

The discourse of *tyag* (renunciation) that is part of the notion of *brahmcharya* is a significant aspect of Hindu religious life both in its historical and contemporary manifestations (see, for example, Das 1977; Dumont 1970; Madan 1987). However, as I will more fully explore in Chapter 5, this is a context where renunciation and consumerism *combine* to produce ideas of masculine identity. For, through a series of juxtapositions, Sharma's novels deftly reproduces a prolix social world that his readers occupy. It is a world where discourses of 'semen loss' (Alter 2005) and the need to 'preserve' semen coexist with consumerist contexts where sexuality is a greatly desired commodity. And one where sexual 'performance' is a context of proving one's masculinity, and non-procreative sex a benchmark of what it is to be modern. A reference to the discussion of the last chapter might make the point clearer. So, while the 'sex clinics' are extremely popular among men of modest economic backgrounds and which purport to provide 'cures' for a variety of 'ailments' such as impotence, premature ejaculation and 'night-fall', just as significantly, however, men also visit the clinics to seek advice on 'sexual satisfaction', an aspect linked to the apotheosis of sexuality within consumer cultures and its representation as possessing a 'truth' (Foucault 1990) that must be grasped in order to become a 'truly' modern subject.

The messages of masculine sexuality that are exchanged between the clinics and their clients are of a hybrid kind. Their hybrid nature lies in the fact that advice on how subaltern urban men might succeed in maintaining their 'traditional' manhood is positioned as a strategy of consumerist modernity; advanced capitalism that produces the lowly 'emasculated' factory worker is also offered as the context of achieving a sense of masculine self-worth. The methods of achieving and maintaining masculine subjectivity are scattered across several registers. It is also at this juncture that we might locate a work such as *Vijay*: its reading pleasures and 'efficaciousness' lie in the constant *relay* of choices established between the world of globalised consumerist modernity and 'traditional' morality. It achieves this through both the extra-narrative device of the letter to the reader and the intra-narrative one that presents celibacy and its antithetical contexts as interwoven states of being. The interweaving of seemingly opposed states of being allows the reader to move between the worlds of sexual adventurism *and* 'traditional' cultural moorings such that he is able to maintain control over both realms: he is not determined by (sexual) modernity and is able to return to 'tradition'. Like Vijay, the (male) reader too is able to overcome the effects of 'Cabricorn' and, metaphorically, maintain his vow of *brahmcharya*. And, also like Vijay, he has the good fortune of being in the company of 'modern' women such as Menaka who, despite their modernity, are also able to return to 'tradition'. This is how one conquers the city, maintaining intact the ways of the masculine self.

In a time of extraordinary social, cultural and economic volatility – where the city is the setting where men both perform masculinity and fear for it – the ability to take part in such change is linked to simultaneously being able to access the moorings of 'tradition'. Tradition – here in the shape of *brahmcharya* – is the shelter and sanity in the tumult of the present. And, as Sharma's next novel, *Naukari Dot Com* (2010b), demonstrates, those who seek to undermine tradition deserve infinite suffering through a denial of its comforts.

Naukari Dot Com: Sons, Lovers and Families

The sexual narrative of *Naukari Dot Com* (henceforth *Naukari*) shares a number of features with *Vijay*. These include the metropolis as a character in its own right, masculine senses of honour and revenge, and the unease over wanton female sexuality, which, subsequently, seeks respectability. The novel is also, as pointed out earlier, about the inviolable bonds of tradition.

The story revolves around Chandraprakash and his son, Avinash; Vishwamohan and his children, Gulshan and Jyoti; and Gayatri (no longer alive), who was earlier married to Chandraprakash but left him for

Vishwamohan. 'Inspector Abodh' of the Mumbai Police is an occasional presence as an investigating officer. The narrative glue that joins the various characters and their stories – Neelima – is, however, someone with no direct relation to any of the characters. The beautiful young Neelima, the daughter of a Mumbai underworld don, is in a relationship with Chandraprakash's son, Avinash. Vishwamohan's son, Gulshan, is also in love with her, but she spurns him. Vishwamohan repeatedly advises Gulshan against pursuing Neelima, and Gulshan is mystified by his father's sympathies for his rival in love. Vishwamohan refuses to say anything further on the matter, except to mention that many years ago, he had been 'unjust' towards Avinash's father and does not now wish any suffering upon Avinash. However, Gulshan persists in pestering Neelima. Infuriated, she decides to 'teach him a lesson'. Gulshan is kidnapped by some *goondas*, imprisoned in a van and warned never to seek her out again. Before being let off, Neelima blows smoke in his face as an act of insult and 'humiliation'. Seething with anger, Gulshan decides on revenge:

> I want to dent her pride, take off her 'polish' and besmirch her honour' [Gulshan said]. I understand, his friend Dilip responded, 'so, you want to rape her'. 'Yes [Gulshan replied]. I want to do it in front of her lover, Avinash. After that, they are free to go, and I will never again as much as look at them. That bitch will then be free to live her life as she pleases, carrying the mark of my desire upon her body. (Sharma 2010b: 82)

This is the first of several 'sexual' turning points. Soon after, Neelima's murdered body is found in her flat. She has also suffered sexual assault. Avinash, Neelima's 'true love', now plans his own revenge. He lures Jyoti, Gulshan's sister (and Vishwamohan and Gayatri's daughter), to an abandoned building site and rapes her. Avinash is unaware that his victim is, in fact, his half-sister (they share the same mother, Gayatri). Jyoti urges her father to file a case against Avinash, but he refuses. Angry and mystified by this reaction, she confronts Avinash with a gun, only to be shot dead by him. Gulshan finds out that Avinash is behind Jyoti's rape. He barges into Inspector Abodh's office, where Avinash has come to claim Neelima's body, and shoots at him. Avinash fires back and Gulshan is killed.

The circle of sexual humiliation and revenge is not, however, complete. For the reader discovers that the web of intrigue and murder can be traced back to an 'original' act of sexual humiliation suffered by Chandraprakash

'twenty-two years ago'. Lower-middle-class Chandraprakash had married
the wealthy Gayatri at his mother's urging. However, Gayatri could never
reconcile to her husband's modest house and income and returned to
her father's palatial dwelling, leaving their son, Avinash, behind with
Chandraprakash. Soon after, Chandraprakash discovers that Gayatri had
been in a relationship with Vishwamohan before their marriage, and Gayatri
reveals that Vishwamohan is Avinash's father and asks that the boy live with
them. Chandraprakash refuses and brings up Avinash as his own son. The
context of humiliation is doubly intense: not only had Gayatri's body been
'sullied' by another man *prior* to Chandraprakash's access to it, but the
consequences of the sexual insult lived on in the form of Avinash. The latter,
it turns out, was reared by Chandraprakash to be the instrument for wiping
out every trace of the insult, and he had been instrumental in arranging for
the circumstances that would lead to the trail of revenge and murder:

> [Chandraprakash to Vishwamohan]: Do you think I love Avinash? Never!
> How can I ever love a baby snake that is the *nishaani* [mark] of my wife's
> boyfriend and her own bad character, infidelity and *ayyashi* [sexual fun]?
> (Sharma 2010b: 156)

Chandraprakash goes on to explain that he had carefully arranged the
chain of events – beginning with Neelima's rape and murder – that would
set different characters against each other, leading to their acts of revenge
and violence, each of these a step in wiping out the ignominy of the original
sexual insult suffered 'twenty-two years ago':

> Chandraprakash to Vishwamohan: Now Avinash has done everything that
> will destroy my greatest enemy [that is, Vishwamohan].... He has killed
> your son, dishonoured your daughter ... your own son has dishonoured
> your own daughter ... and Avinash does not realize that he has done
> all this at my behest, the man he thinks is his father.... (Sharma 2010b:
> 157–158)

But there is a final twist. In the closing pages of the novel, we discover that
Avinash is, *in fact*, Chandraprakash's son with Gayatri:

> Vishwamohan to Chandraprakash: But I have not been defeated, it is you
> who has lost, for Avinash is actually your own son, with Gayatri ... she was

not a fallen woman and had no relations with me till we were married ...
she had lied to you that Avinash was my son, in order to get him back from
you. (Sharma 2010b: 277–278)

Chandraprakash is speechless and pleads with Inspector Abodh that
he, rather than Avinash, be arrested, as 'I am guilty of all the crimes
committed. I must be hanged ... that is the only appropriate punishment'
(Sharma 2010b: 248). Abodh refuses and says that the only suitable
punishment for Chandraprakash's crimes is that he will see his son go to
the gallows. Chandraprakash will then be sentenced to 'saza-e-zindagi',
the punishment of life. This unique justice will, he concludes, be meted
by the 'court of Inspector Abodh' (Sharma 2010b: 284). Inspector Abodh
will not formally charge Chandraprakash with any crime. The impersonal
justice system of the state may well deliver punishment for 'normal' crimes
of murder and rape; however, Chandraprakash's misdemeanour is of a kind
that cannot be addressed by bureaucratic procedure: a suitable riposte is
only available through extra-judicial processes where the true import of
the crime is better appreciated. For Chandraprakash has undermined the
grounds upon which the ability to engage with modernity lies: the Indian
family. Without a stable centre, how can men take *part* in the pleasures
of transnational modernity that is on offer in the metropolitan milieu? It
is the family – as Indian tradition – that allows Indian men to be both
modern and Indian. It is also this aspect that differentiates Sharma's novels
from popular discourses that are a relatively straightforward condemnation
of the 'ills' of 'westernisation': *Vijay Ke Saat Phere* and *Naukari Dot Com*
are formulations for 'better' participation in consumerist modernity
rather than morality tales that advocate withdrawal from it. The city is the
playground of masculinity, but masculinity is also under threat from urban
ways, and the family is the shelter from the storm. In the city of shifting
sands, the family must remain the stable anchor, home to traditional
structures of power and authority where men can 'return' to regain their
senses of masculinity.

Conclusion

Naukari Dot Com and *Vijay Ke Saat Phere* present certain cultural themes
that are familiar to their readers and which have also been part of Indian

masculine common sense. These include the ideas of women's sexuality (Gayatri's 'sexual fun' in *Naukari* as a site of potential slight to men; see, for example, Welchman and Hossain 2005), and the notion that sexual humiliation is the only answer to the slight to one's masculinity. So, when Gulshan is threatened and humiliated by the goons hired by Neelima, she is raped and *then* murdered; Avinash, in turn, rapes his own half-sister. Chandraprakash, who orchestrates these events, is driven by the belief that his 'shame' can only be addressed by directing sexual violence against the *man* (Vishwamohan) who has dishonoured him. Rape, as feminist scholars have suggested, is also a conversation about power between men; "'rape as violation'", Nivedita Menon points out, 'is not only a feminist understanding, it is perfectly compatible with patriarchal and sexist notions of women's bodies and our sexuality (2004: 159). The iconic figure of the 'fast' woman who, despite herself, exercises self-discipline through the overwhelming influence of 'Indian tradition' is also a significant presence: the cigarette-smoking and fast-talking Neelima in *Naukari* who is committed in love to Avinash rather than 'playing the field', and the potential seductress Menaka in *Vijay* who comes to admire Vijay's vow of celibacy, viewing it as an unfailing commitment to Indian traditions; unlike Shirley (Chapter 3), who can never return to tradition, these women are redeemable. And, finally, there is the persistent cultural symbolism of *brahmcharya* itself as an ideal to be emulated.

However, beyond outlining these relatively familiar themes, this chapter has suggested that the novels are an extended tract on the conditions of globalised modernity, and the manner in which men might *take part in* – rather than *withdraw* from – it. The sexual motif in *Vijay* and *Naukari* sits alongside an unstated discourse of 'Indian traditions' – *brahmcharya* and 'the stable Indian family' (Parry 2001) – and the discourse of traditions is established through both narratives *within* the novels and techniques that lie outside them, namely the author's letter to his readers. In these ways, the silent presence of 'Indian traditions' forms the grounds upon which engagements with consumerist modernity is predicated, and the novels outline as a strategy of moral consumption.

But if the city is a site of anxiety and men must constantly guard against threats to masculinity, and if to consume is to both ingest modernity and also be wary of it, men also devise strategies of taming the city. They do this, as the next chapter explains through ethnographic vignettes, by refashioning their identities as fragmented, rather than whole, selves. The political and cultural economies of the city, as I discuss in Chapter 5, are grounds for engaging with the city in ways where masculinity, religiosity and consumerism come together to make the city a place for the all-consuming man.

Notes

1. Pulp fiction, Khair points out, 'is fiction that uses largely fixed generic features to satisfy the largely fixed reading expectations of as large a market as possible' (Khair 2008: 61). However, as he goes on to say, 'a work of fiction can slip from being seen as "pulp" to "literary" by a drastic revaluation of generic features and reader expectations' (2008: 61).

2. The Introduction by Khurram Ali Shafique (2010) to his book of excerpts from the works of Ibne Safi (1928–1980), the pen name for Asrar Ahmed, is an exception. Safi was famous for his Jasusi Duniya (Detective/Spy World) series and, according to his son, 'wrote four novels per month' (Verghis 2011). Born in India, Safi migrated to Pakistan in 1952. He was, however, known as a writer of Urdu fiction. In *Mumbai Fables*, see also Gyan Prakash's (2010) discussion on how Bombay was represented in one particular *late-nineteenth-century* detective novel in English written by a local journalist.

3. As anyone with even a cursory acquaintance with book stalls on footpaths and those at railway stations and major bus depots knows, Hindi detective fiction is one of the significant genres on display. There is an ever-proliferating list of authors and it would be impossible to provide anything like a complete list of these. The pace set by Safi of 'four novels per month' (note 3) appears to be the desirable goal for the current crop as well.

4. This biographical information is based upon a write-up either penned by the author, or written with his approval: http://wikibin.org/articles/ved-prakash-sharma.html, accessed 1 May 2010. A planned meeting with Sharma did not eventuate due to his busy schedule.

5. Even though it is possible that their readership is mixed, it is men who mostly purchase such material. And, while I am unable to provide 'hard' evidence for this assertion, anecdotal accounts suggest that women do not like to be seen to be purchasing detective novels.

6. It should be noted that 'Vijay' was the most common on-screen name for the Bollywood superstar Amitabh Bachchan's characters.

7. 'Alfansey' is also the name of a novel by Ibne Safi and hence a tribute to one of the greats of the genre.

8. Given the London location – as well as spying and 'security' concerns – 'Cobra' may be a play on Cabinet Office Briefing Room A (COBRA), the British government's 'crisis response headquarters'. I am grateful to Steve Legg for the suggestion.

5

Fragmentary Pleasures

Masculinity, Urban Spaces and the Commodity Politics of 'Religious Fundamentalists'

Introduction

This chapter brings together three themes that have been significant throughout the earlier ones – masculinity, urban spaces and consumer culture – to explore the lives of a group of young men who belong to the Bajrang Dal, the all-male organisation of the Hindu right with strong roots in north India. The chapter focuses upon relationships between self-avowed religious and masculine identities to both explore the manner in which the city acts as a template and is shaped by them. The spectacular rise of a Hindu religious consciousness in the Indian public sphere over the past decade is a significant context as far as the Indian present is concerned and has received a great deal of scholarly attention (for example, Basu et al. 1993; Bhatt 2001; Bacchetta 2004; Chakraborty 2011; Anderson and Longkumer 2021). This chapter is not, however, an exploration of men of the religious right and their attitudes towards their putative enemies. Rather, it explores the different ways in which the lives of the so-called religious fundamentalists connect with the processes of contemporary capitalism to produce specific senses of non-middle-class masculine identities. In particular, the chapter investigates the ways in which urban masculine identities are constructed through strategies of the fragmented – or split – self. It suggests that the fragmentary politics of the self is a useful tool for understanding both expressions of male power and its articulation with contemporary consumer culture. In this way, the chapter suggests that the nature of the city – as a site of fragmented spaces and relationships – leads to specific responses in the way that urban masculinities are constructed.

To explore urban 'Hindu masculinities', the chapter engages with those perspectives on Hindu nationalism that take up the central role of the masculine identity of its protagonists and primarily view religious violence as an attempt to regain a 'whole' and 'pure' self, and a desire to return to an 'uncontaminated' past.[1] My argument builds upon theorisations of gender and Hindu nationalism,[2] space and subjectivity,[3] and identity politics in an age of intense and voluminous transnational flows.[4] However, by focusing upon relationships between masculinity and the city – rather than the religiosity of 'religious men' – I continue with the central theme that I have pursued through the book, namely the making (and un-making) of masculine identities and the ways in which the city is 'experienced by working-class men as a reminder of their struggle to accomplish the norm of respectable breadwinner masculinity' (Chowdhury 2019: 15). Hence, while scholars have explored the links between masculinity and Hindu nationalism (Bannerjee 2005), the market and the religious milieu (Kaur 2003; Rajagopal 2001), and spatiality and religious identity (Deshpande 2000; Oza 2006b), this chapter seeks to locate these aspects within the *same* analytical framework to provide an ethnographic account of contemporary meanings of urban masculinities.[5]

'Restoration' is a significant theme on writings on religious nationalism. Within such movements, it is argued, affirmations of identity build upon notions of a 'true people' and an 'authentic nation' (Blom Hansen 1999: 90). Bacchetta notes that 'in the Hindu nationalist framework, the acting out of violence against Muslims is a means for the restoration of the internal Hindu nationalist order' (2004: 80). Further, the destruction of the 'other' is also the remedy for restoring the self to its full manly strength, effacing the sense of 'self-hatred and ... castration' (Blom Hansen 1999: 211). Discussions of 'wholeness' and 'purity' in the context of religious identity can also be found in more explicitly psychoanalytic analyses (for example, Kakar 1990). Most commonly, the urge to wholeness is presented as a 'natural' reaction to processes of intensive change and dislocation. 'To human beings experiencing social mobility, or a loss of socioeconomic and cultural status produced by urbanization or "minoritization"', Blom Hansen says, 'the issue of identity – the urge to eradicate the doubt that splits the subjects – becomes more acute than in situations of relative social stability' (1999: 212); the identity that is under threat of 'splitting' is the masculine one. The idea of 'preserving' the self under conditions of modernity is itself part of a more general understanding of the nature of the 'inner life' in India and occurs in a number of scholarly contexts. These include studies of colonial modernity

(Chatterjee 1993a), post-colonial modernity (Singer 1972) and the 'cultural construction of emotions' (Desjarlais and Wilce 2003: 1184).

This chapter suggests that the broader context within which discourses of 'religious fundamentalism' and masculine violence are situated cannot be characterised as one that speaks exclusively of maintaining the integrity of the whole. Rather, it may simultaneously articulate the desire for the *fragmented and multiple* self. The notion of the 'split subject' – characterised by a 'lack' (Stavrakakis 1999) it seeks to overcome – which forms the cornerstone of theorising about the restorative quest of Hindu fundamentalists – builds upon Lacanian frameworks. However, I suggest below that an *ethnography* of 'splitting' leads us to view it as something other than a context of lacks and absences – to wit, a search for male *plenitude*; and, further, not as a state characterised by 'a lack of *jouissance*' (Stavrakakis 1999: 42), but, rather, as a site of great pleasure. Hence, I argue that the notion of the fragmented self should be considered an aspect of active *self-making* rather than as debris in modernity's wake; and, further, that splitting-as-self-making has particular significance as a strategy of the male self as it negotiates an urban environment.

Fundamentalism, Consumerism, Space

We get a fuller picture of the politics of masculinity that attaches to the young men of the Bajrang Dal if we supplement the 'desire-for-wholeness' perspective by investigating how the pleasures of fragmentation also form a part of the identity projects of 'religious fundamentalists' . In a similar vein, Oskar Verkaaik (2004) has explored the connection between 'fun and violence' among activists of the Muttehida Qaumi Movement (MQM) political party in Pakistan, pointing to the complex nature of motivations that inspire violent public acts by men in associations. My discussion proceeds from the idea that the 'fundamentalist' self is an agent of boundless and multiple capacities and one that is crucially linked to the rise of a new urban consumer culture and the imagination of masculinity within it. And further that foregrounding commodity-consumption as a significant strategy in the making of contemporary identities can broaden the analytical frameworks of 'religious fundamentalism'. My take on consumption follows from the proposition that '[i]nstead of supposing that goods are primarily needed for subsistence plus competitive display', we should 'assume [that] they are needed for making visible and stable the categories of culture' (Douglas and Isherwood 1979: 75).

Further, my argument rests on the idea that contemporary consumerism both valorises and deepens the capacity for engaging with multiple and split strategies of wants and actions (Appadurai 1986; Breckenridge 1995; Campbell 2000; Douglas and Isherwood 1979); as Osella and Osella point out, the 'fragmented or multiple nature of self and subjectivity in *all* ethnographic settings' (2004: 226, original emphasis) is the rule rather than an exception. Therefore, my discussion suggests that the assumption that contemporary self-making is propelled by the *determinative* force of a 'deep' desire for 'wholeness' needs to be re-thought.[6]

In particular, as I argue in this chapter, this departure leads us to a different way of understanding masculinity than is usually the case. This perspective builds upon Marriot's notion of the 'dividual' (Marriott 1990), or the partible – though not an 'essential' and unchanging – self, with the particular dimension of accounting for consumerism as a significant force in contemporary lives. It also draws upon recent ethnographies of consumer cultures around the world that demonstrate that the capacity for self-making develops through capacious engagements with an array of contexts and possibilities (see Farquhar 2002 for China; Freeman 2014 for Barbados; Kemper 2001 for Sri Lanka; and Liechty 2003 for Nepal). As in other parts of the book, this chapter seeks to explore the relationship between masculinity and the city as one that is co-constitutive. It is in this sense that 'fragmentation' is a productive framework of thinking about both men in the city and men *and* the city.

Over the course of the past few decades, the Bajrang Dal has gathered a widespread reputation for violence against religious minorities (Bhatt 2001; Lutgendorf 2007). The Dal is a member of the so-called Sangh Parivar, the 'family of organizations' of the Hindu right consisting of the Rashtriya Swayam Sevak Sangh (RSS), founded by K. B. Hedgewar in 1925, the Vishwa Hindu Parishad (VHP), founded by M. S. Golwalkar in 1964, and the Bharatiya Janata Party (BJP) formed in 1980 by leading members of the RSS (Malik and Singh 1994; van der Veer 1994). Established in 1986 by the VHP as its all-male 'youth wing', the Bajrang Dal was constituted as the 'shock-troop' of Hindu activism whose members, as one senior functionary told me, 'don't much care for ideology, and are mainly interested in action'. The most famous instance of the 'activist' nature of the Bajrang Dal was witnessed in 1992 when its members were at the forefront of the demolition of the 'disputed' Babri Mosque in the city of Ayodhya (Nandy, Trivedy and Mayaram 1995).

The most direct significance of the naming of the Bajrang Dal ('Hanuman's Battalion') is in 'invoking [the god] Hanuman's folksy Hindu epithet of *Bajrang-bali*, or "iron-limbed hero"' (Lutgendorf 2007: 367). Beyond this, there is the modern – and well-documented – history of the making of 'virile Hinduism' within discourses of Hindu nationalism, which 'represents a dense cluster of ideologies of primordialism' (Bhatt 2001: 3). A significant strand within Hindu nationalism relates to the perception that unceasing ideological and cultural assaults upon Hindu society has made it 'weak' and 'degenerate' (Jaffrelot 1996: 71) and turned the Hindu male into a 'frail' being (Chowdhury 1998), unable to protect either his religion or 'his' women. The answer lies in the 're-masculinisation' of Hindu identity.

The Bajrang Dal is a contemporary manifestation of the accumulating discourse on the requirements of 'Hindu masculinity' and the organisation was 'envisioned as a looser, less organized, and less demanding version of the RSS, requiring no uniform or participation in daily drill, but sponsoring ideological and martial training camps' (Lutgendorf 2007: 367). While the 1992 demolition of the Babri Mosque catapulted the Bajrang Dal into global notoriety, there are various other aspects of its public activity that continue to keep it in the news. Among other things, its members have been involved in the killing of a Christian missionary and two of his children in January 1999; attacks on art exhibitions by the acclaimed (Muslim) artist M. F. Husain for 'obscene portrayals of Hindu goddesses' (*Indian Express*, 22 December 2007); public humiliation of couples who take part in Valentine Day celebrations (characterised as 'western' and 'un-Indian'); and preventing 'love jihad' – the putative enticement of 'innocent' Hindu girls into marriage by Muslim men. The Bajrang Dal's reputation for an aggressive approach towards the 'protection' of 'Hindu' culture (equated to 'Indian' culture) is bolstered by the symbolic use of the *trishul* (the trident) in many of its ceremonies to initiate new members (Bhatt 2001), as well as in public demonstrations, when it is brandished as a potential weapon.

The organizational structure of the Dal – expressed through a hierarchical system that stretches across national, regional, city and neighbourhood levels of authority – is clear-cut in principle. However, in practice – and unlike other similar organisations such as the Shiv Sena in Maharashtra (Blom Hansen 1999; Eckert 2003, 2005) – it rarely manifests in its idealised form. And, while the Bajrang Dal has branches in different parts of Delhi (and in other cities), these do not perform the same role as the *shakha*s (branches) of the Shiv Sena, namely acting as '[c]ourts of arbitration, employment exchanges, credit schemes, crèches, infrastructural improvements, and dealing with the police' (Eckert 2005: 48). Their key role is as sites of male sociality and organisational nodes for 'direct action' that might provide street-level support for the political programmes of its parent bodies. Of course, a level of mutual care and self-help *does* manifest itself because of the close association between men of a very similar background, but it does not function in the same organised, consistent and deliberate manner as is the case with the Shiv Sena. The most significant reason for this may be that the Bajrang Dal – unlike the Sena, which is the dominant partner in the coalition that rules Maharashtra – does not aspire to political power. Its key role is as a 'rapid action force' that comes together for specific purposes and then, to some extent, melts away. Basu et al. point out that the Bajrang Dal's recruitment of 'untrained, volatile, semi-lumpen elements' serves to 'absolve the larger front and core organizations from direct responsibility for reckless acts of indiscipline or violence' (Basu et al. 1993: 68).

Interestingly, as Lutgendorf (2007) notes, Hanuman, who is Lord Ram's most loyal *servant*, 'seems to have been considered good for "little" people: children, tribals, Dalits ['the oppressed', referring to 'lower' castes], and unruly urban youths who lack the discipline to join the RSS' (2007: 370). In this sense, then, the Bajrang Dal is not in competition with VHP or RSS activism, positioning these organisations as the realm of those men possessing 'higher' ideological and intellectual capacities. And, just as importantly, it is also in this context that the Bajrang Dal is able to mobilise a constituency of men that cuts across caste lines. While Hinduism may differentiate co-religionists, masculinity provides a glue that brings together the different castes. The significance of this might be inferred from the fact that in various other contexts, masculinity across the caste divide – particularly between 'lower' and 'upper' castes – is frequently a site of competition and hostility (see, for example, Anandhi and Jeyaranjan 2001).

To return to the main argument of this chapter, the apparent quest for 'secure and stable identities' (Blom Hansen 1999: 208) – regarded as characteristic of movements of religious chauvinism – contains an implosive charge that positions the *split* subject at its centre. In the following sections, I explore the nature of the split subject through a series of 'performances' that enunciate a spatial strategy of the urban self. Edward Bruner speaks of the manner in which performances 're-fashion' reality. 'It is in the performance', as he puts it, 'that we re-experience, re-live, re-create, re-tell, re-construct, and re-fashion our culture ... the performance itself is constitutive' (Bruner 1986: 11). I use 'performance' to refer to all those public acts of individuals and collectivities that allow us to identify social processes. So, in this sense, walking in a group along a delimited space to mark that space as 'ours' is an act of performance. Performances include those practices that are not necessarily recognisable as the anthropologist's 'ritual', but which, nevertheless, mark the contours of social life through simply having been carried out. The performances I portray contribute to the 'social construction' of space, a term that captures 'the phenomenological and symbolic experience of space as mediated by social processes such as exchange, conflict, and control' (Low 1999: 112). My discussion is based around three urban contexts that present entangled relations between humans and spaces: streets and street corners, the household and the formulation of an unofficial geography of the city. Through these I investigate how certain performances constitute a series of actions over space as propulsions of the male body across different parts of the city which, in turn, constitute the act of consuming – controlling and mastering – the city.

Masters of Time and Space

The desire to master space is articulated in different ways, and the manner in which *temporal* constraints are flouted is one of these. Bajrang Dal activity takes place around the clock and the men wander the city at various times of the day and night. Meetings that begin in the late afternoon frequently flow into the early hours of the morning and, just as frequently, the group might decide to drop into a member's house across town at, say, one in the morning; usually, the women of the family are woken up, and snacks are hurriedly arranged. In addition, there are impromptu late-night trips – on motorcycles and scooters – along main thoroughfares that are now traffic-less. The convoy usually has no destination and, as the bikers career across the empty roads, stopping at will in order to exchange small talk, the pleasure of occupying the road outside 'formal' time is the key objective. In various conversations, Bajrang Dal members expressed great delight in the fact that their activities escaped the time-discipline expected of the rest of the population, and that *their* map of the city emerged through their power over time. As one young man noted, 'We can be anywhere, anytime ... from

Rajdhani Park [north Delhi] to Tagore Garden [west Delhi], it's our city.'
The gendered temporality of Bajrang Dal sociality translates into a palpable
sense of mastery over space.

The temporal discourses of mastery are complemented by spatial ones.
The Akhil Bharatiya Vidyarthi Parishad (All India Students Council, or
ABVP) is an affiliate of the RSS, and Bajrang Dal members often take part
in its activities. At one of the night-time meetings, we heard from two young
men who had assisted in the organisation of a recently concluded ABVP
rally in Delhi that attracted over seventy thousand students from around
the country. The men took great pride in explaining how well they had
organised the huge event and explained that they spent months minutely
measuring various parts of the route in order to determine the time it would
take to get from one point to another. 'We walked every inch of the route',
as one of them said, 'and have left our imprints (chaap) all over the city.'
The narrators took particular pleasure in explaining how the task represented
an encompassment: 'We measured the route with an "inch tape" ... pushing
all the crowds out of the way ... taking account of every stone. Can you
imagine the scene!' The significance of the imprint the men leave behind is,
of course, debatable. However, it is the desire for – and self-perception of –
mastery that I wish to point to as an aspect of the discourse of self-making.
Furthermore, what may also fuel the discourse is the anxiety and frustration
about an incomplete project, impeded by a variety of hostile forces, including
a 'secular' (or 'pseudo-secular', to use the language of the Hindu right) and
'westernised' intelligentsia.

It is not only the arterial routes that are acted upon; the pleasures of
consuming the post-national city also unfold through a knowledge of
informal passages. So, the men of the Bajrang Dal took great delight in
taking me from one 'posh' locality to another via the lanes and by-lanes
of older villages and neighbourhoods that had been 'pushed' back by the
newer – 'planned' – suburbs. Exiting a main road, we would be plunged
into a maze of narrow passageways that – it appeared to me – could only
be navigated by those experienced in reading the invisible signboards of
the maze. Then, just as suddenly, we would emerge onto a main road in a
different upmarket locality, all the time having travelled within shouting
distance of it, with my companions gleefully commenting on my sense of
disorientation. The knowledge of these 'minor' passageways is like a secret –
mocking – realm through which the Bajrang Dal men represent themselves
as both intimate with and in control of the *multitude* spaces of the city;

their dominion, they would often imply, encompasses both the known and unknown spaces of the city.

Streets and Street Corners: *Prabhat Feri*s and Footpath Performances

Streets

On a freezing and foggy winter morning I stumbled my way to the 'urban village' of Kotla Mubarakpur in south Delhi. I had been invited to take part in a morning prayer ritual known as *prabhat feri* ('dawn circumambulation') organised by the local chapter of the Bajrang Dal, scheduled to begin at 6.30 a.m. We gathered at the temple of Sheetla Mata, the goddess of smallpox. Eventually, the group swelled to about thirty and we readied ourselves to begin our singing, dancing and marching around the locality.

'Urban village' is both an official term (to be found in the Delhi Master Plan of 1962, for example – see Risbud 2002) and part of urban colloquial nomenclature. In the former sense, it refers to village areas that have become surrounded by urban developments and now lie within the city, and which, owing to their 'rural' nature, continue to enjoy certain land-related tax concessions as well as exemptions from planning regulations. 'Urban village' also carries connotations of the 'backwardness' of its inhabitants. As one study on urban planning points out, such localities are characterised by 'rural functions, traditions, character and lifestyle ... [which are surrounded by] modern, sophisticated, cosmopolitan, and high-tech patterns of living and developments' (C. S. Harvey 1996: 9). Kotla Mubarakpur ('Kotla') was originally farming and grazing land, one of the several hundred villages dating from the fifteenth century (Parihar 1999) upon and around which New Delhi had been built (Hoshagrahar 2007; King 1976; Legg 2007) by the British. It earlier contained a mixed population of Muslim landlords and Hindu cattle-rearing castes such as the Gujars. Like the rest of Delhi, contemporary Kotla was shaped by the cataclysmic movement of refugee populations in the wake of the partition of India and Pakistan in 1947. Following the influx of Hindu refugees, much of the Muslim-owned land in the area was bought by the new migrants, their owners having themselves left for Pakistan.

Kotla Mubarakpur has well-defined points of entry and exit, a labyrinthine network of lanes, a haphazard mixture of residential and commercial dwellings, a maze of overhead electrical and cable television wires that dart in and out of buildings, grand façades on incredibly narrow residential structures, shops that spill their wares onto the streets, uncollected garbage heaps, open drains, parks choked with plastic bags, and pathways sometimes ankle-high with mud. There is a variety of shops, but the locality is best known to outsiders as a place for inexpensive timber, sanitary ware and household building products. It is separated by a main road from the exclusive locality of Defence Colony and borders the just as expensive South Extension.

In addition to its permanent residents, the locality has a substantial floating population of working-class men who occupy custom-made dwellings, usually several to a room. There is also a small Muslim population that sometimes relocates upon news of 'communal' (inter-religious) riots in other parts of India, fearing local disturbances. Hence, circulation here unfolds as an often-miserable version of the contemporary global condition (Tsing 2002). As social space, Kotla can also be seen as the palimpsest of the erratic dealings between the state and its citizens, with the latter appearing variously as 'squatters', 're-settlers' and residents of 'unauthorised' colonies. In turn, the state itself appears as a shifting configuration. It can increase or decrease the size of 'legal' dwelling, provide or deny civic amenities and flout urban-planning regulations simultaneously as it seeks to apply them.

For the men about to take part in the *prabhat feri*, the experience of locality is also one of fragmentation, movement and circulation: their grandparents fled Pakistan, the footpath traders come and go according to municipal whims, and people and their livelihoods are displaced according to the latest shift in government policy towards the informal city; even the electricity supply is only erratically present. The chief organiser of the *feri* is Manoj-ji,[7] who also runs two private schools and a 'coaching college' from his home. Within them, young people of modest means obtain unregulated elementary education, while still others prepare for a variety of employment-linked competitive examinations. The masculinity politics that unfolds at Kotla and other localities like it is of a *non-elite* kind, marked by specific relationships between class, consumption, urban space and gender anxieties (on non-elite masculinities, see Rogers 2008; Chowdhury 2019).

Awaiting the march, I stood uncertainly next to a young man holding a *dholak* (drum), who chanted a couplet beginning with 'Jai Ram Shri Ram!' ('Hail to Lord Ram'). As we began our walk around the locality, we were joined by Sameer, who, I was told, was one of the first to climb on top of the

Babri Mosque in 1992 during its demolition by members of the Bajrang Dal and allied organisations. More recently, he had rescued trapped residents of a collapsed building in Kotla. He had also sought election – unsuccessfully – to the Delhi Legislative Assembly. Sameer's family used to own a brass polishing business but that had been shut down owing to a policy change that shifted all small industries out of residential areas. The men I was about to march with ranged in age from early twenties to late forties and many ran their own businesses such as grocery shops.

The procession stopped at various houses and more people joined in. At one house, a woman came out and distributed among the group what she referred to as *prasad* (sanctified offerings). Having made its way around the lanes and streets of the locality – shouting, chanting, singing, stopping and chatting – the march concluded in a park behind the temple that had been the starting point. Here, the group mimicked a routine followed by the RSS: standing in formation, saluting a 'Hindu' flag, and engaging in male camaraderie that also reproduces the bodily postures of the Nazis (Basu et al. 1993). Then tea was served and the marchers fell into friendly banter. Manoj-ji addressed the gathering, repeating a question asked at the start of the *feri*: Had we taken the *sankalp* (vow) that would lead to the construction of the temple at the site of the now demolished mosque in Ayodhya? Small pieces of paper were distributed to all to 'register' for the *sankalp*. Those who had already done so were asked to continue their *jap* (sacred chanting) for the success of the project that the BJP government had recently initiated.[8]

Later, I accompanied some members of the group to Manoj-ji's house for breakfast. We sat in a front room, with the television tuned to FTV, a 'fashion' channel. On top of the television was a Barbie-like doll. We were served a hearty breakfast of fried *pakoras*, bread and tomato sauce, with the women of the household occasionally coming by to replenish the food tray. Much of the conversation concerned the reinvigoration of kin-like relationships within the neighbourhood. So, Manoj-ji noted that since becoming part of the organisation, he had never felt that the Dal men who visited his house were a threat to the women of the family: 'They are more like brothers and fathers,' he said, adding that the mutual respect was enshrined through the practice of addressing each other with the honorific 'ji'. This community of respect, he continued, also produced one of reciprocity. Respect and reciprocity were integrally linked and, in turn, shaped an honourable population that deflected the influences of an otherwise deceitful and fickle urban milieu.

The articulation of masculine citizenship – here linked to men, women and the domestic sphere – reinstitutes locality by reinscribing kin relationships at the level of the neighbourhood. The *mohalla* (neighbourhood) is made a local space through the circulation of kin-like men and by sharing food, sentiment and song. At a time of considerable cultural and economic change – including the greater participation of women in the workforce – the localisation of masculinity allows for its reaffirmation. In a sense, then, masculinity, unable to be satisfactorily managed at the level of the wider public domain – the post-national city – is reinstituted at the level of the domesticated *mohalla* through the workings of the heterosexual homosocial family; a segment of the city withdraws to itself, inscribing *its* space with specific relations of gender, making the *mohalla* an ideological space. So, while nationalist discourse has historically figured India as feminine (as 'Mother India', see Sarkar 2001; Uberoi 2000), at the level of the tactile community – the neighbourhood – space is sought to be populated through the notion of the seminal family: the brotherhood that reproduces culture not through the agency of women, but through each other. While Hinduism's symbolic universe of feminine types can accommodate both the 'fierceness' of, say, Kali and the gentleness of other goddesses, the Bajrang Dal discourse appropriates the former quality as those of the 'ideal' Hindu male (Bacchetta 2004: 27), assigning the latter to the 'proper' Hindu woman (see also Brosius 2005). This derives from perceptions of threats to masculinity in an urban milieu and the appropriate ways of dealing with it.

However, the local is not simply the 'end point' of the national and the global, the space that stabilises the seemingly bewildering circulation of people, ideas and cultures. Rather, it is also a site that takes part in that circulation and is constantly formed and re-formed through this process. While it is true that all localities are unfolding knots of meanings about what it is to belong, the control we have over the capacity to make meanings varies between localities and their inhabitants. Given this, Kotla Mubarakpur is also a site of struggle to define belonging and attachment, rather than conclusive evidence of the resolution of such dilemmas. While the expression of familial masculinity outlined earlier may impart a sense of certainty and continuity regarding the making of locality and gender identity, there are concurrent processes that speak of new ways of constituting the self. The *prabhat feri* is not merely an assertion of Hindu identity over a heterogeneous space, seeking to return it to a state of 'ancient' religious purity; it is also one of several circulatory practices that constitute strategies of *engaging* with the present. I now turn to some of the ways in which such practices enact strategies of multiple and split selves. This will assist in rethinking the performative – 'presentist' – effects of religious routines such as the *prabhat feri*.

Street Corners

Public spaces figure in various other ways in the spatial strategy of the neighbourhood. Every Tuesday (the day dedicated to the worship of Hanuman) Bajrang Dal *karyakartas* (volunteers) from different parts of the city organise performative events in their respective localities. These both publicise Bajrang Dal activity and serve as informal recruitment drives. I accompanied Tapan-ji, a senior Bajrang Dal official, to one such event in the Tagore Garden area in west Delhi. We were driving to the house of Ravi Lakhanpal, a relatively junior official within the Bajrang Dal, who works as an insurance salesman and was overseeing arrangements for the night. Tagore Garden's narrow streets and lanes and the mix of land usage – commercial, residential, light-industrial and squatter dwellings – speak of a realm beyond the regulatory frameworks of the Delhi Master Plan and the Delhi Development Authority (DDA). We drive past the Khan Clinic of Bone and Joint Disease (located next to a pork butchery); Maxwell Academy of Commerce, an 'Open School' that offers an alternative to the board examination system; the local office of the DDA Slum Wing, which houses an Education and Business Training Centre; the premises of Ashtha Tailors and Boutique; and Pargate Educational Centre for 'coaching' in physics and chemistry. The DDA Training Centre, a sign informed us, offers courses in 'Hindi and English typing (120 days)', 'Beauty Culture and Health Care (120 days)', 'Commercial Painting (80 days)', 'Jute Work (60 days)' and 'Dress Making (80 days)'.

We were warmly welcomed into the Lakhanpal residence, a narrow single-fronted three-storied dwelling whose upper stories sat precariously above the ground. We sat in the front room and dinner was served. This, Tapan-ji had earlier told me, was common practice when Bajrang Dal members visited each other. As we ate, Lakhanpal and Tapan-ji talked about the assistance that could be offered during the forthcoming wedding of one of the local members of the Bajrang Dal. Tapan-ji also narrated two instances of 'threatening behaviour' of Muslims. In the first, the daughter of a Bajrang Dal *karyakarta* stopped going to school because of harassment by local

Muslim boys, and the second related to 'encroachment' upon government land to build a mosque.

The sharing of food and stories of (Hindu) family life in the Lakhanpal house reinforced both the already established meaning of that space as well as the sense of the gathering as one of (male) kin-like subjects. It also served to undercut – for the limited purpose of forming a male coterie – the differences of caste. In this way, then, the physical spaces of the city, the more abstract spaces of the nation and the embodied subjectivity of male presence coalesced at the site of the family; and, further, the Muslim threat – personal and spatial – became a challenge to the Hindu male body as encroachments upon it. However, in the *wider* public sphere of urban India, discourses regarding the family are not as constrained as they once might have been. In particular, the 'norms for women in Hinduism' (Wadley 1988: 34–35; see also Lamb 2018), where 'male-dominated literature prescribes control and subordination of the woman' (1988: 34–35), are in the process of being reformulated in the context of new commodity cultures where women's sexuality has become a frequent topic of discussion. As I have noted in Chapter 4, a variety of mainstream Hindi-language 'women's' magazines – whose circulation, according to the annual *Indian Readership Survey* conducted by the Readership Studies Council of India (RSCI), is rapidly outstripping that of their English-language counterparts – devote considerable space to discussions of female sexuality.

In these publications, articles on virginity are presented alongside those on a 'successful honeymoon', advertisements for Revlon and Lakme cosmetics, and Today lubricants and contraceptives ('Why choose Today? Not one, two reasons. Exactly the lubricant I wanted. In seven minutes Today lubricates the vagina. This leads to maximum pleasure during intercourse. Just the contraceptive he wanted; Today is easy to use and has no side-effects. So, when you and yours come together, there is nothing between the two of you').[9] These discussions are part of the emerging commodity culture of the *vernacular* public sphere and are connected to the idea of choice in personal life. The targeting of women as consumers and as 'individuals' can, however, as Tanika Sarkar (1995) points out, alter familial dynamics in quite specific ways. Most perceptibly, this might be in terms of their 'claim to a larger share of the family budget' (Sarkar 1995: 212) to facilitate new forms of consumption practices. Hence, '[o]lder ways of feminine domesticity and patriarchal control face new strains' (Sarkar 1995: 212).

It is in localities such as Kotla Mubarakpur and Tagore Garden, rather than the up-market Defence Colony, say, that Hindi 'women's' magazines such as *Meri Saheli* and *Grihasobha* find their largest readership. Notwithstanding the risk of some generalisation, it could be said that Kotla Mubarakpur and Tagore Garden belong to a cultural circuit predominated by *Hindi*-language sources such as these magazines. Magazine articles reflect the social and cultural concerns characteristic of such (social) spaces. So, in stories such as 'Nevta' (The Wedding Invitation) (*Meri Saheli*, December 1998), the 'sacred' brother–sister bond comes under severe strain owing to the brother's financially straitened circumstances, and in 'Dusri Subah' (A New Dawn) (*Meri Saheli*, November 2017), the *mise-en-scène* is an *economy*-class train compartment. Other common topics of discussion include 'arranged versus love' marriages, and the many different ways of obtaining diplomas and degrees.

The potential that the magazines' 'sexual' material offers for generating masculine anxiety within spaces of relatively stable gender hierarchies need hardly be laboured. If Muslims threaten the nation-space, the recent upsurge of public discussion of the sexuality of (Hindu) women might be seen to hold a similar threat to that most cherished (because controllable) of all spaces, the home. So, though Tanika Sarkar's discussion of the speeches of the female Hindutva ('Hinduness') ideologue Sadhavi Rithambara is limited to the latter's exhortations to Hindu men to recuperate and 'exercise' their masculinity in relation to the Muslims who would 'emasculate' them (Sarkar 2001), the conjunction of consumption culture and Hindu womanhood ought not be left out of the analyses of the sources of Hindu male anxiety.

This anxiety is of particular analytical significance since its sources include *Hindi*-language magazines whose readership is not the 'alienated' and 'westernised' groups that are the object of considerable Hindu right-wing scorn. In fact, it is this 'unalienated' group – small business families, lower-level government functionaries, and so on – that provides the Bajrang Dal with its greatest support base. We might now locate the dinner gathering at Ravi Lakhanpal's house in the wider cultural economy of the city in the following manner. While, on the one hand, high-circulation Hindi magazines publish articles – widely read in places such as Kotla Mubarakpur and Tagore Garden – that question the necessity of virginity before marriage for women, there are parallel processes within the city through which men seek to anchor masculinities. And, in a time of rapid change, neighbourhood-level Bajrang Dal–related activity provides for many men a sense of continuity and stability. The key to this is moral consumption: men (and women) both take an active part in the new consumer cultures of the city, and also exercise strategies of consumption that keep intact their masculine and 'feminine' identities; women – as suggested in the last chapter – take part in consumer culture but 'balance' it with attention to domestic duties and, as this chapter suggests, men band together in performances of kinship that reinforce masculinity. Men might accede to the allurements of the city, but they are not overwhelmed by them. That is the key to managing the politics of space.

After dinner at the Lakhanpal residence, we left to attend the evening performance, arriving at the location at around 8.30 p.m. A small stage had been constructed on the footpath, with carpets spread out on the street itself, converting it into a sitting area. On the stage, there was an upright statue of Hanuman holding a *gada* – a mace – and dressed in *contemporary* Indian clothing. The stage had been decorated with banners for the Bajrang Dal, others for Hindu unity, and posters of *ugra*-Ram, the 'fierce' images of the god-king Ram used by the Hindutva forces. Young men draped in saffron scarves occupied the footpath and sang a variety of religious songs, many based on Bollywood tunes. Each song ended with a clenched-fist salute. Then, Tapan-ji, the chief guest, addressed the gathering on the importance of worshipping arms and the necessity of Hindus responding in kind to 'Muslim violence'. He also talked about the destruction of the '*rakchason ki* building ('the building of the demons', the mosque) in Ayodhya and the hundred-day vigil that was to take place in order to protect the *sant*s (saints/holy men) and the workers who were going to construct a temple at the site.

We were about to leave the venue when a ruckus directed our attention to a man dressed as the god Shiva who began a dance set to film music, a rubber Cobra swaying on his shoulders. His exaggerated camp movements seemed to impart a frisson of excitement among the crowd. And even though the dancer looked somewhat bored and appeared merely to go through the motions, there was about him a homoerotic aura that borrowed from the transgendered culture of *hijra*s ('eunuchs'; Reddy 2005), and the playful teasing behaviour of female impersonators. The dance ended with a semen-like spurting of a jet of water from Shiva's hair to signify the birth of the river Ganges. The crowd applauded enthusiastically, drenched to various degrees by the spurting fluid. This, Lakhanpal whispered, was the *tandav nritya* (dance of destruction). The *tandav nritya* was, in fact, full of soft flowing gestures, with a sensuous homoerotic quality, quite unlike the *ugra*-Ram posters surrounding us. Later, Lakhanpal, Nitin (another local member) and I discussed the performance in some detail. Lakhanpal mentioned that these had always been great crowd-pullers and that the male audiences really 'enjoyed' them. 'Yes,' Nitin joined in, adding that the man was a 'beautiful' dancer. The strident masculine 'heterosexual matrix' (Osella and Osella 2006: 187) of the previous hour or so was, as if, leavened with a highly ambiguous form that combined fragments from Bollywood cinema and commodity and urban cultures at the edge of the city. This, in turn, gestured at 'a horizon of possibility' (Halperin 1995: 62) that might be understood as the blurring of the boundaries of homosociality and homoeroticism.

The gendered unfolding of Dal activities no doubt provide a way of re-emphasising (and valorising) the bonds of fraternity. However, the 'shoring-up' of masculinity – whether against Muslims or women – may not be a straightforward matter, able to rely on an 'undiluted' template of maleness. For, as I have suggested in Chapter 3, urban male subjectivity is constituted from diverse materials through a strategy of *indiscriminate* consumption. Hence, the tableau of choice that the Bajrang Dal men might seek out as everyday practice includes the 'Hindu soldier and the warrior monk' (Bannerjee 2005: 76) of the militant right, as well as the ambiguous sexuality of the Shiva performance and the accompanying Bollywood music. Rather than attempt to recuperate and consolidate a clearly definable 'Hindu' masculinity (notwithstanding Tapan-ji's exhortations), actions on the street – marked by pedestrian excess and footpath surplus – take a number of different avenues.

Domestic Spaces: Sitting Rooms

The common practice within the Bajrang Dal is for senior members to visit the juniors. In a sense, this produces a 'reverse hierarchy' – in terms of caste, class and age – though without a substantive change in structure. Dal activity unfolds upon urban spaces classified – as discussed later – into distinct administrative regions within which the *mohalla* plays an important role as the irreducible unit that supports the entire network at various levels above it. This allows for the making of localised spaces for the performance of masculinity. So, rather than abstract regional and national-level spaces of solidarity and action, the rigorous binding of male bodies – visible, willing, and incitable – to concrete spaces within the grasp of localised authority restores the possibilities of being men and taking control.

Ravi Lakhanpal's house was also the site for another meeting involving three young men of the Bajrang Dal from Tagore Garden. Nitin (whom we met earlier) owned an aquarium business, Keshav was the 'managing director' of a 'yellow-pages' publication called Blockbuster, and Rakesh ran a printing business. Between cups of tea, we talked about a number of things: their goals and aspirations, disappointments, ideals, pastimes, the nature of television, fashion, and the cost of living. Towards the end of the meeting, Nitin distributed invitation cards to his brother's wedding. The *mohalla* is re-inscribed through such processes of domestic affiliation: senior men ('fathers') visit their juniors and join in common dining; marriage invitations are handed out; and young men act as brothers, sons and grandsons. This constitutes the process of the making of the seminal family, where men reproduce men, without the agency of women. To be sure, the women are there, but as auxiliaries: as cooks, as taking over the business of child-care and as recipients of male protection through which the men achieve their sense of maleness.

However, the making of a delimited, spatialised and gendered community is not necessarily a reaction to the 'destruction' of neighbourhood and 'community' life by the forces of globalisation (cf. van Wessel 2004). Rather, it is also a way of seeking accommodation with them. When I asked the group gathered in Lakhanpal's house what they thought of the hypothesis that economic liberalisation and the rise in consumption culture have led to a decline in religious and 'spiritual' interest, they replied as one that such a conclusion was completely unwarranted, and that the 'economic' and the 'religious' were not in any way in competition. The strategy of identity that operates within this context seeks to *connect* various worlds – that of the family, community, as well as consumption and commerce – into a mutually reinforcing complex, rather than abolish them in favour of a unified Hindu identity that exists apart from the market. It is in this sense, then, that the production of the ideal subject of neoclassical economics – the all-consuming man – is as much the grounds for 'Hindu fundamentalist' identity as any easily isolatable religious drive. If anything, the market is perceived as the source of empowerment and control over one's identity and destiny, an aspect that the post-colonial – 'socialist' – state is seen to have consistently stymied; the state is both alienated and corrupt, whereas the market is the touchstone for the acts that are 'true' to one's self-interest. The market – as with the city where the allure of consumerism is the greatest – is a possible threat but also the site where moral consumption facilitates the ability to negotiate such threats. There is an interesting parallel here with quite a different context. Speaking of an African-American Muslim community, Starrett suggests that '[g]iven their predominantly positive view of commerce, communities like this, which construct their identities through the market, experience the market as liberating, empowering, and creative' (2003: 96; see also Rajagopal 1999; Srivastava 2007).

At another Bajrang Dal gathering in the upmarket south Delhi locality of Gulmohur Park – the residence of a businessman who is also an RSS supporter – we were addressed by a very senior member of the RSS, the parent body of the Bajrang Dal. Like many others who work for the RSS as *pracharak*s (propagandist/ideologue), Rasbihari-ji is a bachelor and embodies the religious notion of *tyag*, or renunciation towards a greater goal. The 'renouncer' has an important place within Hinduism and its sects (Bacchetta 2004; Das 1977; Dumont 1970; Madan 1987), and it has been suggested that 'the ideal of the wandering ascetic ... [is] an image of extraordinary power and persistence in most South Asian religious cultures' (Babb 2003: 818). This came across as a substantial aspect of Rasbihari-ji's authority as he admonished the gathering for not doing enough towards the construction of the temple in Ayodhya. Within this milieu, the most admired men were those whose lives had been touched by *tyag*. The RSS *pracharak*, totally committed to his vocation, liable to be moved to any part of the country according to the requirements of the organisation, and usually leading the life of a celibate, falls into this category. *Tyag* also produces discipline, and the discipline of *tyag* makes for an honourable and esteemed masculinity.

Tyag – renunciation – in a time of hyper-consumption provides an interesting entry into the idea of masculine identity. The most active members of the Bajrang Dal are also seen to embody aspects of *tyag* in the smaller measure that it is seen to attach to householders and non-ascetics: the householder active in the service of the *sangh* (organisation) is a superior man and a better head of the household through the discipline and character resulting from his organisational work. *Tyag* – renunciation as a way of generating and expending 'positive' energy – is the trope through which the power of gender relationships is maintained, and it competes with the popular discourse of 'semen conservation' in generating notions of manhood.[10] Bajrang Dal activity is an expression of *tyag*, where men perform 'selfless' tasks towards a greater goal, so the Bajrang Dal male identity is configured as inherently superior to women, as well as to other men who are either not involved in such work or oppose it. I had noted in Chapter 3 that sex clinics advised their clients on the 'proper' course of consumption such that men could take part in the pleasures of the city but also guard against threats to masculinity, a theme that also repeats in the narratives of the detective novels analysed in Chapter 4. Similarly, in the context of the discussion of this chapter, the care of Hindu masculinity in the age of hyper-consumption requires appropriate training in order to consume in a 'proper' manner.

What is of particular significance is the way in which Dal activists position *tyag* within the wider framework of globalisation and contemporary capitalism. *Tyag* is the local act through which the crusading Hindu male comes to defend Indian maleness at a time of numerous attacks upon it through national and global processes that weaken its hold on the family and say in society. *Tyag*, then, is the site at which the politics of the domestic, the tension between contemporary capitalism and 'spiritualism', and the production of the local space as the realm of the seminal family are brought together.

Hence, the *tyag* discourse expressed in the Gulmohur Park sitting room is not in the nature of an exhortation to capture a pre-modern ideal, or a wish to return to a pre-modern past. Rather, it gains its significance through its location within a *disjunctural* spatial strategy that speaks to *contemporary* masculine identities. In the sitting room where Rasbihari-ji lectured, several different contexts combined to produce the dialogue of *tyag* as an effective strategy of the *present*. The domestic space within which Rasbihari-ji spoke of 'sacrifice' was one that embodied combinations of chastity *and* conjugality, Spartan lifestyle *and* ostentatious Gulmohur Park living, and the desire to 'give up' *along with* the desire for material wealth represented by the exclusive surroundings. 'Hindu identity' at Gulmohur Park did not consist in the articulation of an exclusivist notion of *tyag* that unambiguously *demarcated* it from the life of the householders present as audience. Rather, it ever so firmly tied *tyag* to their lives as non-renouncers *who could concurrently aspire to giving up*. It is of these conjoined worlds of being and desire that Osella and Osella speak through their observation that '[t]he world of the renouncer and that of the householder are not incompatible but continually impinge and spill over onto each other' (Osella and Osella 2003: 743).

After the Gulmohur Park meeting, I went to the house of Rakesh Mishra, a Bajrang Dal functionary from Kotla Mubarakpur. Rakesh is an engineer by training but currently runs his own business exporting semi-precious gems. A few years ago, he had spent a year in Russia. He mentioned that in the future, perhaps another six or seven years, he may become a full-time worker for the RSS or the Bajrang Dal. We discussed the reasons for 'European success' (the ability to 'analyse'), the suitability of democracy for India, his admiration for the Chinese system of state-sponsored capitalism, the export potential of Indian industries and the need for 'population control'. We had dinner in the sitting room of his house, decorated with photos of his deceased father and grandfather, books on engineering, religious imagery, a large silver eagle and a variety of medals and trophies. Rakesh's family own the building in which they live, their ground-floor residence coexisting with shops and rental accommodation. Recently, Rakesh told me, a 'developer' had been contracted to convert a portion of the rambling house into a 'mini shopping centre'.

Another Geography

The final context of my discussion concerns the Bajrang Dal's administrative and ideological geography of the city, one that is counterpoised to the 'official' one of the state. The latter's administrative framework is elaborated, among other categories, through states, districts, cities, electoral constituencies, wards, municipalities, policing zones and blocks. However, one night, while explaining the structure of the Bajrang Dal, Ravi Lakhanpal outlined an alternative geography formulated by the Bajrang Dal. According to its administrative scheme, he said:

> Delhi is a Prant [region], and this is divided into eleven Vibhags [sections], and within each Vibhag there are Zillas [districts], and beneath that there are Prakhands, so there approximately three or four Zillas within each Vibhag and a similar number of Prakhands within each Zilla; then below the Prakhand the *rachna* [set-up] is the Khand, and below that the Upkhand ... this is the most local level of operation ... Tagore Garden is a Prakhand, and there are three Khands beneath that ... and this is C block, which is an Upkhand ... C, B, E ... all these make a Khand ... so there are three Khands here: Tagore Garden Extension, Tagore Garden and Rajouri Garden, all these make up the Tagore Garden Prakhand.

Lakhanpal's explanation – replete with the Sanskritised lexicon of an 'ancient' Hindu past as well as a term of Arabic provenance – imagines an urban space of lanes and by-lanes distinct from the 'highway' discourse of the state; it is a space imagined as the realm of the 'people'. However, it is not that the men of the Bajrang Dal are anti-statist; indeed, they take an active part in that realm. Rather, here as well, their strategies speak of a deep familiarity and comfort with split selves that occupy split spaces. It is a context where local spaces and localised bodies speak the language of contemporary capitalism and globalisation, unfolding through fragmentary and fragmenting processes. In other words, what is being expressed is not – or not simply – the desire for a return to a pre-colonial – 'purified' – past, but rather the willingness for a fuller engagement with contemporary modernity with its promise of the neoclassical consuming identity: the promise to have it all.

During my interactions with the men of the Bajrang Dal, I accompanied them to a number of 'state-sponsored' spaces. These included war memorials and those for national heroes, leisure parks and reserves, government housing areas, the surrounds of the Parliament House and the Presidential Estate, and the imposing thoroughfare (Raj Path) that leads to the Estate.[11] The most common reaction from my fellow visitors was one of great pride in these symbols of national 'achievements' and development. Evidence of statism – inscribed upon a variety of spaces – is, indeed, greatly admired. What the men seek to do, however, is *supplement* existing ways of engaging with space, and add to the menu of everyday life choices, by drawing upon other regimes of their familiarity. In so doing, they participate in the possibilities of global modernity – particularly those relating to expanded consumption – through *additional* recourse to local-level strategies. Hence, the state's classification and that of the Bajrang Dal sit side by side, not as substitutes, but as supplements, utilised according to different desires.

Conclusion

The discussion of this chapter has suggested that the Hindu male self, as expressed through the Bajrang Dal discourse and activity, though seemingly articulated through the idea of a unified Hindu identity, is ensconced within strategies of the split self, expressive of the male desire to engage more fully with a social world where the ability to choose – goods, strategies – presents itself as the way to self-realisation. The sitting rooms, lanes, shop fronts, street corners, footpaths, temples, parks, passageways to houses and the pseudo-filmic spaces of the dancing Shiva articulate a strategy that seeks to *bind* together such spaces through performative acts such that contemporary male subjectivity can be constructed as spread over *all* of them: a bit here and a bit there, but able to encompass – consume – the *multiplicity* of spaces on offer. The pleasures of fragmentation – the scattering of the male body across a number of spatial registers – are fundamental to the making of Bajrang Dal identities, signifying, as they do, the capacity for greater consumption *and* control. In their engagements with contemporary capitalism, 'Hindu fundamentalists' fashion themselves by embracing fragmentary consumption practices rather than resisting the threat of fragmentation. The multiple spatial strategies of the *prabhat feri*, sitting-room conversations and commensality, footpath performances and 'vernacular' geography make the entire city a conjoined neighbourhood, appropriated through these strategies by the all-consuming *man*. Most significantly, as a key thread in this book has argued, the man-of-the-city remains in control of his masculinity through an exercise of proper – moral – judgement regarding his relationship to the world of goods. He moves among shopping malls, new real-estate developments and FTV shows as a choice-making subject: splitting himself as both a hyper-consumer and also someone who can exercise *tyag*.

The substantive discussion of the book began, in Chapter 2, with a discussion of the early-twentieth-century nationalist imagination of masculinity and the city. The twentieth and twenty-first centuries have seen an extraordinary churn in ideas of nationalism where, as I have discussed elsewhere (Srivastava 2015), the national emotion is increasingly entangled with cultures of consumption, a context I refer to as post-nationalism. The present discussion of the 'religious nationalism' of the Bajrang Dal men in a time of consumerist modernity is an exploration of the changes in ideas of male-hood since the days of 'high' nationalism of the early parts of the twentieth century. It outlined how older identities are remade in the era of consumerist modernity. In the final two chapters of the book, I investigate this question in order to reunite discussions of masculinity and the city to those of national identity. For the streets, footpaths and homes that have formed the backdrop of the discussion in this and the earlier chapters are also enfolded within questions of national identity. Masculinity and the city are important entry points towards understanding contemporary forms of nationalist discourse with, as the final chapter will demonstrate, considerable consequences for the refashioning of contemporary life through new ideas regarding the political leadership most suitable for a 'new' India.

If men establish command over urban spaces through multiple acts of regulating, patrolling and roaming – becoming, in turn, the all-consuming male subject – their presence has increasingly encountered another one. The public visibility of women – particularly young, single women – as workers, leisure-seekers and consumers, for example, is also a significant aspect of the changing nature of urban life in India (see, for example, Bernroider 2018; Brosius 2016; Phadke, Khan and Ranade 2011). The next chapter explores how urban discourses of masculinity deal with this co-presence through narratives of technology-in-the-city.

Notes

1. There is a voluminous body of scholarly literature on 'religious fundamentalism' in India. It includes writings on colonial history (Pandey 1994), historiography and 'communalism' (Thapar, Mukhia and Chandra 1977), Hindu nationalism (Chatterjee 1993b; Jaffrelot 1996; Nandy, Trivedy and Mayaram 1995), gender and 'communalism' (U. Chakravarty 1998; Sarkar and Butalia 1995), religious violence (Brass 2003) and the media and the rise of 'Hindu' programming (Mitra 1993; Rajagopal 2001).

2. See, for example, Bacchetta (2004), Bannerjee (2005), U. Chakravarty (1998); Kaur (2003) and Sarkar and Butalia (1995). Given the voluminous nature of writings of topics related to the social and political processes and effect of 'Hindutva', I provide references to the relevant material in the endnotes. This will save disrupting the flow of the discussion in the main text.

3. See Foucault (1980), Lefebvre (1991), Massey (1994), Rofel (1999) and Soja (1993).

4. See Derné (2008) and Oza (2006a).

5. Other relevant works include psychological and psychoanalytic approaches that have explored 'obsessive fear' of the physical effects of 'semen loss', the spiritual effects of sexual desire, and the role of the mother in engendering early male identity (Carstairs 1958; Kakar 1990); and research focusing upon pre-colonial and colonial contexts (O'Hanlon 1997 and Omissi 1991, respectively), imperial stereotypes (Sinha 1997), and Indian nationalism and 'physical culture' (Rosselli 1980). Anthropological contributions include explorations of 'traditional masculinities' (Alter 1992), and films and manhood (Derné 2000; Osella and Osella 2004).

6. Osella and Osella (2004) build their discussion on young men in Kerala 'and their movie heroes' around a similar idea: 'Acknowledgement of the fragmented or multiple nature of self and subjectivity in *all* ethnographic settings' , they point out, 'alert us to the possibility that identities are neither bounded and set, once and for all, nor internally consistent' (2004: 226, original emphasis).

7. Not his real name.

8. Fieldwork on which the discussion is based was conducted in the years prior to the construction of the temple that began in 2021.

9. This topic is more fully explored in Srivastava (2007, especially chs. 7 and 8).

10. As noted in Chapter 3, 'semen conservation' was also a topic of discussion among sex-clinic owners and their clients. It has a long history in India-related scholarship, where it is regarded as an important cultural expression of male sexuality and identity (see Alter 1992; Carstairs 1958; Kakar 1990).

11. In an interesting act of remaking the heart of the city, Raj Path is currently being dug up as part of the government's Central Vista Project. I address this in the final chapter as an aspect of the refashioning of the city as an expression of the new masculinity politics of the state.

6

Technotopias

Masculinity, Women, the City and the Post-national Condition

Introduction

This chapter focuses on the politics of gender as it relates to young single women in the city. The rise of the youthful, unattached female consumer is an important aspect of contemporary urbanism. It both fuels the new economies of commerce and urbanism and is a site of masculine anxiety. Both in terms of a new readership for 'women's magazines' that carry explicit discussion of female sexuality (Chapters 4 and 5) and landscapes of leisure such as the Akshardham Temple complex in Delhi where 'female visitors … move seamlessly between roles as consumers *and* devoutly religious persons' (Srivastava 2017: 100), the city is increasingly the site of an alternative to the 'self-sacrificing' woman that has been the staple of Indian cultural discourse.

However, as the earlier chapters of the book have discussed, contemporary ideas of masculinity continue to draw upon long-standing ideas of male honour, family life and inviolable Indian traditions that lend stability to men's identities. The persistence of male identities of considerable vintage *along* with apparently altered notions of female behaviour calls for an understanding of the relationship between urban masculinity and women in the public sphere. The earlier chapters have suggested this in a tangential manner and the present one takes up this thread in a more focused way. The chapter explores contemporary narratives of urbanism, masculinities and women by explicitly utilising the two concepts – post-nationalism and moral consumption – that form the book's overarching analytical frameworks. Through these concepts, I explore the side-by-side existence of older cultures of masculinities and new forms of female identities and presence. I suggest that a significant way this otherwise hostile relationship is resolved is through imagining the city as a 'technotopia': a place made 'better' – and its problems resolved – through the intensive application of multiple technologies, including those of communication and surveillance. Within this context, my broader discussion is about the ways in which the urban technotopia is part of a masculinist imagination of making cities, and the 'technological turn' that I investigate in this chapter is the refashioning of a contemporary politics of masculinity.

In particular, the chapter investigates how an array of processes – of regional, national and global scales – play out as grounds for imagining the place of women's bodies across urban spaces at a time of significant social and cultural change. The discussion seeks to locate the relationship between the city and gender within new notions of citizenship, the social meanings of consumer cultures and the changing relationships between citizenship, the state and the market. The focus on the relationship between technology, urbanism and masculinity is significant in the light of the contemporary salience of technological forms and processes in the city. 'Smart City' planning, apps that facilitate different activities and closed-circuit television (CCTV) cameras that capture urban life at multiple junctures are just a few of the ways in which technological tools are being deployed as everyday aspects of governance and surveillance and have become normalised as aspects of urban life (Datta 2015; Arunima 2020). As this chapter will suggest, they are also implicated in new relationships between discourses of masculinity, women and city life.

Ideas of family life and the role of men within it, as previous chapters have shown, have been significant in the making the politics of masculinities. This chapter gathers some of those arguments to connect them to salient discourses about urban life and the role of technology within it. The shifting imagination of city-ness, where solutions to social problems that relate to gender relations are being cast as amenable to technological fixes, is rich grounds for exploring re-inventions of ideologies of masculinity. This, as I will discuss, can be fruitfully explored by theorising the changing nature of the citizen–state relationship ('post-nationalism') and local inflections on consumerism ('moral consumption').

A key aspect of the *discursive* spaces created by processes of post-nationalism and moral consumption concerns a specific manner of viewing relationships between private and public spaces. Furthermore, this translates into certain ways in which a social relation such as gender is imagined as playing out across such spaces. I will illustrate this through three specific examples. The first of these, regarding 'smart cities' lays the groundwork for the later discussion of relationships between masculinity, technology and women in the city.

Technotopias 1: Smart Cities

I begin with a context that relates to concerns about urban spaces and processes at a very broad level. This refers to the so-called Smart Cities project launched by the Government of India. The document called 'Smart Cities: The MoUD's (Ministry of Urban Development) Note for the Parliamentary Panel on Urban Development' outlines the following definition for Smart Cities:

> Smart Cities are those that are able to attract investments and experts and professionals. Good Quality infrastructure, simple and transparent online business and public services processes that make it easy to practice one's profession or to establish an enterprise and run it efficiently without any bureaucratic hassles are essential features of a citizen centric and investor-friendly smart city. (Lok Sabha Secretariat 2014: 4)

Discussions that surround the Smart City programme in India proceed from the perspective that technology as a tool of urban planning is 'gender-neutral' – and that it, in fact, can have a positive outcome on gender inequality by promoting women's safety in public places. The discussion of this chapter will explore the ways in which it is entangled with practices of gender.

One hundred cities across India have been selected to be converted into smart cities. The smart cities idea is built around a host of technological processes that, it is suggested, will address issues of infrastructure, housing, 'IT connectivity', 'e-governance and citizen participation' and safety and security, particularly that relating to 'women, children and the elderly' (MoUD 2015: 4–5). The 'safety and security' aspects relate mainly to the provision of a greater number of surveillance devices, such as CCTV camera in public places, as well as street lighting. Each selected smart city will receive around 100 crore rupees (1 crore = 10 million) per year for five years. Further funds are to be raised via municipal bonds, 'leverage borrowings from financial institutions', both Indian and global, and public–private partnership schemes. Most significantly, smart cities are to be developed through 'constituted boards' to be known as special purpose vehicles (SPVs), each of which will have a chief executive officer (CEO) as well as nominees from the central government, the state government and urban local bodies. The Smart Cities project, Ayona Datta (2015) suggests, is characteristic of an era of 'technocratic nationalism ... in which to be patriotic is to believe in the power of technology' (Datta 2015: 50). The Smart Cities plan was developed through the assistance of Bloomberg Philanthropies, which also assisted the MoUD in selecting cities for funding. Among other global corporations, IBM and Cisco SmartCity Dubai have either expressed strong interest or signed agreements to convert selected cities into 'smart' ones.

There are specific aspects to the post-national moment, as it relates to the conceptualisation and planning of smart cities. First, there is the changing relationship between the state, private capital, and imagined urban citizens. This relationship is being recast, as I have noted elsewhere (Srivastava 2020), by imagining the state as a friend of the middle classes and refashioning the idea of the 'ordinary' person such that this identity now attaches to the middle classes, a category of significant self-definition (Baviskar and Ray 2011). This is a significant new development, since in the post-colonial period the state's project of 'postcolonial development' (Gupta 1998) was primarily focused on the poor. To begin with, there is the potentially troubling relationship between the SPV, elected bodies, and *non-professional* and non-middle-class citizens. If the city – the smart city – is imagined as a corporation, then how does this imagination engage with its social and economic asymmetries? I will later suggest that the smart cities idea is an entirely novel form of governmentality that lays the grounds for future thinking about relationships between spaces and subjectivities and, particularly in the case of this chapter, gendered subjectivities.

The next rung of my argument and my second example comes from a variety of surveillance mechanisms suggested for making Delhi safe and the proliferation of mobile apps that seek to contribute towards women's safety in urban spaces.

Technotopias 2: CitySafe

In early 2015, the Delhi government floated a tender to install 18,300 'smart poles' in the New Delhi area. These smart poles 'would have CCTV cameras, WiFi and LED bulbs' (Mathur 2015). The idea of public safety for women has had valence in Delhi after the brutal – and globally reported – rape of a young woman, Jyoti Singh, in Delhi on 16 December 2012. City-wide surveillance through CCTV cameras has found great favour with the Delhi government, which (irrespective of the party in power) is frequently confronted with media reports that play up the idea of Delhi as the 'rape capital' of India. While there is no reliable data on the number of CCTV cameras installed around the city as part of *official* efforts at ensuring public safety (and other aspects, such as traffic management), a recent interview with a senior employee at a Delhi government body responsible for the city's digital infrastructure indicates that this is a major preoccupation.[1] The official pointed out that there are 'thousands of cameras around Delhi, installed on a variety of buildings'. He added, however, that a very large number of these are not operational due to a lack of payment of dues by the government to the private companies contracted to install and maintain the equipment. Apart from state-sponsored measures – such as 'smart poles' and CCTVs on government-owned buildings – there has also been a proliferation of non-state activity that seeks to address concerns of public safety for women through electronic surveillance and tracking mechanisms. A mobile application that was launched in Delhi in 2013 is one example. This app, which I will refer to as CitySafe, is a

> map based ... app ... the core of which ... [is] the Safety Audit ... which consists of a set of nine parameters that together contribute to the perception of safety. Each audit results in a pin on the specific location where the audit was performed and also records the time and date.[2]

Further, 'citizens can view (and contribute) information and comments on Audits, Harassment, Hazards and Places'. There are nine parameters that 'citizens' can report on. These include lighting, 'openness in the area', 'visibility', 'people density', 'gender diversity', and 'feeling'.

The advisory group for the CitySafe app consists of software developers, an urban planner, a self-described 'technocrat and entrepreneur', global consultants on 'women's issues' and the head of a prominent Indian NGO that also focuses upon women's issues. Localities that are audited receive a score and there are red and green pins to indicate levels of safety and danger. There are 'heat maps' that indicate 'your city's safe and unsafe clusters ... [a]nd the safest locations and routes in your city. Green color in the heatmap is for safe, amber for less safe, and red for unsafe'.[3] Users are invited to compare the safety score of their locality with that of others. The application's promoters have been requested by the police and various residents' welfare associations (RWAs), among other groups, to demonstrate its functions. The development of the app and various activities to support its popularisation has been funded by international corporate philanthropies as well as government-funded aid-giving bodies. CitySafe 'provides information about infrastructure to promote safety for women and other groups, to citizens at large and important stakeholders including the government, NGO's, corporations and RWAs'.[4]

In line with my argument about technotopias and consumer cultures, I suggest that the Smart Cities discourse is part of a broader context where state and non-state discourses combine to interpret the idea of urban safety in the language of the consumer-citizen (Fernandes 2006) who has access to the goods of high-tech modernity. This subject is able to demarcate dystopic – 'red pin' – urban spaces. This version, or vision, of urban safety emerges from both a technologisation of feminist concerns and an overwriting of the asymmetries of Indian urban life by producing 'heat maps' that visualise certain localities as dangerous. In most cases, it is not difficult to predict what kinds of localities might become identified as risky ones. This manner of mapping the city as a series of more or less dystopic spaces is also based on a set of relationships between the state and its organs (such as the police), constituents of civil society (such as RWAs and NGOs), and private capital of local and global scales. While the professed aim of CitySafe is to contribute towards improving urban infrastructure to lead to greater safety of women in public spaces, the app – and the gloss that accompanies it – institutionalises and normalises long-standing power relations.

The broader point is that the combined politics of gender and urban spaces is produced through an alignment of specific social and class formations that contain the seeds of an exclusionary vision of the city. The key aspect that undergirds this aspect of safety for women is a version of 'urban fear' (Low 1997) that is based upon the logic of identifying populations under threat and spaces from where such threat might emanate. Even if unwittingly, gender becomes the site of an unspoken fragmentation of the city into its 'dangerous' and 'safe' spaces, rather than a social critique of the cultures of urban masculinity and uneven development of urban spaces. That is to say, a technological imagination of the city – and how to make it 'safe' – serves to efface the *actual* nature of gender relations in the city, one that is not related to the culture of public spaces per se but, rather, the cultures of masculinity that join the domestic sphere to non-domestic ones. This is not, to reiterate an earlier point, the logic of 'neoliberal urban development'. Rather, I seek to capture a process where ideas of 'technological nationalism' (Datta 2015), the role of global capital and technologies, the safety of 'good citizens' and the efforts of a concerned state combine to produce a deeply problematic view of urban life. This complex landscape of action and behaviour is also an aspect of post-nationalism. I will build upon the discussion of this section in the next one to further illustrate the entanglement of technology, consumer culture and 'women's safety' as they relate to contemporary cultures of masculinity.

Technotopias and Moral Consumption: 'UGC Guidelines for Safety on Campus'

The invariable backdrop to recent discussions about gender and safety in public places – particularly discussions that refer to single young women – is the rape and brutal violence inflicted upon the young woman known as Jyoti Singh in Delhi on 16 December 2012. The rape and the protests that followed in various towns and cities across the country were widely covered by the Indian as well as the global media. Two weeks later, Singh died from her injuries (see Chapter 1). In early 2013, in the wake of the massive outcry over the rape, the University Grants Commission (UGC), the government body charged with overseeing the higher education system, established a committee to engage with universities about ways of improving security at university campuses. The committee – consisting of academics from a variety of social science disciplines – consulted widely at university campuses across the country and provided its report towards the end of 2013. Among other things, the report included discussions on 'the nature of power, the problem of violence, countering sexual harassment and issues of equality and freedom' (Saksham 2013: 4); the 'entrenched patriarchal practices/structures and mind sets and the corresponding cultures of impunity and silence that sustain them, and conspire/militate against gender justice and perpetuate pervasive violence in society' (Saksham 2013: 19–20); the 'multiple fault lines of caste, class, community, religion and disability' (Saksham 2013: 82); and discourses of 'protection' and policing of young women, and cultures of masculinity. In thinking about urban spaces and young women in particular, the report sought to rethink the relationship between being single and personal autonomy by imagining different kinds of freedoms as rights rather than concessions made by different authority figures such as parents and college principals.

The fate of the Saksham ('Enabled') report prepared by the UGC-appointed committee is unclear and it does not seem that its recommendations were either debated by the Commission or implemented by it. In 2015, however, the Commission released a document entitled *UGC Guidelines on Safety of Students On and Off Campuses of Higher Educational Institutions* (UGC 2015). The contents of this document are at significant variance with the recommendations contained in the Saksham report. A familiarity with some aspects of the *UGC Guidelines* might provide some clues as to why the UGC thought it prudent to release a report of this nature, rather than be seen as endorsing the Saksham report as a means towards gender rights. I begin by quoting some of its the key parts:

1. Any physical infrastructure housing students, whether HEI [Higher Education Institutions] or hostels, should be secured by a boundary wall of such height that it cannot be scaled over easily. In order to further fortify it, a fence of spiralling barbed wires can be surmounted [*sic*] on the wall so that unauthorized access to the infrastructure is prevented effectively. The entry points to such housing units should be restricted to three or less and they should be manned by at least three security guards, sufficiently armed, CCTV cameras, identity verification mechanism and register of unknown entrants/visitors with their identity proofs and contact details. At least one woman security personnel should be deployed at such entry points so that physical security check of girl students or visitors can be undertaken. The bags and other belongings of students/visitors can also be examined, manually and/or by metal detectors, in order to secure a weapon-free and violence-free campus.

2. Biometric way of marking student attendance, both in HEI as well as hostels, can be an effective way to overcome proxy. Such digital mechanism can enable HEIs to keep an eye on a student's movement and whereabouts in a failsafe manner.

3. Setting up a university police station *within* the premises of the HEIs, wherever feasible, can go a long way in instilling a sense of security amongst students and scare amongst nuisance makers and petty criminals. [Emphasis added]

4. HEIs should organize quarterly parents-teachers meet (PTM) so that grievances and gaps in system can be addressed and resolved. Online complaint registration system can also be launched so that issues can be addressed before they slip out of hands of authorities.

5. It is mandatory for institutions to elicit consent letters from the parents/guardians of the Students who are embarking on tour. (UGC 2015: 2–5)

Beyond an obvious context of anxiety – where the discourse of care masks fears regarding young and single women's autonomy – it is worth locating the document within the broader process of moral consumption. This, I suggest, allows us to think about the imbrication of gender with the multiple processes of contemporary modernity and post-nationalism.

Moral consumption is a process of dealing with consumerist modernity. In the Indian context, it particularly refers to the imagined, potentially destabilising effects of consumerism. Consumer culture presents a double bind in the context of gender: consumerism is both a structure of desire that marks the making of new identities and also a site of anxiety inasmuch as it carries the promise of individuation for both men *and* women. The *UGC Guidelines* address this *masculine* anxiety – additionally stoked by the Saksham report that explored the gendered nature of urban life – through a discourse of moral consumption. The guidelines create specific notions of an 'outside' and an 'inside' that single young women are expected to traverse: they travel between consuming cultures of the *world* while, ultimately, being commanded to return to the spatialised gaze of traditional structures of power at or of *home* – consumption is good, but it must move along specified moral contours. The *UGC Guidelines* address the nature of the fraught territory that lies between the disembedding effects of contemporary modernity – new forms of technology, changing norms of young women's sexuality, for example – and the embedding processes of power and authority. The *Guidelines* occupy a very specific discursive space. They present the following question as one of fundamental importance: what are the most 'appropriate' ways of allowing young women who may choose to occupy streets and other public spaces as part of emerging cultures of consumerism, but also countering the potentially threatening culture of publicness through a process of controlling such 'freedom'? 'Moral consumption' is the answer: it fashions a mode of behaviour in line with the politics of masculinity.

The *Guidelines* provide a solution to the problem of finding the 'balance' between the home and the world (Ponniah 2018). Young women should be of the world, one that is marked by changing relations between the state and the middle classes; 'technocratic nationalism'; exclusionary urban processes exemplified by gated communities; and the rise of consumerist nationalism. However, the unpredictable manner in which these, either singly or in combination, might produce 'uncontrollable' female subjects can be managed through a discourse of moral consumption: there should be an *Indian* way of being in the world. Urban young women must strike a balance between being and behaving, going out but also obeying the strictures of 'home'.

Discussions about changes in the nature of the family in India are significant contexts for debates regarding gendered subjectivities and life in the metropolis. In particular, within popular discourse, putative changes in the family form – from joint to nuclear, say – are frequently invoked both as signifiers of a change from older ways and traditions and the changing role of women in society (Kaur and Palriwala 2014; Parry 2001). They are also, in some instances, utilised as a context of discussions about transformations in attitudes regarding unmarried women:

> Singles form part of a new demographic that is changing the way women are perceived in India. They are either never-married or divorced, unabashedly celebrating their singledom, not giving into either the arranged marriage conundrum or the ticking biological clock. (Balakrishnan 2019)

However, celebratory – or, perhaps, just hopeful – narratives do not usually match the far more complicated situation that characterises the quotidian experiences of single-ness marshalled by other observers. The Indian city, while offering certain freedoms that are absent in non-urban environments, is a long way off from being a utopia of solitary life for women. It is important to remember, for example, that far-reaching changes in urban living that concern the nature of work, leisure, residence, mobility and commerce have also been accompanied by a national-level movement towards religious and social conservatism. Hence, while, on the one hand, gated communities and their 'modern' lifestyles proliferate, they are also, on the other, sites of an efflorescence of Hindu religious ritual activities that take their cue from a national mood marked by Hindutva politics. The recent proliferation of the Karva Chauth ritual, where women pray for the well-being of their husbands (see Srivastava 2015, especially chs. 5 and 7; Radhakrishnan 2009), is a case in point. The rise of religious conservatism as political strategy has also led the re-fashioning and consolidation of new forms of social conservatism where gender continues to play an important role in the making of 'Indian traditions'.

Urban spatial transformations – that might give off an air of a new world of possibilities – are, in fact, circumscribed by wider social norms that continue to affect how women are regarded. Specifically, gender continues to be a site of expression of 'Indian traditions' and 'morality' (see, for example, Bernroider 2018 on single women as tenants in Delhi), and 'urban-ness' itself is just *one* context affecting women's lives. As Patricia Uberoi points out, while bridal magazines in India narrate stories of 'modern relationships', they circulate in contexts 'where descent, succession and inheritance are in the male line; post-marital residence is "patrivirilocal" ... and authority resides with the senior males of the family or lineage' (Uberoi 2008: 245).

Notwithstanding media boosterism that speaks of new worlds of opportunities for women, ideas of national traditions and morality continue to hold fast and 'choice' is usually about the goods to consume rather than, say, spousal choice (Uberoi 2008). The moral life of the nation now finds expression *through* consumer culture rather than against it. And debates on westernisation and perceptions regarding transgressions of normative gendered comportment and spatial etiquette – such as those expected within private and public life (Brosius 2016: 245) – are part of a new context that I refer to as moral consumption.

Conclusion

I will conclude with an account of the urban past to contextualise the urban present. The colonial era in India, as historians have noted, was marked by attempts to specify the kinds of public spaces that the British knew where, unlike in India, there was no confusion between the 'private' and the 'public' (Kaviraj 1997). Urban populations in the Indian context, on the other hand, did not appear to have rules and regulations of social order, hence presenting a problem for a clear differentiation of the private and the public that lay at the heart of the 'domestic values of bourgeoise privacy' (Kaviraj 1997: 98). The colonisers set about, then, to create clearly demarcated public spaces that would erase the blurring of boundaries between the public and the private. The western notion of 'public' in the Indian context has translated into a history of public spaces that, since the colonial period, has been about lessons in civility and an education in modernity. This was an also attempt to distinguish the public as a population that was imagined to be rational from the 'crowd', imagined as irrational. *Contemporary* discourses on space move us to an interesting context of the making of new publics and the educational discourses of space in a time of post-nationalism. Whereas the colonial and early post-colonial discourse emerged out of a dialogue between the state and elite citizens, the provenance of the current one is wider and more complex and involves a greater number of interlocutors.

The three contexts outlined earlier in this chapter – the Smart City programme, the CitySafe app and the *UGC Safety Guidelines* – are overlapping ones. They seek to produce a new kind of urban spatial discipline: one that is anchored to the imperatives of post-national modernity and moral consumption. The Smart City programme seeks to create a public out of the changing relationship between the state and national and global capital through intensive deployment of technology. This public is to be distinguished from the crowd that might disrupt this relationship. It lays the groundwork, in turn, for a *techno-politics* of population management. This techno-politics is the context for addressing a specific section of that population, that is, women. This is where we might locate the CitySafe app, which refracts techno-politics at an oblique angle to institute women's safety as a relationship between civic citizens and bodies. It refracts the problems related to urban cultures of masculinity as one of technical and infrastructural shortcomings. In the process, it institutionalises a colonial map of the city that imagines it as a place of 'crowds' (identified through red pins) and 'publics' (via green pins). Finally, the recently released *UGC Guidelines* on the safety of women seeks to insert the social back into techno-politics. However, this is on the terms of techno-politics itself. The *Guidelines* seek to address and engage with the unintended consequences of a technological cornucopia: the effect of new public cultures that accompany consumerism and discourses around personal autonomy. It addresses the issue through the vocabulary of techno-politics inasmuch as it seeks to promote the 'appropriate' use of techno-modernity through the model of moral consumption. The *Guidelines* approve participation in techno-modernity, but the approval is circumscribed by the rules of propriety and properness. In the context of women, the *Guidelines* provide an answer to the question of how to be of the world but also return home when required; consumerist modernity is, here, set on course to being 'appropriate' *Indian* consumerist modernity.

This chapter has attempted to point to the interlocking processes through which meanings of urban spaces, autonomy and gender are produced and the specific ways by which a politics of masculinity – the relationship between genders – is implicated in apparently 'neutral' discourses of technology. First, there is a national-level discourse – that of smart cities – that imagines spaces as a collaborative venture between different forms of capital, governmentality, technologies and 'knowledge-workers'. At this level, the discourse of gender is absent as contemporary processes of producing cities are seen as necessarily 'untainted' by the messiness of the social. The smart cities idea, though ostensibly about a reorganisation of the relationship between populations and technologies, concerns the establishment of a de-socialised – that is to say, de-politicised – subject at the heart of urban life. The second level is that of the CitySafe app. This is where the politics of the city – already redefined by smart city discourses – is instituted as another version of techno-politics that speaks of 'danger' and 'safety' in terms of relationships between Indian NGOs, International NGOs, technocrats, the corporate sector, RWAs, government bureaucracies and the police. Finally, the *UGC Guidelines* document provides a guide to local action and behaviour in a time of technotopias. In particular, it seeks to outline the manner in which contemporary female bodies might occupy the spaces and processes created by modernity. It seeks to address the following issue: if contemporary modernity creates or accommodates heterotopias, what are the ways through which meanings of space are reduced to manageable proportions within existing structures of masculinist power? The management of space through an invocation of time – 'our modernity' –is a specific task of power in the contemporary period. It is in this sense that I speak of moral consumption as a specifically Indian way of dealing with the disembedding processes of the present.

Moral consumption is, then, a 'chronotope' of modern life in India. It finds play in the actions – actual or proposed – of both men and women. A chronotope, as the literary and cultural critic Mikhail Bakhtin pointed out, 'is a way of understanding experience; it is a specific form-shaping ideology for understanding the nature of events and actions' (Morson and Emerson 1990: 36). The name chronotope, Bakhtin says, 'is given to the intrinsic connectedness of temporal and spatial relationships that are artistically expressed in literature' (Bakhtin 2011: 84). Bakhtin speaks of several types of chronotopes that might populate a novel and signify different types of experiences. So, in novels where the road serves as a chronotope, 'the image of the road [comes to signify] … "the course of a life," "the course of history" and so on' (Bakhtin 2011: 243–244). I take the liberty of utilising a literary method towards analysing non-literary contexts in the light of its inherent power as a tool of social analysis. Moral consumption comes to signify the fusing of putative Indian and western spaces and times to produce an idea of propriety in a time of change. It produces this notion through a relationship with the concurrently circulating discourses of Smart Cities and CitySafe.

This discussion does not suggest an 'iron cage' of deterministic action where behaviours across spaces can be characterised as resulting from meta-discourses about spaces. Movements across space and actions upon space take place in socially determined but also erratic, 'extra-social' ways. The chapter has outlined the ways in which relationships between spaces – here, urban spaces that are both objects and processes (Lefebvre 1991) – and the history and politics of a specific post-colonial present plays out in the Indian case. This allows us to interrogate the relationships between processes connected to economic and cultural globalisation, changes in the form of the state and changes in its relationship with private capital, new policy formulations, and older structures of power through which masculinity speaks, such as the family. In order to think about the meta-discourses of urbanism and the meaning they hold for an understanding of masculinity-in-the-city, I have outlined certain relationships between society and economy, rather than rely upon characterising the present as a 'neoliberal' one which, perhaps, has come to mean a 'conceptual trash heap capable of accommodating multiple distasteful phenomena without much argument as to whether one or the other component really belongs' (Boas and Gans-Morse 2009: 156, quoted in Flew 2014: 53).

Finally, in this context, the relationship between the masculinity politics of the Smart City and that of the footpath (Chapter 3) is also worth considering. While, on the one hand, the techno-masculinity discussed in this chapter emerges from middle-class preoccupations with technology and its role in 'protecting' women, they also, on the other, would appear to stigmatise non-middle-class men (and localities); dangerous masculinity lurks elsewhere – in slums, on the footpath – and the Smart City, armed with apps, biometric identification procedures and CCTVs, is the urban *deux ex machina* to deal with it. However, notwithstanding the differentiating effects of technology, the varying class contexts are united through the discourses of post-nationalism and moral consumption.

The urban technotopia as well as the city of the footpaths both constitute worlds where historically valorised masculinity and global processes are enfolded within each other. At both sites, masculinity is seen to be under threat from processes of the city. However, engaged with, resulting in ways of guarding against the threats. In the post-national city, the cultural boundaries of 'national' life are secured through global processes, objects and technologies; goods, commodities, magical potions that are converted into goods and commodities, CCTV cameras and biometric surveillance combine to produce contexts of engaging with a world in flux. And, further, negotiations with an unstable social environment – which one must engage with *and* be on guard against – are best done through moral consumption. Technology, in this instance, is *both* a site of anxiety (where young women might use dating apps) and also the resolution of the anxiety (an app can guarantee their safety from strangers and CCTV cameras ensure that they return 'home' as required).

In the concluding chapter, I focus attention on a specific person to explore how the several themes explored in the book – and positioned within the frameworks of post-nationalism and moral consumption – coalesce into palpable ways of being and believing. During the 2014 general elections in India, a variety of media narratives – both within independent journalism and advertisements – addressed a very specific aspect of Prime Minister Narendra Modi's public representation, that relating to his 'forceful' masculinity. The chapter explores the coming together of discourses of masculinity, the city and populist politics. I explore an Indian version of political populism – more generally understood as a movement 'in which personalistic leaders seek to gain and retain power by establishing unmediated links with mass constituencies, who are otherwise relatively free of existing party and institutional ties' (Kenny 2017: 179) – as a narrative of urban masculinity that seeks to both refashion and consolidate older structuers of power. The concluding chapter suggests that 'Modi-masculinity' is a potent reformulation of older versions of Indian masculinist discourse in a time of consumerist modernity. Standing at the juncture of the politics of 'Indian traditions' and the re-fashioning of masculine identities, while Modi-masculinity represents a version of 'muscular nationalism' (Banerjee 2012), the chapter also argues that it presents a very specific strategy of dealing with 'threats' to masculinity (and muscular nationalsim) that urban life and consumerism might potentially carry. And, in this way, it crystallises the key ideas regarding the post-national politics of masculinity and the city explored throughout the book.

Notes

1. To preserve confidentiality, I have omitted both his name and that of his organisation.
2. The description, along with that which follows, is taken from the *CitySafe Information Booklet*. As I have anonymised the name of the app itself, I will only refer to it by this title.
3. From the *CitySafe Information Booklet*.
4. From the *CitySafe Information Booklet*.

7

Conclusion

Masculine Body Politics

Introduction

Cultures of the city, the previous chapters have suggested, have been the contexts of the making of a masculine national culture (Chapter 2) as well as the anxieties regarding the imagined threats to it (Chapters 3–6). The city is a place of the double bind: it is both desired and feared. And masculinity-in-the-city consists of different strategies of being a man who is not just in the city but able to exert control over its processes. This self is, as I have argued, the forceful agent of encompassment, seeking dominion over many different realms, including the home, the neighbourhood and wider public spaces, religious identity and the world of goods.

The gender politics of Indian modernity has primarily been traced through the exploration of the discourses surrounding women. The female body and feminine chastity have had significant careers within feminist historiography as well as sociological and anthropological studies that seek to track the complex contours of power in the making of sociality. India-related scholarship has produced a rich body of work relating to topics as diverse as women as repositories of Indian traditions (Chatterjee 1993a; Mani 1993; Sunder Rajan 1993), the nation as a goddess (Ramaswamy 2010), televisual femininity (Mankekar 1999; Munshi 2010), women and Hindu nationalism (Bacchetta 2004; U. Chakravarty 1998; Sarkar and Butalia 1995) and women and new middle-class identities (Donner 2011; Ponniah 2018; Bhandari 2020). This book has sought to utilise these frameworks of analysis towards a different end: an analysis of the entanglements between urban and masculine cultures.

This chapter brings together many of the themes cited above – which have also informed the discussion of the book – to explore how abstract ideas about society and culture take concrete human form and influence action. The chapter suggests that the 2014 Indian general election constitutes a rich context for thinking about the ways in which various dispersed popular discourses on masculinity came together. The deployment of discourses of masculinity as a significant electoral strategy was unprecedented, as was the role of the media. The imbrication of these two contexts produced a vision of an *actual* man-of-the-city figure – one that has been explored in the earlier chapters – that has significant lessons for the ways in which we understand the Indian present.

This concluding discussion focuses on discourses of masculinity that gathered around the person of India's current (2022) prime minister, Narendra Modi. I suggest that though couched in the language of 'traditional' – and corporeal – manhood, 'Modi-masculinity' is a recension in a time of consumerist modernity and represents a sharply delineated version of the urban man who has, finally, learned to both live in the city and exercise control over its processes. Modi-masculinity stands at the juncture of new consumerist aspirations, the politics of Indian traditions and gender, and the re-fashioning of masculine identities. Some idea of the peculiarity of Modi's mediated image can be derived from the fact that his masculinity was *counterpoised* to that of a political opponent, the incumbent prime minister, Manmohan Singh, whose ethnic identity as a Sikh (should have) positioned him in the ranks of the 'martial races' (Omissi 1991).

Masculinity as Campaign Strategy

The 2014 election was significant for the investments made by political parties in campaigning through various media. The dividends of such investment were recognised slightly earlier, during the 2011 anti-corruption campaign led by the ex-bureaucrat Arvind Kejriwal. The latter successfully used traditional electronic as well as social media to garner massive support. Soon after joining Twitter in November 2011, Kejriwal gathered a following of 1.5 million. In 2012, he launched the Aam Admi Party (AAP), which gained unprecedented success in the state elections in Delhi in 2013. Kejriwal was the chief minister of Delhi until his resignation in February 2014, being re-elected to the post in February 2015. In the 2014 general election, and then again in 2019, the Bharatiya Janata Party (BJP) utilised a sophisticated and massively funded campaign that centred around its prime ministerial candidate, Narendra Modi, demonstrating deft media-management skills. Modi was quick to set up his own website and establish a Twitter account. Of particular importance was his projected self in mainstream print and electronic news media.

A significant aspect of the media discourse that gathered around what was hailed as Modi's US-style 'presidential' campaign, focused on his 'forceful' masculinity. Modi's election campaign – as well as popular narratives that surrounded his personality – significantly focused upon his 'manly' leadership style, identifying this as efficient, dynamic, potent and capable of overcoming the 'policy-paralysis' that had putatively afflicted the previous regime. In this, he was implicitly counterposed to Manmohan Singh, his 'impotent' predecessor, and more generally against an 'effeminate' Indian type who is unable to strike hard at both external enemies (Pakistan and China, say) and internal threats ('Muslim terrorists', most obviously). His manly '56-inch chest' – able and willing to bear the harshest burdens in the service of 'Mother India' – was a frequently invoked metaphor in the election.

The following statement by fashion writer Shefalee Vasudev (2014) exemplifies the recognition that Modi's image has been specifically crafted for the media:

If we can read nationalism in Modi's dressing, Obama's look is about accessible glamour, just as Kennedy's was about spirited decadence. If Libya's Colonel Gaddafi was the most garishly dressed politician in the world, former French first lady Carla Bruni was about Parisian sophistication and nonchalant sexiness. Each made a different statement. (Vasudev 2014)

Others, such as blogger Vrinda Gopinath (2014), also recognised that masculinity was a significant aspect of Modi's media image in specific ways:

Modi's Empire Line is most flattering to himself – of opulent turbans adorned with pearls and feathers, rath chariots of gold and chrome, a machismo swagger with his self-proclaimed 'chappan chatti' (56-inch chest), giant cut-outs in every street, to 3D virtual images that walks, talks and eats; mammoth road shows of pomp and pageantry; flashy showmanship and stagecraft at public meetings; it's an intoxicating cocktail of hyper masculinity, virility, and potency. Good Grief, Narendrabhai does sound like a Mughal Emperor in Modern India! (http://www.altgaze. com/?p=753, accessed 14 July 2017)

Further, as the sociologist and media commentator Shiv Vishwanathan noted,

[o]riginally Modi appeared in the drabness of white kurtas, which conveyed a swadeshi asceticism. Khadi is the language for a certain colourlessness. Modi realized that ascetic white was an archaic language. His PROs forged a more colourful Modi, a Brand Modi more cheerful in blue and peach, more ethnic in gorgeous red turbans.... Hair transplants and Ayurvedic advice served to grow his hair.... He senses he has to sustain himself as both icon and image of a different era. (Vishwanathan 2013: 54)

The *political* significance of media discourses of 'Modi-masculinity' was recognised by his opponents through their efforts to dispute it. Little by little, they cast their criticism in terms of questioning his claims to 'real' manhood. In October 2013, a Congress party minister told a Hindi newspaper that Modi could never become prime minister as he had not married and hence lacked 'manhood'.[1] And, in February 2014, TV news reports quoted leading Congressman Salman Khurshid referring to Modi as *napunsak* (impotent) for not preventing the anti-Muslim violence that took place in Gujarat in 2002 when the latter was the chief minister of the state. Masculinity came to be invoked to describe both personal and political choices.

Notwithstanding the 'traditionalist' casting of the discussion – including invocations of family life and virility – Modi-masculinity should, in fact, be seen as a specific effect in the times of urban consumerist modernity; it is about the negotiations required of men in the city, to both be of the city and overcome its possible dangers and risks to the capacities of manhood. And, while it directly addresses men, Modi-masculinity also contains suggestions regarding ways of being in the city for women. In this, it gathers ideas around women's safety and autonomy – discussed in Chapter 6 – around the agency of a specific masculine type who might implement the dictates of urban gendered behaviour. Further, while borrowing from pre-national and nationalist ideas, Modi-masculinity's peculiar characteristic lies in its judicious presentation of Indian manhood as both deeply national (and hence territorialised) and also global (and de-territorialised). It offers a model of choice that derives from conditions created by post-national discourses as well as those of moral consumption. Within these contexts, as explained earlier, there is no condemnation of consumption as illegitimate grounds of identity-formation (cf. van Wessel 2004: 104) or emphases on the morality of the savings-behaviour of the Five-Year Plan hero (Chapter 3). Rather, the concern is with 'appropriate' participation in consumerist activities that the new city, the one with gated communities and shopping malls, offers (Srivastava 2015). In this way, the populist politics that forms the context of Modi's success moves beyond ethnocentric narratives, anti-Mulsim rhetoric and nativism to offer a vision of the future that converts apparent binaries into a seamless narrative of control and power. It is a narrative of the Hindu-male-of-the-city who is master of both the home and the world. In this, it builds upon the meanings of family and 'tradition' in a time of change (Chapter 4) and the tendencies and notions of the all-consuming man (Chapter 5).

Post-nationalism Moral Consumption and Modi-masculinity

Post-nationalism and moral consumption are important contexts for a fuller engagement with the meanings of Modi-masculinity. To begin with, these allow for an understanding of the two different audiences of Modi-masculinity, namely territorialised and de-territorialised Indians. The former consists of older and newer (or, in Modi's own terminology, 'neo') middle classes within India, whereas the latter refers to the Indian diaspora. Post-nationalism, as noted earlier in the book, is the context of entanglements between nationalist ideologies and new cultures of consumerism, including emergent ideas around privatisation and individuation. It indexes a situation where it is no longer considered a 'betrayal' of the dreams of 'nation-building' to either base individual subjectivity within an ethic of consumption (as opposed to savings) or to think of the state's statism in a context of cooperation with private capital (as encapsulated by public–private partnerships). Moral consumption is the site of a civilisational debate that seeks to accommodate older social identities – wife, mother, husband, son, sister, for example – within the newer individualising tendencies of consumerism. Most significantly, it does not constitute a rejection or critique – it is important to re-emphasize – of consumption (cf. Lim Chua 2014 and van Wessel 2004) but, rather, an attempt to situate new forms of subjectivities (for example, individualism) within existing social structures and hierarchies.

Taking up the thread of how long-established identities have come to be articulated through the language of consumer cultures, I suggested in Chapter 6 that the commoditisation of religious and ritual contexts allows for a situation where women can be both hyper-consumers (subjects of the world) and also 'good' wives (able to return home to 'tradition'). New ways of combining religious and national identity *through* the consumerist trope of 'choice' have led, as I also explained (citing the case of Delhi's Akshardham religious complex), to a reinstitution of masculinist discourses of control and constraint; the potentially disruptive consequences of consumerism have been tamed through the dictates of moral consumption.

Modi-masculinity stands at the crossroads of post-nationalism and moral consumption and, in this, combines the continuing imperatives of long-standing power structures and relations of deference with the evolving processes of capitalism. That is to say, it combines the idea of an Indian essence with the notion of global comity to produce a discourse about relationships between men, women, the home and the urban world. Modi-masculinity is, in the most obvious way, the counterpoint to the figure of the Five-Year Plan hero – the idealised protagonist of the economic planning regime that held sway in an earlier 'Nehruvian India' – of the 1960s and 1970s. The Five Year Plan hero was also, as I have pointed out in Chapter 1, a man of the city. The decades since the 1980s have witnessed dramatically new forms of urban development, one where the role of private capital has become dominant (Guiu Searle 2017; Srivastava 2015; Sud 2016). This new 'post-liberalisation' urban context is, as the book has explored, one where ideas of family life, intimacies, religious belief, class, caste and gender identities – among other aspects – are undergoing dramatic change. Modi-masculinity is the epochal symbol of a new urban era, just as the Five-Year Plan hero was of an earlier one. The former speaks the language of the political and cultural economies of the twenty-first century – summarising the desires and anxieties of a post-national present as far as gender relations are concerned – just as the latter articulated narratives of mid-twentieth-century modernity. Modi-masculinity both transcends territorially defined notions of national identity and disavows 'savings' in favour of consuming as an act of citizenship. It represents, in this way, a (masculine) way of being in the post-national city.

Inasmuch as Modi-masculinity presents the case for a dominant and domineering male figure who can *forcefully* champion the cause of 'minimum government, maximum governance' (one of Prime Minister Modi's favourite election slogans), it speaks to a middle-class constituency that has, in recent times, sought to disengage from state mechanisms (Jaffrelot 2008) in favour of private enterprise. In terms of urban developments, this has translated into specific spaces such as DLF City in Gurugram district in the state of Haryana. Gurugram, it will be remembered, was discussed in Chapter 1 in the context of the banning of *namaaz* prayers in public spaces. As also mentioned earlier, over the past three decades, the locality has been a site of intense real estate activity, led by several private companies, the most significant of which is the Delhi Land and Finance (DLF) Corporation. Beginning from the early 1980s, vast tracts of agricultural land have been transformed into shopping malls, gated residential communities, independent houses, private hospitals, theme parks and a variety of other leisure-related spaces. The 'Millennium City', as Gurugram (earlier called Gurgaon) is known in both real estate advertising and lay discourse, has increasingly become divided into two quite distinct parts: New Gurugram (containing privately public infrastructure, malls and gated enclaves) and Old Gurugram (marked by state-funded and creaking infrastructure, unruly traffic and poor infrastructure). New Gurugram is the product of sustained private investments since the 1980s (Searle 2017; Srivastava 2015) And the newly created spaces of habitation, commerce and leisure are also connected to new ideas regarding family life, class and national identity. The political economy of recent urbanism is inextricably enmeshed with the social and cultural economies of everyday life in the city.

Modi-masculinity builds upon the processes and anxieties of masculinity-in-the-city that have been discussed in different chapters of the book and also offers a template for how (heterosexual) masculinity might relate to the home and the world. In order to *outline* the nature of the template, however, it is important to return to aspects of the discussion of previous chapters.

The discussion of Chapter 3 ended with my meeting with Ramesh Vishwakarma, a rural migrant to Mumbai and client of the Kaya Kalp sex clinic. I had suggested that men of Ramesh Vishwakarma's background – economically marginal, desirous of 'another' life but also fearful that 'too much modernity' might be the undoing of their already precarious manhood – were characterised by a masculine identity marked by both fragility and uncertainty. The detective stories analysed in Chapter 4 offered 'solutions' to the uncertainties of the city. They are narratives about wanting to be part of its risky fun – seeking the company of sexually adventurous women, for example – but also being able to manage the risks; 'adventurous' women who slighted masculinity deserved punishment, of which the most appropriate type might be rape. The novels, as the chapter suggested, are also tracts on the palliative effects of Indian traditions upon the destabilising consequences of urban processes: 'fast' women might be calmed through self-discipline, and *brahmacharya* (celibacy) might provide a centring principle for men.

Through an ethnography of young men belonging to the Hindu right-wing Bajrang Dal organisation, Chapter 5 suggested that the search for a centring principle may not, in fact, be a straightforward one, involving a rejection of global modernity in favour of variously imagined local traditions. The chapter argued, instead, that even the apparently most 'essential' of all selves – the religious one – might best be thought of as not particularly essential or unified after all. Rather, that Hindu 'self-realization' – whether through *brahmacharya* or acts of building communities of self-interest – involved traversing multiple urban spaces and participating in varied activities, and that this behaviour mimicked the nature of the city and the dictates of consumerism to produce an 'all-consuming' urban man. It was this, the chapter suggested, that characterised the nature of contemporary masculinity-in-the-city. Its significance lies, I argued, in concocting a strategy of 'fragmentation' rather than maintaining 'wholeness' – as is commonly suggested in discussions that seek to capture reactions to change and turmoil (Blom Hansen 1999) – as an aspect of power and control.

Finally, I noted in Chapter 6 that the background to discourses of women's safety in public lay in 'technotopic' imaginations of the city. That is, a way of thinking about deep-rooted social problems regarding gender relations that came to be presented as having technological solutions: apps and CCTV cameras, for example, as a solution to gender norms and behaviours with multiple roots within familial and institutional contexts. Narratives of how young, single women might be kept safe became entangled, I suggested, with ideas of urban spaces that were either inherently safe or unsafe, control and autonomy, how women might be of the world but also of the home, and 'proper' and 'improper' participation in consumerist activity.

I will now build upon these aspects – returning also to post-nationalism and moral consumption – to draw together the various strands in the book to reflect upon the constructed masculinity of Narendra Modi. The contents and processes of the 'public man' that is Modi are of considerable significance for the discussion of this book.

Conclusion: Modi-Masculinity and Our Times

In Chapters 1 and 6, I have suggested that the term 'neoliberalism' was inadequate to the task of coming to grips with contemporary relationships between the state, its citizens and forms of capital, and the ways in which these continue to shape life in the city. The manner in which these three contexts relate to each other can best be understood, I pointed out, through attention to local histories of interaction rather than seeking to produce universal theories of capitalism. The latter process flattens distinct social contexts into an undifferentiated 'global' whole. The key task of the book has been to demonstrate that an attention to *a* city and its processes need not imply a lack of engagement with the broader – global – processes that characterise urbanism around the world. It is in this sense that the ideas of post-nationalism and moral consumption have something to tell us about how *local* social and economic histories produce ways of being in the *world*.

Let us now return to consider how the various themes explored in the book – that link the city and masculinity – gather about Modi-masculinity, making it a productive site for exploring the times we live in. To begin with, Modi-masculinity offers not only the possibilities of worldliness but also the promise that men might continue to maintain their hold on both the home and the world. The men who visit sex clinics experience the city as a space of extraordinary social and economic precarity. As they desperately seek to make a home within it, the city barely offers a foothold; instead, consigning them, as workers, to the ranks of the labouring-immiserated and, as inhabitants, slums and shantytowns. To this group, Modi-masculinity's 'strong masculinity' offers a strategy of negotiating a hostile city and, subsequently, a world that one must both be part of and yet also guard against. This is well illustrated through the following example of a discussion between an anthropologist and one of his subjects.

Outlining a conversation with a private security guard at a Delhi hospital on relationships between politics, religion and everyday life, Irfan Ahmad suggests that the discussion contains themes that are significant to an understanding of 'contemporary India from the perspective of an "ordinary" or "common" man' (2017: 57). For my purposes, the following excerpts also tell us something about the appeal of Modi-masculinity for those who occupy the city's spatial, social and economic margins. At one point in their conversation, Ahmad expresses confusion regarding his interlocutor Dharmendra Panchal's comment that though India is passing through Kaliyuga (a period of darkness and untruth, according to the Hindu worldview), Modi represents a king of the Satya Yuga (age of truth):

> Panchal: Try to understand the issue (*bāt kō samajhyē*). In Kaliyuga too there are individuals with qualities characteristic of people in Satya Yuga…. Not each and every one is a sinner (*pāpī/kukarmī*). God (*Bhagvān*) makes someone a king only when he possesses some qualities (*gun*). See, before he became the Prime Minister and when he was the Chief Minister of Gujarat what a spectacular development of the state he achieved. He made Gujarat shine. In the whole world – from America to Japan – he won applause for his work in development.
>
> He secured development for all (*sab ka vikaās kiya*). He has determination. It is not only people from the BJP who praise Narendra Bhai Modi. Even his rivals from the Congress Party and Aam Admi Party admit that he has those qualities. After becoming the Prime Minister, he travelled to many countries – Canada, the US, and the UK – and brightened the name of India. He made the world realize the importance and might of Bhārat (*lōha manvāya*). Obama and leaders like him pay attention to and respect Narendra Bhai Modi.
>
> Narendra Bhai Modi pursues *bhaktī* (devotion) not only in the domain of politics but equally in his personal life. Whenever and wherever he comes across a temple of Bhōlē bāba [Shiva] he offers his prayer. Notwithstanding that he is the Prime Minister he keeps fasts (*varat*) in the [Hindu] months of Chaitra and Kartika. Have you seen such a Prime Minister before? Compare Narendra Bhai Modi with impotent (*napunsak*) leaders from the Congress Party. You will notice a significant difference. (Ahmad 2017: 68–69)

For men at the bottom of the urban hierarchy, Modi-masculinity offers strategies of both taking part in its *Kaliyuga* processes – inescapable in order to secure livelihoods that rural realms no longer provide – and also preserving something of one's true self; *bhakti* (devotion) here has something more than religious connotations: it is also a commitment to maintaining masculinity in a constantly threatening environment. It is this – control over both the home and the world – that is recognised as the mark of a 'true' man as distinct from one who is *napunsak* (impotent).

'The aspirations and disappointments of working-class Bengali men in Kolkata', Romit Chowdhury points out, 'are driven by [the] master discourse of respectable [middle-class] masculinity' (2021: 14). And, he adds, 'from their location on the margins of the urban labour market and in an urban milieu which refuses to acknowledge them as men worthy of respect' (Chowdhury 2021: 14), they take part in acts that seek 'to accomplish the norm of respectable breadwinner masculinity' (Chowdhury 2021: 15). For men such as Dharmendra Panchal, struggling to make a life in an urban environment that is experienced as both economically and socially hostile, the 'norms of respectable breadwinner masculinity' indexed by Modi-masculinity provide a context of establishing identity. Modi-masculinity is the bulwark against a milieu that constantly challenges Panchal's ability 'to approximate key indices of a socially valued form of masculinity' (Chowdhury 2021: 14).

Let us return one last time to Ahmad's conversation with Panchal, the security guard, about the nature of the world and what ails it:

DP: Dharma [religious duty] says that one must get married.… There is no home where the rule of dharma prevails. Look at the world: son is against father; daughter-in-law is against mother-in-law; brothers are against each other. Women have become like men. Look at Mayawati,[2] Sonia Gandhi [widow of the former Prime Minister Rajiv Gandhi and President of the Congress Party], Mamta Banarjee [sic] [Chief Minister of West Bengal], Pratibha Patil [former President of India]. According to our dharma the job of women is not to rule but to take care of the home (grih). (Ahmad 2017: 65)

Ved Prakash Sharma's detective stories tackle this world of urban *adharma*, a situation where religious tenets (*dharma*) no longer hold. Yet the city is an unavoidable site of belonging. In new places of work and through uncontrollable mechanisms of governance, undomesticated women appear as co-workers and administrators respectively. Here too, Modi-masculinity provides the template for urban masculinity. Potentially tempestuous women – with possibly overpowering tendencies – are put into dialogue with a manhood that is able to define the contours of the home and the world, keeping them apart while holding them in an appropriate relation. Public development and private *bhakti*, the capaciousness of national might and the asceticism of individualised sacrifice through *varat* (fasting) maintain social balance and an equilibrium in gender identities. The city is manageable.

But not just manageable, it is also open to conquest. The young men of the Bajrang Dal (Chapter 5) encompass and conquer multiple urban spaces by taking part in the pleasures of fragmentation; these actions reproduce the nature of a city that is deeply segmented and split across lines of class, caste, religious identity and gender norms. Modi-masculinity represents the pleasures of fragmentation, as discussed in Chapter 6, an anthropomorphic form of the strategies required to meld with the spatial character of the city – consuming and resisting consumption; material desires and *bhakti*; being of the home but also the world; feasting and fasting; adventurous and respectable; of the *mohalla* (neighbourhood community) but also of a wider comity. The exercise of male agency requires actions across multiple urban spaces (and times), each disparate one representing various realms of the city to be brought under control. To scatter is to encompass, and to splinter is to experience the gathering of a male essence.

The strategies of locating male 'essence' are – as the book has argued – as varied as those of making a life in the city. Technotopic imaginations of the city are also crucibles of masculinist discourses and ideas of a masculinist technotopia lie at the heart of Modi-masculinity. The issue of 'women's safety', as pointed out in Chapter 6, is firmly ensconced within a discourse of the intensive application of technology to urban life. So, for example, the Indian government's 100 Smart Cities Mission – closely associated with the prime minister's 'visionary' plan for Indian cities (Smart Cities Mission 2021: 8) – seeks 'to improve efficiency in service delivery through software-driven technological solutions' (Shetty and Gupte 2017: 121). This, in turn, is linked to the consolidation of ideas around 'technocratic governance' and 'technocratic citizenship' (Datta 2015). Within these discourses, there is a sense that technology can 'cut through' the messiness of social structures. This, indeed, is also the promise of Modi-masculinity, to robustly do away with the *napunsak* (impotent) strategies of past leaders.

In the post-national city, then, while both men and women have opportunities of taking part in the life of capitalist modernity and becoming consumers, masculine anxieties over female consumption – the woman as the sacrificing figure who facilitated male consumption rather than herself being a consumer has been a long-standing cultural discourse – are, in effect, assuaged through Narendra Modi's 'strong' masculinity. He takes part in the activities of the world – as men must – while not effacing the world of 'tradition'. He is the advocate of moral consumption; ergo, consumption is good as long as it is 'appropriate' to the Indian cultural context. Modi-masculinity is the site of both worldliness – 'development', consumerism, technological force – and an unwaivering allegiance to traditions of the home and the family.

It is in this way that Modi-masculinity, while aligned to an emerging discourse of 'enterprise culture' (Gooptu 2013), is not quite neoliberalism's self-regulating, autonomous individual spoken of in analyses of neoliberalism in the west (see, for example, Urciuoli 2008; Freeman 2014). Instead, it imagines an individualised subject who is encouraged to make (his) own enterprise, though not exactly as he pleases but, rather, through the dictates of social structures, such as family and kin networks. It is this logic at play in recent Indian television advertisements for personal insurance – a significant index of 'subjectivity and sociality and neoliberal financing' (Patel 2006: 29) – where high-achieving (and enterprising) children are shown purchasing policies for their parents rather than themselves.

National visions of the city – such as the Smart Cities Mission – speak through the language of technology and conjure urban spaces as 'improved' by it while leaving intact social relations, such as those between genders. That, we might say, is precisely their *raison d'être*. There is, however, an even more graphic example of an ongoing project of urban transformation that contributes to the discourse of Modi-masculinity, explicitly positioning it as the power to domesticate the city. The Central Vista Project in Delhi, inaugurated in 2020 and due for completion in 2024, involves the 'redevelopment' of a 3 kilometre stretch of road between the president's residence (Rashtrapati Bhavan) and the India Gate monument in central Delhi. This part of New Delhi – designed by Edward Lutyens and Herbert Baker and completed during the second decade of the twentieth century – contains some of the most significant architectural expressions of colonial power. The post-colonial state populated this landscape with its own personnel and processes as a conscious act of inaugurating a new era of governance. The Central Vista Project extends the logic of power by drawing an explicit association between Narendra Modi's 'masculine' personality and the refashioning of urban spaces.[3]

When completed, the project will – among other things – encompass a new parliament house, a remodelled central vista, new residences and offices for the vice-president and prime minister and combined office facilities for several of the ministries currently housed in different buildings. The estimated cost of the project is around 1.8 billion US dollars (most likely to increase over time, given that cost overruns are the norm in infrastructure projects of this magnitude). The project was described by Modi as the urban makeover that is part of India's journey towards 'aatmanirbhar Bharat [self-reliant India]'. The idea of a self-sustaining India became a particularly important part of the political discourse after the prime minister used the term in 2020 to describe the government's strategy of post-COVID economic recovery.[4]

State narratives and supporters of the Central Vista Project variously describe it as a pathway to 'defining a new India' (Bimal Patel, the project's chief architect) (Sharma 2021), an expression of India's position as a 'rising power' (Darda 2021) and characterised by architecture that is 'modern while celebrating India's rich tradition' (Sharma 2021). Underlining the close interest Modi had in the project, Chief Architect Patel pointed out that though 'the prime minister is not involved in the details of the project, ... his guidance is crucial to defining [its] overall character' (Sharma 2021). The project faced a great deal of public criticism. These included charges of destruction of 'heritage' buildings, misplaced public expenditure priorities during a health emergency, lack of public consultation and violation of laws that prevent the change of land use without permission from relevant bodies (Ahsan 2021). The public outcry was accompanied by legal challenges as well as petitions to the Delhi Development Authority (DDA), the central body authorised to make changes in land use. Notwithstanding the controversy, the project received bureaucratic and legal approval and, at the time of writing (2022), construction proceeds apace.

The close association between the re-fashioning of the symbolic heart of India's capital city – ensconced within the geographies of colonial and post-colonial power – and Narendra Modi is another eloquent chapter in the story of masculinity and the city that, as this chapter has suggested, can be summarised through the idea of Modi-masculinity. The Central Vista Project gathers at one place the most significant themes explored in this book: the city as a site of expressing masculine prowess; masculine desire and ability to control and re-fashion urban spaces; and the re-fashioning of – 'self-reliant' – nationalism in the era of globalisation and consumerism, a context I have referred to as post-nationalism. While there is no necessary relationship between masculinity and urbanism (that is, it cannot be automatically assumed), I have argued that there exists a symbiotic relationship between the two as far as the Indian situation is concerned. And further, in the context of this chapter, this relationship is graphically illustrated through the public persona of Prime Minister Narendra Modi.

There are three key themes around which the arguments of the project's protagonist's coalesce. First, it is presented as marking a clear break from the past, with one commentator describing the old parliament building as 'decrepit, ... malodorous and uninhabitable' (Operajita 2021). Second, the severance is not seen to imply that the past is irrelevant – rather, the salience of a specific past and its judicious combination with strategies of the future. And, finally, the project is presented as the result of Modi's efficient style as represented by the sweeping away of the putative barriers of legal, political and bureaucratic obstructionism that – by implication – have also stood in the way of a greater national destiny.

The city imagined as the site of the re-fashioning of 'national destiny' through the actions of a leader who is both presented and perceived through narratives of masculinity – in stark contrast to those who preceded him – is an apt precis for the key concern of this book. The break from the past that Modi effects is the promise to both transform and domesticate urban futures that only a 'real' man might be able to achieve – perhaps like Vijay in Ved Prakash Sharma's novels. The future that is promised is, however, tethered to a past that is 'appropriate' to an Indian present, one where the 'traditions' continue to guide it and – by extension – older structures are not displaced. In addition, the making of an 'Indian' future – even if built upon foundations laid by 'Hindu' masculinity – entails an engagement with the world rather than a withdrawal from it, much like the actions of the young men of the Bajrang Dal. And, finally, the city and urban futures are to be secured through the efficiency of action that only Modi-masculinity can marshall. In this way, the nature of masculine power articulated through the persona of Narendra Modi goes to the heart of both being a man in the post-national city and providing an outline of masculine actions upon the city. It seeks to overturn historical 'emasculation', those caused by different kinds of 'invaders' as well as post-colonial rulers who paid insufficient attention to shoring up masculine capacities. It engages with the world of urban flux in order to domesticate its unsettling nature through discourses of gendered power. For men, the city is a promise, possibility, risk and fulfilment.

Notes

1. Modi is married but has lived separately from his wife.
2. A prominent Dalit politician and ex-chief minister of Uttar Pradesh.
3. As there are no academic studies on the project so far, my discussion draws upon a number of media reports.
4. See https://aatmanirbharbharat.mygov.in, accessed 30 August 2021.

Bibliography

Ahmad, Irfan. 2017. 'In Conversation with an Ordinary Indian: Kaliyuga, War, End of the World and Hindutva'. *Journal of Religious and Political Practice* 3 (1–2): 57–74.

Ahsan, Sofi. 2021. 'Justice Khanna Dissent on Central Vista Project: Must Make Intelligible Information Public'. *Indian Express*. 6 January. Accessed 30 August 2021. https://indianexpress.com/article/india/central-vista-project -justice-sanjiv-khanna-parliament-building-7134350/.

Alter, Joseph. 1992. *The Wrestler's Body*. Chicago: University Press.

———. 2005. 'Celibacy, Sexuality, and Nationalism in North India'. In *Bodies in Contact: Rethinking Colonial Encounters in World History*, edited by Tony Ballantyne and Antoinette Burton, 310–320. Durham, NC: Duke University Press.

———. 2011. *Moral Materialism: Sex and Masculinity in Modern India*. New Delhi: Penguin.

Anandhi, S. and J. Jeyaranjan. 2001. 'Masculinities and Domestic Violence in a Tamil Nadu Village'. Research paper published by Institute for Development Alternatives, Chennai.

Anderson, Benedict. 1986. *Imagined Communities. Reflections on the Origins and Spread of Nationalism*. London: Verso.

Anderson, Edward and A. Longkumer, ed. 2020. *Neo-Hindutva: Evolving Forms, Spaces, and Expressions of Hindu Nationalism*. Abingdon: Routledge.

Appadurai, Arjun. 1986. 'Theory in Anthropology: Centre and Periphery'. *Comparative Studies in Society and History* 28 (2): 356–361.

———. 1990. 'Disjuncture and Difference in the Global Cultural Economy'. *Public Culture* 2 (2): 1–24.

————. 1993. 'Patriotism and Its Futures'. *Public Culture* 5 (3): 411–429.

————. 1996. *Modernity at Large: Cultural Dimensions of Globalization.* Minneapolis: University of Minnesota Press.

————. 1997. 'Introduction: Commodities and the Politics of Value'. In *The Social Life of Things: Commodities in Cultural Perspective*, edited by A. Appadurai, 3–63. Cambridge: Cambridge University Press.

Arunima, G. 2020. 'Cameras, Campuses and the Future of Politics in an Era of Imaging Technologies'. *Contributions to Indian Sociology* 54 (1): 1–26.

Athique, Adrian. 2012. *Indian Media.* Cambridge: Polity Press.

Baas, Michiel. 2020. *Muscular India: Masculinity, Mobility and the New Middle Class.* Delhi: Context Books.

Babb, Lawrence. 2003. 'Sects and Indian Religions'. In *The Oxford India Companion to Sociology and Social Anthropology*, vol. 1, ed. V. Das, 802–826. Delhi: Oxford University Press.

Bacchetta, Paola. 2004. *Gender in the Hindu Nation: RSS Women as Ideologues.* New Delhi: Kali for Women.

Bakhtin, M. M. 2011. 'Forms of Time and of the Chronotope in the Novel: Notes Towards a Historical Poetics'. In *The Dialogic Imagination. Four Essays by M.M. Bakhtin*, edited by. M. Holquist, 84–258. Austin: University of Texas Press.

Balakrishnan, Rekha. 2019. 'Why Single Women above 35 in India Are Saying "Yehi Hai Right Choice, Baby"'. Yourstory.com, 25 November. Accessed 13 December 2019. https://yourstory.com/herstory/2019/11/single-women-india-dating-sex-life.

Bandyopadhyay, Ritajyoti. 2016. 'Institutionalizing Informality: The Hawkers' Question in Postcolonial Calcutta'. *Modern Asian Studies* 50 (2): 675–717.

Bannerjee, S. 2005. *Make Me a Man! Masculinity, Hinduism and Nationalism in India.* Albany: State University of New York Press.

————. 2012. *Muscular Nationalism: Gender, Violence and Empire in India and Ireland, 1914–2004.* New York: New York University Press.

Basu, Srimati. 2015. 'Gathering Steam: Organizing Strategies of the Indian Men's Rights Movement'. *Economic and Political Weekly* 50 (44): 67–75.

————. 2019. 'The Cinematic Pleasures of Indian Men's Rights Activists'. *Queer Legal Studies* 6 (1): 63–81.

Basu, T., P. Datta, S. Sarkar, T. Sarkar and S. Sen. 1993. *Khaki Shorts and Saffron Flags: A Critique of the Hindu Right.* New Delhi: Orient Longman.

Batra, Lalit. 2009 'A Review of Urbanization and Urban Policy in Post-independent India'. Working Paper Series. Centre for the Study of Law and Governance, Jawaharlal Nehru University, New Delhi.

Baviskar, Amita and Raka Ray, ed. 2011. *Elite and Everyman: The Cultural Politics of the Indian Middle Classes*. New Delhi: Routledge.

Benjamin, Walter. 1992. 'On Some Motifs in Baudelaire'. In *Illuminations*, translated by Harry Zohn, edited by H. Arendt, 152–196. London: Fontana.

Berger, John. 1965. *The Success and Failure of Picasso*. Harmondsworth: Penguin Books.

Berger, John and Jean Mohr. 2010. *A Seventh Man: Migrant Workers in Europe*. London and New York: Verso

Bernroider, Lucy. 2018. 'Single Female Tenants in South Delhi: Gender, Class and Morality in a Globalizing City'. *Gender, Place and Culture: A Journal of Feminist Geography* 25 (5): 758–774.

Bhandari, Parul. 2020. *Matchmaking in Middle Class India: Beyond Arranged and Love Marriage*. Singapore and New Delhi: Springer.

Bhatt, C. 2001. *Hindu Nationalism: Origins, Ideologies and Modern Myths*. Oxford: Berg.

Blackwood, Evelyn and Saskia Wieringa. 1999. *Same Sex Relations and Female Desires: Transgender Practices across Cultures*. New York: Columbia University Press.

Blom Hansen, T. 1999. *The Saffron Wave: Democracy and Hindu Nationalism in Modern India*. Princeton: Princeton University Press.

Boas, T. and J. Gans-Morse. 2009. 'Neo-liberalism: From New Liberal Philosophy to Anti-Liberal Slogan'. *Studies in Comparative International Development* 44 (1): 137–161.

Bourdieu, Pierre. 1977. *Outline of a Theory of Practice*. Cambridge: Cambridge University Press.

———. 1984. *Distinction: A Social Critique of the Judgement of Taste*. Translated by Richard Nice. London and New York: Routledge.

———. 1986. 'The Forms of Capital'. In *Handbook of Theory and Research in the Sociology of Education*, edited by J. G. Richardson, 241–258. New York: Greenwood Press.

Brass, Paul. 2003. *The Production of Hindu–Muslim Violence in Contemporary India*. Seattle: University of Washington Press.

Breckenridge, C. A. 1995. *Consuming Modernity: Public Culture in a South Asian World*. Minneapolis: University of Minnesota Press.

Breman, Jan. 1996. *Footloose Labour: Working in India's Informal Economy*. Cambridge: Cambridge University Press.

Brenner, N. and C. Schmid. 2015. 'Towards a New Epistemology of the Urban?' *City* 19 (2–3): 151–182.

Brosius, Christiane. 2005. *Empowering Visions: The Politics of Representation in Hindu Nationalism*. London: Anthem Press.

———. 2012. *India's Middle Class: New Forms of Urban Leisure, Consumption and Prosperity*. New Delhi: Routledge.

———. 2016. 'Regulating Access and Mobility of Single Women in a "World Class"-City: Gender and Inequality in Delhi, India'. In *Inequalities in Creative Cities. Issues, Approaches, Comparisons*, edited by Ulrike Gerhard, Michael Hoelscher and David Wilson, 217–238. New York: Palgrave Macmillan.

Bruner, E. M. 1986. 'Experience and its Expressions'. In *The Anthropology of Experience*, edited by V. Turner and E. M. Bruner, 3–32. Urbana: University of Illinois Press.

Bulsara, J. F. 1948. *Bombay: A City in the Making*. Bombay Citizenship Series. Bombay: National Information and Publications Ltd.

Butler, Judith. 1999. *Gender Trouble: Feminism and the Subversion of Identity*. London and New York: Routledge.

Campbell, C. 2000. 'The Puzzle of Modern Consumerism'. In *The Consumer Society Reader*, edited by J. L. Martyn, 48–72. Oxford: Blackwell.

Carstairs, M. G. 1958. *The Twice Born*. London: Hogarth.

Chakraborty, Chandrima. 2011. *Masculinity, Asceticism, Hinduism: Past and Present Imaginings of India*. Ranikhet: Permanent Black.

Chakravarthy, Pritham, trans. 2008. *The Blaft Anthology of Tamil Pulp Fiction*, vol. 1, Chennai: Blaft.

———, trans. 2010. *The Blaft Anthology of Tamil Pulp Fiction*, vol. 2. Chennai: Blaft.

Chakravarty, Sumita S. 1993. *National Identity in Indian Popular Cinema, 1947–1987*. Austin: University of Texas Press.

Chakravarty, Uma. 1998. 'Inventing Saffron History: A Celibate Hero Rescues an Emasculated Nation'. In *A Question of Silence? The Sexual Economies of Modern India*, edited by M. John and J. Nair, 243–268. New Delhi: Kali for Women.

Chandbagh I: A Doon School Miscellany. Dehradun: Doon School, 1954.

Chandoke, Neera. 1991. 'The Post-colonial City'. *Economic and Political Weekly* 26 (50): 2868–2873.

Chandra, Nandini. 2008. *The Classic Popular: Amar Chitra Katha, 1967–2007*. New Delhi: Yoda Press.

Chatterjee, Partha. 1993a. 'The Nationalist Resolution of the Woman Question'. In *Recasting Women: Essays in Colonial History*, edited by K. Sangari and S. Vaid, 233–253. New Delhi: Kali for Women.

————. 1993b. *The Nation and Its Fragments: Colonial and Postcolonial Histories.* Princeton: Princeton University Press.

————. 2004. *The Politics of the Governed: Reflections on Popular Politics in Most Parts of the World.* Delhi: Permanent Black.

Chopra, Radhika. 2007. *Reframing Masculinities: Narrating the Supportive Practices of Men.* New Delhi: Orient Longman.

Chowdhury, Indira. 1998. *The Frail Hero and Virile History: Gender and the Politics of Culture in Colonial Bengal.* Delhi: Oxford University Press.

Chowdhury, Romit. 2021. 'The Social life of Transport Infrastructures: Masculinities and Everyday Mobilities in Kolkata'. *Urban Studies* 58 (1): 73–89.

Cohen, Lawrence. 1995. 'Holi in Banaras and the Mahaland of Modernity'. *GLQ: A Journal of Lesbian and Gay Studies* 2: 399–424.

Connell, R. W. 2005. *Masculinities.* Cambridge: Polity Press.

Constitution of the Indian Public Schools Society (1986 [1936]). Dehradun: Indian Public Schools Society.

Darda, Vijay. 2021. 'Let's Not Politicise the Central Vista Project'. *Indian Express*, 7 July. Accessed 30 August 2021. https://indianexpress.com/article/opinion/columns/narendra-modi-govt-central-vista-project-7392272/.

Das, Veena. 1977. *Structure and Cognition: Aspects of Hindu Castes and Rituals.* Delhi: Oxford University Press.

————. 1995. *Critical Events: An Anthropological Perspective on Contemporary India.* Delhi and New York: Oxford University Press.

Datta, Ayona. 2015. 'A Hundred Smart Cities, A Hundred Utopias'. *Dialogues in Human Geography* 5 (1): 49–53.

De Alwis, M., S. Deshpande. P. Jeganathan. M. John, N. Menon, A. Nigam and S. A. Zaidi. 2009. 'The Postnational Condition'. *Economic and Political Weekly* 44 (10): 35.

Derné, Steve. 2000. *Movies, Masculinity, and Modernity: An Ethnography of Men's Filmgoing in India.* Westport: Greenwood Press.

————. 2008. *Globalization on the Ground: New Media and the Transformation of Culture, Class, and Gender in India.* New Delhi: Sage.

Deshpande, S. 2000. 'Hegemonic Spatial Strategies: The Nation-space and Hindu Communalism in Twentieth-century India'. In *Community, Gender and Violence. Subaltern Studies XI*, edited by P. Chatterjee and P. Jeganathan, 167–211. London: Hurst.

Desjarlais, R. and J. Wilce. 2003. 'The Cultural Construction of Emotion'. In *The Oxford India Companion to Sociology and Social Anthropology*, edited by Veena Das, 1179–1204. Delhi: Oxford University Press.

Devika, J. 2009. 'Bodies Gone Awry: The Abjection of Sexuality in Development Discourse in Contemporary Kerala'. *Indian Journal of Gender Studies* 16 (1): 21–46.

Dey, Abhishek. 2018. '"Pray in Mosques": Why Gurgaon's Muslims Might Not Be Able to Follow the Haryana CM's Advice'. *Scroll.in*, 7 May. Accessed 10 January 2019. https://scroll.in/article/878081/pray-in-mosques-why-gurugrams-muslims-might-not-be-able-to-follow-the-haryana-cms-advice.

Donner, Henrike. 2011. 'Gendered Work, Domestic Work and Perfect Families: New Regimes of Gender and Food in Bengali Middle-Class Lifestyles'. In *Being Middle Class: A Way of Life*, edited by Henrike Donner, 47–72. London: Routledge.

Doon School Book (DSB). 1948. Dehradun: Doon School Old Boys' Society.

Douglas, M. and B. Isherwood. 1979. *The World of Goods*. London: Routledge.

Dumont, Louis. 1970. 'World Renunciation in Indian Religions'. In *Religion, Politics and History in India*, edited by Louis Dumont, 33–60. Paris: Mouton.

Dwyer, Rachel. 2000. *All You Want Is Money, All You Need Is Love: Sex and Romance in Modern India*. London: Cassell.

Eckert, J. 2003. *The Charisma of Direct Action: Power, Politics, and the Shiv Sena*. Delhi: Oxford University Press.

———. 2005. 'Whose State Is It? Hindi Nationalist Violence and Populism in India'. In *The Dynamics of States: The Formation and Crises of State Domination*, edited by K. Schlichte, 41–70. Aldershot: Ashgate.

Farquhar, J. 2002. *Appetites: Food and Sex in Post-Socialist China*. Durham, NC: Duke University Press.

Fernandes, Leela. 2006. *India's New Middle Class: Democratic Politics in an Era of Economic Reform*. Minneapolis: University of Minnesota Press.

Flew, Terry. 2014. 'Six Theories of Neoliberalism'. *Thesis Eleven* 122 (1): 49–71.

Foucault, M. 1979. *Discipline and Punish: The Birth of the Prison*. New York: Vintage Books.

———. 1980. 'Questions on Geography'. In *Power/Knowledge: Selected Interviews and Other Writings 1972–77*, edited by C. Gordon, 63–77. Brighton: Harvester.

———. 1990. *The History of Sexuality*, vol. 1: *An Introduction*. London: Penguin.

Fraser, Nancy. 1992. 'Rethinking the Public Sphere: A Contribution to the Critique of Actually Existing Democracy'. In *Habermas and the Public Sphere*, edited by C. Calhoun, 109–142. Cambridge: MIT Press.

Freeman, Carla. 2014. *Entrepreneurial Selves: Neoliberal Respectability and the Making of a Caribbean Middle Class*. Durham: Duke University Press.

Gandhi, M. K. 1928. 'True and False Industrialisation'. *Young India*, 24 May, 756–757.

Gooptu, Nandini. 2013. 'Introduction'. In *Enterprise Culture in Neoliberal India: Studies in Youth, Class, Work and Media*, edited by N. Gooptu, 1–24. London: Routledge.

Gooptu, Nandini (with Rangan Chakravarty). 2018. 'Skill. Work and Gendered Identity in Contemporary India: The Business of Delivering Home-Cooked Food for Domestic Consumption'. *Journal of South Asian Development* 13 (3): 293–314.

Gopinath, Vrinda. 2014. 'Does Narendra Modi's Grand Image of Himself Come from His Roots, Asks Vrinda Gopinath'. Altgaze.com, 24 December. Accessed 21 February 2015. http://www.altgaze.com/?p=753.

Guha, Atulan. 2009. 'Labour Market Flexibility: An Empirical Inquiry into Neoliberal Propositions'. *Economic and Political Weekly* 44 (19): 45–52.

Gupta, Akhil. 1998. *Postcolonial Development. Agriculture in the Making of Modern India*. Durham: Duke University Press.

———. 2012. *Red Tape: Bureaucracy, Structural Violence, and Poverty in India*. Durham: Duke University Press.

Gupta, Akhil and James Ferguson. 1992. 'Beyond "Culture": Space, Identity and the Politics of Difference'. *Cultural Anthropology* 7(1): 6–23.

Gupta, Charu. 2002a. '(Im)possible Love and Sexual Pleasure in Late-Colonial North India'. *Modern Asian Studies* 36 (1): 195–221.

———. 2002b. *Sexuality, Obscenity, Community: Women, Muslims, and the Hindu Public in Colonial India*. New York: Palgrave Macmillan.

Habermas, Jürgen. 1987. *The Philosophical Discourse of Modernity: Twelve Lectures*. Cambridge, MA: MIT Press.

Halperin, D. 1995. *Saint Foucault: Towards a Gay Hagiography*. Oxford: Oxford University Press.

Hansen, Kathryn. 2004. 'Theatrical Transvestism in the Parsi, Gujarati and Marathi Theatres (1850–1940)'. In *Sexual Sites, Seminal Attitudes. Sexualities, Masculinities and Culture in South Asia*, edited by Sanjay Srivastava. New Delhi: Sage.

Harriss, John, 2007. 'Antinomies of Empowerment Observations on Civil Society, Politics and Urban Governance in India'. *Economic and Political Weekly* 42 (26): 2716–2724.

Harvey, C. S. 1996. 'Housing Transformation in an Urban Village in Delhi'. MA thesis, Department of Housing, School of Planning and Architecture, New Delhi.

Harvey, David. 1989. *The Urban Experience*. Oxford: Basil Blackwell.

———. 2005. *A Brief History of Neoliberalism*. Oxford: Oxford University Press.

Hochschild, Arlie Russell. 1983. *The Managed Heart: Commercialization of Human Feeling*. Berkeley: University of California Press.

Hoshagrahar, Jyoti. 2007. 'Negotiated Modernity: Symbolic Terrains of Housing in New Delhi. In *Colonial Modernities: Building, Dwelling and Architecture in British India and Ceylon*, edited by P. Scriver and V. Prakash, 219–240. London: Routledge.

Jaffrelot, Christophe. 1996. *The Hindu Nationalist Movement and Indian Politics*. New Delhi: Viking.

———. 2008. '"Why Should We Vote?" The Indian Middle Class and the Functioning of the World's Largest Democracy'. In *Patterns of Middle Class Consumption in India and China*, edited by Christophe Jaffrelot and Peter van der Veer, 35–54. New Delhi: Sage.

Jain, Kajri. 2007. *Gods in the Bazaar: The Economies of Indian Calendar Art*. Durham, NC: Duke University Press.

John, Mary E. and Janaki Nair, eds. *A Question of Silence? The Sexual Economies of Modern India*. London: Zed Books, 1998.

Kakar, Sudhir. 1990. *Intimate Relations: Exploring Indian Sexuality*. Chicago: University of Chicago Press.

Kamath, Lalitha and M. Vijayabaskar. 2009. 'Limits and Possibilities of Middle Class Associations as Urban Collective Actors'. *Economic and Political Weekly* 44 (26–27): 368–376.

Kaur, Raminder. 2003. *Performative Politics and the Cultures of Hinduism: Public Uses of Religion in Western India*. New Delhi: Permanent Black.

Kaur, Ravinder and Rajni Palriwala, eds. 2018. *Marrying in South Asia: Shifting Concepts, Changing Practises in a Globalising World*. New Delhi: Orient Blackswan.

Kaushik, Divya. 2019. 'Security or Moral Policing? RWAs and Working Women Lock Horns over Locked Gates'. *Times of India*, 6 August. Accessed 23 December 2020. https://timesofindia.indiatimes.com/city/delhi/security-or-moral-policing-rwas-and-working-women-lock-horns-over-locked-gates/articleshow/70534386.cms.

Kaviraj, Sudipta. 1997. 'Filth and the Public Sphere: Concepts and Practices about Space in Calcutta'. *Public Culture* 10 (1): 83–113.

Kemper, S. 2001. *Buying and Believing: Sri Lankan Advertising and Consumers in a Transnational World*. Chicago: University of Chicago Press.

Kenny, Paul D. 2017. *Populism and Patronage: Why Populists Win Elections in India, Asia, and Beyond*. Oxford: Oxford University Press.

Khair, Tabish. 2008. 'Indian Pulp Fiction in English: A Preliminary Overview from Dutt to De'. *Journal of Commonwealth Literature* 43 (3): 59–74.

King, A. D. 1976. *Colonial Urban Development: Culture, Social Power, and Environment*. London: Routledge and Kegan Paul.

Kinkley, Jeffrey C. 2000. *Chinese Justice, the Fiction: Law and Modern Literature in China*. Stanford: Stanford University Press.

Kishan Lal, Hakim Hari. N.d. *The Message of Youth*. Delhi: Khandani Shafakhana.

Kopytoff, Igor. 1997. 'The Cultural Biography of Things: Commoditization as a Process'. In *The Social Life of Things: Commodities in Cultural Perspective*, edited by Arjun Appadurai, 63–91. Cambridge: Cambridge University Press.

Kulkarni, Mangesh, ed. 2019. *Global Masculinities: Interrogations and Reconstructions*. Abingdon and New York: Routledge.

Kumar, Krishna. 1991. *Political Agenda of Education*. Delhi: Sage Publications.

LaDousa, Chaise. 2014. *Hindi Is Our Ground, English Is Our Sky: Education, Language and Social Class in Contemporary India*. New York: Berghahn Books.

Lamb, Sarah. 2018 'Being Single in India: Gendered Identities, Class Mobilities, and Personhoods in Flux'. *Ethos* 46 (1): 49–69.

Lefebvre, H. 1991. *The Production of Space*. Translated by D. Nicholson-Smith. Oxford: Blackwell.

Legg, S. 2007. *Spaces of Colonialism: Delhi's Urban Governmentalities*. Oxford: Blackwell.

Liechty, M. 2003. *Suitably Modern: Making Middle-Class Culture in a New Consumer Society*. Princeton: Princeton University Press.

Lim Chua, Jocelyn. 2014. *In Pursuit of the Good Life: Aspiration and Suicide in Globalizing South India*. Berkley: University of California Press.

Lok Sabha Secretariat. 2014. 'The MoUD's (Ministry of Urban Development) Note for the Parliamentary Panel on Urban Development'. Government of India, New Delhi.

Low, Setha M. 1997. 'Urban Fear: Building the Fortress City'. *City and Society* 9 (1): 53–71.

———. 1999. 'Spatializing Culture: The Social Production and Social Construction of Public Spaces in Costa Rica'. In *Theorizing the City: The New Urban Anthropology Reader*, edited by S. M. Low, 111–137. New Brunswick, NJ: Rutgers University Press.

Lutgendorf, P. 2007. *Hanuman's Tale: The Message of a Divine Monkey*. New York: Oxford University Press.

Lynch, O. M. 1990. 'Introduction: Emotion in Theoretical Contexts'. In *Divine Passions. The Social Construction of Emotion in India*, edited by O.M. Lynch, 3–36. Berkeley: University of California Press.

———, ed. 1990. *Divine Passions: The Social Construction of Emotion in India*. Berkeley: University of California Press, 1990.

Madan, T. N. 1987. *Non-Renunciation: Themes and Interpretations of Hindu Culture*. Delhi: Oxford University Press.

Mains, Daniel. 2007. 'Neoliberal Times: Progress, Boredom, and Shame among Young Men in Urban Ethiopia'. *American Ethnologist* 34 (4): 559–672.

Malik, Y. K. and V. B. Singh. 1994. *Hindu Nationalists in India: The Rise of the Bharatiya Janata Party*. Boulder, CO: Westview.

Mangan, J. A. 1986. *The Games Ethic and Imperialism: Aspects of Diffusion of an Ideal*. Harmondsworth: Viking Press.

Mani, Lata. 1993. 'Contentious Traditions: The Debate on Sati in Colonial India'. In *Recasting Women: Essays in Colonial History*, edited by Kumkum Sangari and Sudesh Vaid, 88–126. New Delhi: Kali for Women.

Mankekar, Purnima. 1999. *Screening Culture, Viewing Politics: An Ethnography of Television, Womanhood, and Nation in Postcolonial India*. Durham: Duke University Press.

Marriott, M. 1990. 'Constructing an Indian Ethnosociology'. In *India through Hindu Categories*, edited by M. Marriott, 1–39. New Delhi: Sage.

Marx, Karl. 1978. *Capital*, Vol. I. Moscow: Progress Publishers.

Massey, Doreen. 1994. *Space, Place and Gender*. Cambridge: Polity Press.

Mathur, Aneesha. 2015. 'Smart Poles in Central Delhi: NDMC to Issue Fresh Tender'. *Indian Express*, 22 August.

Mazzarella, William. 2001. 'Citizens Have Sex, Consumers Make Love'. In *Asian Media Productions*, edited by Brian Moeran, 168–196. Honolulu: University of Hawaii Press.

———. 2003. *Shoveling Smoke: Advertising and Globalization in Contemporary India*. Durham: Duke University Press.

McLain, Karline. 2009. *India's Immortal Comic Books: Gods, Kings, and Other Heroes*. Bloomington: Indiana University Press.

Menon, Nikhil. 2022. *Planning Democracy. How a Professor, an Institute and an Idea Shaped India*. New Delhi: Penguin.

Menon, Nivedita. 2004. *Recovering Subversion: Feminist Politics Beyond the Law*. Urbana: University of Illinois Press.

Metcalfe, Andrew. 1989. *For Freedom and Dignity: Historical Agency and Class Structure in the Coalfields of NSW.* Sydney: Allen and Unwin.

Ministry of Urban Development (MoUD). 2015. *Smart Cities. Mission Statement and Guidelines.* New Delhi: Ministry of Urban Development.

Mishra, Vijay. 2002. *Bollywood Cinema: Temples of Desire.* New York and London: Routledge.

Mitra, A. 1993. *Television and Popular Culture in India: A Study of the Mahabharat.* New Delhi: Sage.

Morson, G. S. and C. Emerson. 1990. *Mikhail Bakhtin: Creation of a Prosaics.* Stanford: Stanford University Press.

Mubarki, Meraj Ahmed. 2018. 'Looking beyond Post-Colonial Modernity: Subaltern Masculinity and the Mumbai Cinema'. *South Asia: Journal of South Asian Studies* 41 (4): 723–743.

Munshi, Shoma. 2010. *Prime Time Soap Operas on Indian Television.* New Delhi: Routledge.

Nandy, A., S. Trivedy and S. Mayaram. 1995. *Creating a Nationality: The Ramjanmbhumi Movement and the Fear of the Self.* Delhi: Oxford University Press.

National Readership Studies Council. 2006. *National Readership Survey (2006).* Mumbai: National Readership Studies Council.

O'Hanlon, R. 1997. 'Issues of Masculinity in North Indian History'. *Indian Journal of Gender Studies* 4 (1): 1–19.

Ojha, Abhilasha. 1999. 'RWAs Will Soon Have Direct Control over Sanitation and Community Halls'. *Indian Express*, 12 January. Accessed 11 December 2015. www.indianexpress.com/res/ple/ie/daily/19991201.

O'Neill, Deirdre and Mike Wayne. 2017. 'On Intellectuals'. In *Considering Class. Theory, Culture and the Media in the 21st Century*, edited by Deirder O'Neill and Mike Wayne, 166–184. Leiden and Boston: Brill.

Ong, Aiwa. 2006. *Neoliberalism as Exception: Mutations in Citizenship and Sovereignty.* Durham, NC: Duke University Press.

Omissi, David. 1991. '"Martial Races": Ethnicity and Security in Colonial India 1858–1939'. *War and Society* 9 (1): 1–27.

Operajita, Oopalee. 2021. 'A Fact Check for Anish Kapoor and Other Central Vista Project Critics'. *Indian Express*. 12 June. Accessed 31 August 2021. https://indianexpress.com/article/opinion/columns/central-vista-project-critics -fact-check-anish-kapoor-covid-crisis-7355169/.

Orsini, Francesca. 2004. 'Detective Novels: A Commercial Genre in Nineteenth-Century North India'. In *India's Literary History: Essays on the Nineteenth*

Century, edited by Vasudha Dalmia and Stuart Blackburn, 435–483. Delhi: Permanent Black.

Osella, C. and F. Osella 2003. 'Ayyappan Saranam': Masculinity and the Sabarimala Pilgrimage in Kerala'. *Journal of the Royal Anthropological Institute* (N.S.) 9 (4): 729–754.

———. 2004. 'Young Malayalee Men and Their Movie Heroes'. In *South Asian Masculinities: Contexts of Change, Sites of Continuity,* edited by R. Chopra, C. Osella and F. Osella, 224–261. New Delhi: Kali for Women.

———. 2006. *Men and Masculinities in South India.* London: Anthem Press.

———. 2009. 'Muslim Entrepreneurs in Public Life between India and the Gulf: Making Good and Doing Good'. *Journal of the Royal Anthropological Institute* 15 (1): S202–S221.

Oza, R. 2006a. *The Making of Neoliberal India: Nationalism, Gender and the Paradoxes of Globalization.* New Delhi: Women Unlimited.

———. 2006b. 'The Geography of Hindu Right-Wing Violence in India'. In *Violent Geographies: Fear, Terror and Political Violence,* edited by D. Gregory and A. Pred, 153–173. London: Routledge.

Pal, Bipin Chandra. 1973. *Memories of My Life and Times.* Calcutta: Bipinchandra Pal Institute.

Pandey, Gyan. 1994. *The Construction of Communalism in Colonial North India.* Delhi: Oxford University Press.

Parihar, S. 1999. *Some Aspects of Indo-Islamic Architecture.* New Delhi: Abhinav.

Parry, Jonathan. 2001. 'Ankalu's Errant Wife: Sex Marriage and Industry in Contemporary Chattisgarh'. *Modern Asian Studies* 35 (4): 783–820.

Patel, Geeta. 2006. 'Risky Subjects: Insurance, Sexuality and Capital'. *Social Text* 89 (24): 25–65.

Pateman, Carol. 1989. *The Disorder of Women: Democracy, Feminism, and Political Theory.* Stanford: Stanford University Press.

Phadke, Shilpa. 2007. 'Dangerous Liaisons: Women and Men, Risk and Reputation in Mumbai'. *Economic and Political Weekly* 42 (17): 1510–1518.

Phadke, S., S. Khan and S. Ranade. 2011, *Why Loiter? Women and Risk on Mumbai Streets.* New Delhi: Penguin Books.

Pigg, Stacey Leigh. 2005. 'Globalizing the Facts of Life'. In *Sex in Development: Science, Sexuality, and Morality in Global Perspective,* edited by Vincanne Adams and Stacey Leigh Pigg, 39–65. Durham, NC: Duke University Press.

Pigg, Stacey Leigh and Linnet Pike. 2004. 'Knowledge, Attitudes, Beliefs and Practices: The Social Shadow of AIDS and STD Prevention in Nepal'. In

Sexual Sites, Seminal Attitudes: Sexualities, Masculinities and Culture in South Asia, edited by Sanjay Srivastava, 271–299. New Delhi: Sage.

Pinto, Jerry. 2006. *Helen: The Life and Times of a Bollywood H-Bomb*. New Delhi: Penguin Books.

Plain, Gill. 2001. *Twentieth-Century Crime Fiction: Gender, Sexuality and the Body*. Edinburgh: Edinburgh University Press.

Ponniah, Ujithra. 2018. 'Managing Marriage through "Self-Improvement": Women and "New Age" Spiritualities in Delhi'. *South Asia. Journal of South Asian Studies* 41 (1): 137–152.

Pradhan, Kanu Charan. 2017. 'Unacknowledged Urbanisation: The New Census Towns in India'. In *Subaltern Urbanisation in India: An Introduction to the Dynamics of Ordinary Towns*, edited by Eric Denis and Marie-Hélène Zèrah, 39–66. Springer: New Delhi.

Prakash, Gyan. 2010. *Mumbai Fables: A History of an Enchanted City*. Princeton: Princeton University Press.

Prasad, Madhava. 1998. *Ideology of the Hindi Film: An Historical Construction*. Delhi: Oxford University Press.

Radhakrishnan, Smitha. 2009. 'Professional Women, Good Families: Respectable Femininity of a "New' India"'. *Qualitative Sociology* 32 (2): 195–212.

Rajagopal, A. 1999. 'Thinking about the New Indian Middle Class: Gender, Advertising and Politics in an Age of Globalization'. In *Signposts: Gender Issues in Post-Independence India*, edited by R.S. Rajan, 57–100. Delhi: Kali for Women.

———. 2001. *Politics after Television: Hindu Nationalism and the Reshaping of the Public in India*. Cambridge: Cambridge University Press.

Rajan, S. Irudaya and R. B. Bhagat. 2021. 'Internal Migration in India: Integrating Migration with Development and Urbanization Policies'. https://www. knomad.org/publication/internal-migration-india-integrating-migration-development-and-urbanization-policies. Accessed 15 August 2021.

Ramaswamy, Sumathi. 2010. *The Goddess and the Nation: Mapping Mother India, Durham*, NC: Duke University Press.

Reddy, Gayatri. 2004. 'Crossing "Lines" of Subjectivity: The Negotiation of Sexual Identity in Hyderabad'. In *Sexual Sites, Seminal Attitudes: Sexualities, Masculinities and Culture in South Asia*, edited by Sanjay Srivastava, 147–164. New Delhi: Sage.

———. 2005. *With Respect to Sex: Negotiating Hijra Identity in Hyderabad*. Chicago: University of Chicago Press.

Report of the Education Commission (1964–66). 1966. *Education and National Development*. New Delhi: Ministry of Education, Government of India.

Risbud, Nilima. 2002. 'Policies for Tenure Security in Delhi'. In *Holding Their Ground: Secure Land Tenure for the Urban Poor in Developing Countries*, edited by A. Durand-Lasserve and L. Royston, 59–74. London: Earthscan.

Ritzer, George. 1993. *The McDonaldization of Society: An Investigation into the Changing Character of Contemporary Social Life*. London: Sage.

Rofel, L. 1999. 'Rethinking Modernity: Space and Factory Discipline in China'. In *Culture, Power, Place: Explorations in Critical Anthropology*, edited by A. Gupta and J. Ferguson, 155–178. Durham, NC: Duke University Press.

Rogers, Martyn. 2008. 'Modernity, "Authenticity", and Ambivalence: Subaltern Masculinities on a South Indian College Campus'. *Journal of the Royal Anthropological Institute* (N.S) 14 (1): 79–95.

Rose, Nikolas. 1990. *Governing the Soul: The Shaping of the Private Self*. London: Free Association Books.

Roselli, J. 1980. 'The Self-Image of Effeteness: Physical Education and Nationalism in Nineteenth-century Bengal'. *Past and Present* 86 (February): 121–148.

Roy, Kumkum. 2000. 'Unravelling the Kamasutra'. In *A Question of Silence? The Sexual Economies of Modern India*, edited by Mary E. John and Janaki Nair, 52–76. London: Zed Books.

Roy, Satyaki. 2020. *Industrialisation in India: India's Neoliberal Path of Industrial Development*. New Delhi: Oxford University Press.

Roy, Srirupa. 2007. *Beyond Belief: India and the Politics of Postcolonial Nationalism*. Durham and London: Duke University Press.

Rudra, Ashok. 1996. *Prasanta Chandra Mahalanobis: A Biography*. Delhi: Oxford University Press.

Saksham. 2013. *Measures for Ensuring the Safety of Women and Programmes for Gender Sensitization on Campuses*. New Delhi: University Grants Commission.

Samaddar, Ranabir. 2020. 'Borders of an Epidemic'. In *Borders of an Epidemic. COVID-19 and Migrant Workers*, edited by R. Samaddar, 1–23. Kolkata: Calcutta Research Group.

Sarkar, Sreela. 2008. 'The New Middle Class, Technology and Modernity in Seelampur'. National Center for Digital Government Working Paper Series 08-001. National Center for Digital Government, Amherst, MA.

Sarkar, Tanika. 1995. 'Heroic Women, Mother Goddesses: Family and Organization in Hindutva Politics'. In *Women and the Hindu Right: A Collection of Essays*, edited by T. Sarkar and U. Butalia, 181–215. New Delhi: Kali for Women.

———— . 2001. *Hindu Wife, Hindu Nation: Community, Religion and Cultural Nationalism*. Bloomington: Indiana University Press.

Sarkar, Tanika and Urvashi Butalia. 1995. *Women and the Hindu Right: A Collection of Essays*. New Delhi: Kali for Women.

Schindler, Seth. 2017. 'Towards a Paradigm of Southern Urbanism'. *City* 21 (1): 47–64.

Searle, Llerna Guiu. 2017. *Landscapes of Accumulation: Real Estate and the Neoliberal Imagination in Contemporary India*. Delhi: Primus Books.

Seidler, Victor 1994. *Unreasonable Men: Masculinity and Social Theory*. London: Routledge.

Sengupta, Mitu. 2008. 'How the State Changed Its Mind: Power, Politics and the Origins of India's Market Reforms'. *Economic and Political Weekly* 43 (21): 35–42.

Sennett, Richard. 1976. *The Fall of Public Man*. New York: Knopf.

Sethi, Aman. 2009. 'The Price of Reforms.' *Frontline* 22 (19) (10–23 September): 4–5

Shafique, Khurram Ali. 2010. *Psycho Mansion: Ibne Shafi*. Karachi: Fazleesons.

Sharma, Pandey Bechan, 'Ugra'. 2009. *Chocolate and Other Writings on Male Homoeroticism*. Translated by Ruth Vanita. Durham, NC: Duke University Press.

Sharma, Niharika. 2021. 'The Chief Architect of Central Vista Thinks Modi's Project Will Define "New India"'. *Quartz India*, 14 July. Accessed 30 August 2021. https://qz.com/india/2032660/chief-architect-explains-why-modis-central -vista-is-important/.

Sharma, Ved Prakash. 2010a. *Vijay Ke Saat Phere* (Vijay's Wedding Rituals). Meerut: Tulsi Paper Books.

————. 2010b. *Naukari Dot Com* (Careers Dot Com). Meerut: Tulsi Paper Books.

Shatkin, Gavin. 2014. *Contesting the Indian City: Global Vision and the Politics of the Local*. Oxford: Wiley Blackwell.

Shetty, Prasad and Rupali Gupte. 2017. 'Cities and Smartness'. In *The Contemporary Urban Conundrum*, edited by Sujata Patel and Omita Goel, 116–127. *India International Centre Quarterly*. New Delhi: India International Centre.

Simmel, Georg. 1971. 'The Metropolis and Mental Life'. In *On Individuality and Social Forms. Selected Writings*, edited by D. Levine, 324–339. Chicago: University of Chicago Press.

Simone, AbdouMaliq. 2019. *Improvised Lives: Rhythms of Endurance in an Urban South (After the Postcolonial)*. Cambridge: Cambridge University Press.

Singer, Milton. 1972. *When a Great Tradition Modernizes. An Anthropological Approach to Indian Civilization*. New York: Praeger.

Singh, Sumer B. 1985. *Doon: The Story of a School*. Dehradun: Indian Public Schools Society.

Singh, Karan. 1982. *Heir Apparent: An Autobiography*. Delhi: Oxford University Press.

Singh, Vikash. 2017. *Uprising of the Fools: Pilgrimage as Moral Protest in Contemporary India*. Stanford: Stanford University Press.

Sinha, Mrinalini. 1997. *The 'Manly Englishman' and the 'Effeminate Bengali' in the Late Nineteenth Century*. New Delhi: Kali for Women.

Sirari, Tanvi. 2006. 'Civil Uprisings in Contemporary India'. Centre for Civil Society Working Paper No. 161. New Delhi: Centre for Civil Society.

Smart Cities Mission. 2021. *Making A City Smart: Learning from the Smart Cities Mission*. New Delhi: Ministry of Housing and Urban Affairs.

Soja, E. W. 1993. *Postmodern Geographies: The Reassertion of Space in Critical Theory*. London: Verso.

Srinivas, Deepa. 2010. *Sculpting a Middle Class: History, Masculinity and the Amar Chitra Katha in India*. New Delhi: Routledge.

Srivastava, Sanjay. 1998. *Constructing Post-Colonial India. National Character and the Doon School*. London: Routledge.

———. 2004. 'The Masculinity of Dis-Location: Commodities, the Metropolis, and the Sex-Clinics of Delhi and Mumbai'. In *South Asian Masculinities: Change and Continuity*, edited by Radhika Chopra, Caroline Osella and Filippo Osella, 175–223. New Delhi: Kali for Women.

———. 2006. 'The Voice of the Nation and the Five-Year Plan Hero: Speculations on Gender, Space, and Popular Culture'. In *Fingerprinting Popular Culture: The Mythic and the Iconic in Indian Cinema*, edited by Vinay Lal and Ashis Nandy, 122–155. New Delhi: Oxford University Press.

———. 2007. *Passionate Modernity: Sexuality, Class, and Consumption in India*. New Delhi: Routledge.

———. 2010. 'Fragmentary Pleasures: Masculinity, Urban Spaces and Commodity Politics in Delhi'. *Journal of Royal Anthropological Institute* (N.S.) 16 (4): 835–852.

———. 2011. 'Urban Spaces, Disney-divinity and Moral Middle Classes in Delhi'. In *Elite and Everyman. The Cultural Politics of the Indian Middle Classes*, edited by Amita Baviskar and Raka Ray, 364–390. New Delhi: Routledge.

———. 2012. 'National Identity, Kitchens and Bedrooms: Gated Communities and New Narratives of Space in India'. In *The Global Middle Classes:*

Theorizing through Ethnography, edited by Mark Liechty, Carla Freeman and Rachel Heiman, 57–84. Santa Fe: School of Advanced Research Press.

———. 2015. *Entangled Urbanism. Slum, Gated Community and Shopping Mall in Delhi and Gurgaon*. Delhi: Oxford University Press.

———. 2017. 'Divine Markets: Post-nationalism, Religion and Moral Consumption in India'. In *Religion and the Morality of Markets*, edited by Filippo Osella and Daromir Rudnyckyj, 94–115. Cambridge: Cambridge University Press.

———. 2018. 'Masculinity Studies and Feminism: Othering the Self, Engaging Theory'. In *Men and Feminism in India*, edited by Romit Chowdhury and Zaid Al-Baset, 35–49. Delhi, London and New York: Routledge.

———. 2020. 'Hindu Majoritarianism, Forms of Capital, and Urban Politics: The Making of a New Ordinary Citizen in India'. *HAU: Journal of Ethnographic Theory* 10 (3): 742–749.

Starrett, G. 2003. 'Muslim Identities and the Great Chain of Buying'. In *New Media in the Muslim World: The Emerging Public Sphere*, edited by D. F. Eickelman and J. W. Anderson, 80–100. Bloomington: University of Indiana Press.

Stavrakakis, Y. 1999. *Lacan and the Political*. London: Routledge.

Stoler, A. Laura. 1995. *Race and the Education of Desire: Foucault's History of Sexuality and the Colonial Order of Things*. Durham: Duke University Press.

Sud, Nikita. 2016. 'State, Scale and Networks in the Liberalisation of India's Land'. Working Paper no. 207. Queen Elizabeth House, University of Oxford.

Sunder Rajan, Rajeshwari. 1993. *Real and Imagined Women. Gender, Culture and Post-colonialism*. London: Routledge.

School of Women's Studies Jadhavpur University (SWSJU). 2010. *Re-Negotiating Gender Relations in Marriage: Family, Class and Community in Kolkata in an Era of Globalisation*. Kolkata: Jadhavpur University.

Tahir-Gürçağlar, Şehnaz. 2008. 'Sherlock Holmes in the Interculture: Pseudotranslations and Anonymity in Turkish literature'. In *Beyond Descriptive Translation Studies: Investigations in Homage to Gideon Toury*, edited by Anthony Pym, Miriam Shlesinger and Daniel Simeoni, 132–151. Philadelphia: John Benjamins.

Taussig, Michael. 1980. *The Devil and Commodity Fetishism in South America*. Chapel Hill: University of North Carolina Press.

Thapar, R., H. Mukhia and B. Chandra. 1977. *Communalism and the Writing of Indian History*. New Delhi: People's Publishing House.

Trawick, Margaret. 1990. *Notes on Love in Tamil Family*. Berkeley: University of California Press.

Tsing, A. 2002. 'The Global Situation'. In *The Anthropology of Globalization: A Reader*, edited by J. X. Inda and R. Rosaldo, 453–486. Oxford: Blackwell.

Tyagi Singh, Amita and Patricia Uberoi. 1994. 'Learning to "Adjust": Conjugal Relations in Indian Popular Fiction'. *Indian Journal of Gender Studies*1 (1): 93–120.

Uberoi, P. 2000. 'Feminine Identity and National Ethos in Indian Calendar Art'. In *Ideals, Images, and Real Lives: Women in Literature and History*, edited by A. Thorner and M. Krishnaraj, 322–346. New Delhi: Sangam Books.

———. 2008. 'Aspirational Weddings. The Bridal Magazine and the Canons of "Decent Marriage"'. In *Patterns of Middle-Class Consumption in India and China*, edited by C. Jaffrelot and P. van der Veer, 230–262. New Delhi: Sage.

University Grants Commission (UGC). 2015. *UGC Guidelines on Safety of Students On and Off Campuses of Higher Educational Institutions*. Delhi: University Grants Commission.

Urciuoli, Bonnie. 2008. 'Skills and Selves in the New Workplace'. *American Ethnologist* 35 (2): 211–228.

van der Veer, Peter. 1994. *Religious Nationalism: Hindus and Muslims in India*. Berkeley: University of California Press.

van Wessel, Margit. 2004. 'Talking about Consumption: How an Indian Middle-Class Dissociates from Middle-class Life'. *Cultural Dynamics* 16 (1): 93–116.

Vasudev, Shefalee. 2014. 'The Wear Tear of the Modi "Kurta"'. Livemint.com, 14 June. Accessed 21 February 2015. http://www.livemint.com/Leisure/ 78cC1RJF8eGlUNBqnDPhqJ/Essay-The-wear-and-tear-of-the-Modi-kurta .html?utm_source=copy.

Venkatachalapathy, A. R. 1997. 'Domesticating the Novel: Society and Culture in Inter-War Tamil Nadu'. *Indian Economic and Social History Review* 34 (1): 53–67.

Verghese, B. G. 1965. *Design for Tomorrow: Emerging Contours of Indian Development*. Delhi: Sterling Publishers.

Verghis, Shana Maria. 2011. 'Before Mogambo, There Was Ibne Safi'. *The Pioneer*, 25 April.

Verkaaik, Oskar. 2004. *Migrants and Militants: Fun and Urban Violence in Pakistan*. Princeton: University Press.

Vishwanathan, Shiv. 2013. 'The Remaking of Narendra Modi'. *Seminar* 641 (January): 52–58.

Wadley, Susan. 1988. 'Women and the Hindu Tradition'. In *Women in Indian Society: A Reader*, edited by R. Ghadially, 23–43. New Delhi: Sage.

Weinstein, Liza, Neha Sami and Gavin Shatkin, 2014. 'Contested Developments Enduring Legacies and Emergent Political Actors in Contemporary Urban India'. In *Contesting the Indian City: Global Vision and the Politics of the Local*, edited by Gavin Shatkin, 39–64. Oxford: Wiley Blackwell.Welchman, Lynn and Sarah Hossain, eds. 2005. *Honour Crimes, Paradigms, and Violence Against Women*. London: Zed Books.

Williams, Raymond. 1975. *The Country and the City*. St Albans: Paladin.

Index